THE GREAT BOOK OF

CHICAGO
SPORTS LISTS

THE GREAT BOOK OF

CHICAGO
SPORTS LISTS

DAN MCNEIL AND ED SHERMAN

RUNNING PRESS
PHILADELPHIA · LONDON

9   8   7   6   5   4   3   2   1
Digit on the right indicates the number of this printing

Library of Congress Control Number: 2009921677
ISBN 978-0-7624-3709-2

Designed by Joshua McDonnell
Edited by Greg Jones

Running Press Book Publishers
2300 Chestnut Street
Philadelphia, PA 19103-4371

Visit us on the web!
www.runningpress.com

CONTENTS

DEDICATIONS

Dan McNeil: Over the past 20-plus years, the most constant characteristic I've observed about Chicago sports fans is they have an unparalleled passion for their teams. I'd like to dedicate this project to them, with whom I have engaged in spirited debates over topics like these here.

Ed Sherman: To my favorite Chicago sports fans: My father, Jerry, and my sons, Matthew and Sam. From generation to generation. *L'dor Vador*.

ACKNOWLEDGEMENTS

The authors would like to thank Len Shapiro for recommending us to the publisher to do the Chicago book. Thanks to Greg Jones at Running Press for working with us and shepherding the project to conclusion. We received valuable advice from Jody Rein and Shari Wenk.

Special thanks to all the contributors who provided their time and insights in compiling their lists.

We would like to thank John McDonough, Jay Blunk and Brandon Faber for allowing us access to the Blackhawks lockerroom to shoot the cover photo.

Thanks to Norman Cohen of Diamond Photography for taking the picture.

Ed would like to thank his old grade-school friend Ira Cohen for checking out many of the lists and making suggestions on what should be added. All those hours watching games and pouring over statistics as kids finally paid off.

Thanks to Ed's son, Sam, a fellow White Sox fan who pitched in doing research. Thanks also to my son Matthew, my favorite Cubs fan. Yes, we are a house divided. Isn't that what Chicago sports are all about?

Thanks for the love and support from my wife, Ilene, the heart and soul of our sports-obsessed family. Yes, we're also thankful to her for the occasional reminder that there are more things to life than sports.

And finally, thanks to my mother, Sue, for her unwavering support. To my father, Jerry, I know wherever he is, he is getting a kick out of this book.

INTRODUCTION

Both of us cut our teeth on Chicago sports growing up in the late 60s and into the 70s. That was long before his Airness took flight, and before the Bears Shuffling Crew had its year of terror and glory. We were well into our 40s before our beloved White Sox delivered us a World Series title, something we never thought we would see in our life-times.

When we first started our obsession with sports, titles were something teams won in Los Angeles, New York, Boston, and other places. The Second City rarely was first- or even second-best in anything.

It was a bleak period for Chicago sports. Many of our teams were mediocre, and the good ones left us with heartbreak. There was the Hawks' Game 7 loss in the Stanley Cup Finals to Montreal; the Bulls' Mother's Day defeat to Golden State in the playoffs; Kermit Alexander ending Gale Sayers' greatness with one hit to the knee; and of course, the 1969 Cubs.

Yet we became hooked as kids because we learned early on that sports runs through our blood in Chicago. Win or lose, these are our teams. Our loyalty is unflinch-ing. Our suffering made us appreciate the championships even more.

In our travels throughout this vast land, one thing is abundantly clear: Chicago is the best sports town in the country. We don't buy titles here. We earn them.

This book is a celebration of Chicago sports. These lists are our boiled-up passion exploding on the pages. Stuff that made us glad, thrilled, irritated, frustrated, and downright pissed—it's all in here.

These are many of the same lists that sports fans argue about at bars throughout the city. We recruited several of our town's biggest sports personalities to contribute to the debate with their own lists.

And for fun, since sports conversation often leads to other topics, we spiced up the book with observations from McNeil on pop culture, ranging from the best pizza places in town and favorite local bands, to overrated things about Chicago. As listeners to his radio show know, McNeil is at his best when he gets on a rant. He is in his full glory in these pages. You'll know his lists when you see the "DM" initials after the List Title. Lists with "ES" were penned by Ed Sherman. And our esteemed contributors' lists are given complete bylines.

We hope this book sparks some brisk debate among Chicago sports fans. These are just our opinions. Do we think we're right on everything? Hardly. Is there a chance we missed a name here and there? Perhaps. We don't claim to be perfect.

Feel free to disagree early and often, and call us blithering idiots a time or two. However, always keep in mind that we have one thing in common: We're all Chicago sports fans, for now and forever.

Where to begin? You could pick any of 100 games that Jordan dominated, and you wouldn't be wrong. I'm sure fans are going to look at this list and wonder why I didn't include so-and-so game. Everyone has their list of Jordan's best games. Here's mine.

10. Broadway debut. This was Jordan's statement game. On November 8, 1984, he made his first appearance at Madison Square Garden. He was incredible with one highlight move after another in scoring 33 points in just his seventh NBA game. In the ultimate sign of respect and admiration the jaded New Yorkers, who know a thing or two about basketball, gave Jordan a standing ovation when he came out of the game. A star was born.

9. 1988 NBA All-Star Game. Sure, nobody plays defense in All-Star games. Still, that shouldn't take away from what Jordan did in his showcase game at Chicago Stadium. He scored 40 points, including 16 in the fourth quarter. He hit 17 of 23 shots from the field. It was quite a display from the game's ultimate star.

8. Burning the Suns. The Bulls opened a quick 2-0 lead on the road in the 1993 Finals, but Phoenix abruptly changed the momentum with a triple-overtime victory in Game 3. Then it was Jordan to the rescue again. He took over in Game 4, pouring in 56 points, the second most ever in an NBA Finals game. Thanks to Jordan, the momentum was back in the Bulls' favor again and they went on to win the title.

7. Welcome back to New York. Madison Square Garden always did bring out the best in Jordan. His biggest New York moment came on March 28, 1995 in his first game back to the Garden following his first retirement. Despite playing only four games, Jordan astonished Spike Lee and the other Knicks fans by pouring in 55 points. For the grand finale, he feathered a great pass to Bill Wennington for an easy game-winning layup.

6. The big 69. Jordan always managed to torture the Cleveland Cavaliers in so many different ways. He just bludgeoned them on March 28, 1990. Jordan scored a career high 69 points on 23 of 37 shooting from the field and 21 of 23 from the line. Poor Craig Ehlo, who must be having nightmares to this day about having to guard Jordan.

5. Raining threes. Even Michael Jordan astonished himself in Game 1 of the 1992 Finals. He couldn't miss from beyond the arc, hitting an amazing six three-pointers in a 16-minute stretch in the first half. After the last three, Jordan turned to Magic Johnson, who was working the game as an analyst for NBC, and offered a shrug as if to say, "I don't know how I'm doing this." All told, Jordan scored 35 points in the first half and 46 for the game.

4. "The Shot." Of all the clutch shots Jordan hit, the one against Cleveland in Game 5 of the first-round series in 1989 remains as the defining moment. With three seconds left, Jordan somehow got open and hit a 15-footer over Craig Ehlo (him again) at the buzzer to give the Bulls a 3-2 series victory over the Cavaliers. "The Shot" will be replayed for eternity.

3. The final shot. There was only one way Jordan should have finished his career—hitting the final shot to win an NBA title. Sure enough, the scenario was set in Game 6 of the 1998 NBA Finals when Jordan canned the game-winner to give the Bulls their sixth championship. Perhaps sensing the history of the moment, he held his follow-through for a few seconds. It should have been the last shot of his career, but Jordan had to ruin it with that weird final two seasons with Washington.

2. Feeling sick. There was no way Jordan could play in Game 5 of the 1997 Finals. When he wasn't throwing up, he spent the rest of the day of the game hooked to an IV moaning in bed. Miraculously, a half-dead Jordan played and made the Jazz feel sick. Somehow he mustered the energy to hit 38 points in leading the Bulls to a crucial victory. Afterwards, there was the memorable image of Jordan hanging on to Scottie Pippen for support as he walked off the court. Considering what he had to overcome, many people feel it was Jordan's best performance.

1. 63 is not enough. For my money, Jordan's best game occurred in Game 2 of the 1986 first-round series against Boston. This was a 1-on-5 performance against a Celtic team that had three Hall of Famers in Larry Bird, Robert Parish and Kevin McHale. Boston, though, couldn't stop Jordan, as he poured in an unthinkable 63 points at the Boston Garden. It wasn't enough, as the Bulls lost in double overtime. But Jordan was the clear winner. Afterward, a stunned Bird said it all: "That was God disguised as Michael Jordan."

In Chicago, we are not steeped in memories of postseason baseball thrill rides. That changed, however, when Ozzie Guillen's White Sox blitzed the pack and won the '05 World Series. It was an improbable run after the Sox stumbled and saw their 15-game lead dissipate before getting hot in late September and winning the AL Central. The Sockos went 11-1 in that magical October, tying the '99 Yankees for the fewest games required to win it all since baseball went to divisional realignment in '95. These are the most defining moments of that October.

10. Chasing Roger Clemens in the World Series Opener at US Cellular Field. I've hated Clemens long before the rest of the world caught on to his act. And I do mean hated. Eventual Series MVP Jermaine Dye homered off Clemens in the first and, with the White Sox leading 3-1, Clemens limped off the mound with a bad hamstring after just two innings. He did not return. The White Sox won the game 5-3 to take Game 1 against Houston.

9. The 5th inning of Game 2 against Boston. Keyed by a Tadahito Iguchi home run, the White Sox scored all five of their runs in the fifth inning and muscled out a 5-4 win to take a commanding two-game lead in their best-of-five AL division series against the Red Sox. David Wells, who was a bust in his one year in a Sox uniform in '01, took the hard-luck loss, due largely to an error by former Chicago utility man Tony Graffanino.

8. The famous dropped third strike. After dropping the opener in the ALCS against Los Angeles, the White Sox and Angels appeared to be headed for extra innings in Game 2. Knotted at 1-1, A.J. Pierzynski seemingly had struck out for the final out in the ninth. Home plate umpire Doug Eddings signaled strike three, but did not execute what he later called his "out mechanic." Pierzynski recognized that and chugged to first after Angels catcher Josh Paul rolled the ball back to the mound. After a lengthy debate, play resumed. Pablo Ozuna pinch ran for Pierzynski and stole second. Joe Crede delivered an RBI double and the White Sox headed to Anaheim with the series tied.

7. White Sox shell Red Sox in ALDS Opener. It is uncommon for a Chicago baseball fan to relax during a playoff game. Not with this one. If it were a fight, they would have stopped it. To the delight of a huge US Cellular crowd on a sun-splashed day, the Sox hit five home runs, three of which were off Boston starter Matt Clement, a former Cub, and cruised to a 14-2 win to take the first game.

6. Geoff Blum's 14th-inning HR in Game 3 in Houston. The game took more than five hours—the longest game in World Series history. The White Sox and Astros employed 17 pitchers collectively. Those pitchers combined to throw 482 pitches. My favorite was the one thrown by Houston's Ezequiel Astacio, duck-hooked over the right field wall by pinch hitter Geoff Blum. Acquired in mid-season, Blum, my favorite sociology major in baseball history, parked a two-run job that gave the Sox a 7-5 lead, the eventual final score. Mark Buehrle, whose business card says "starter," finished the 14th to earn the save and the Sox were only 27 outs away from their first championship since 1917.

5. Four complete games in the ALCS. Obviously, a four-game stretch does not constitute a "moment," but it would be foolish not to recognize the collective contributions from the White Sox staff in the club's four straight victories to close the ALCS. It marked the first time a staff rattled off four consecutive complete games in postseason play since '56. Buehrle got it started with a five-hit gem in the Sox's 2-1 win in Game 2. Jon Garland was a 5-2 winner over John Lackey in Game 3 in Anaheim. Freddy Garcia beat Ervin Santana 8-2 in the fourth game, and Jose Contreras closed it out with a 6-3 win over Kelvin Escobar on October 16th.

4. Juan Uribe's catch in the stands. October 26, 2005. Game 4 of the World Series. In the eighth, Dye's single up the middle scored Willie Harris to give the Sox a 1-0 lead. Big Bobby Jenks was working the ninth, gunning for another save and the most important one in his young life. With the Astros down to their final two outs, pinch hitter Chris Burke slapped a pop foul down the left field line. Both Crede and Uribe gave chase, but it was shortstop Uribe who left his feet and reached deep into the stands to snare the pop for the second out in the inning. Fittingly, Uribe would assist in the game's final out on a lazy chopper.

3. Orlando Hernandez's hocus pocus. Game 3 of the ALDS in Fenway Park. The Sox were gunning for the sweep and their first postseason series win since they won the championship in '17. Boston cut the White Sox lead to 4-3 on Manny Ramirez's second homer of the game. As the skies darkened, Guillen had a tough decision to make with the bases loaded and nobody out in the Boston sixth. He summoned "El Duke," the right-hander who had been a starter all season. Hernandez came out of the pen and got Jason Varitek and Graffanino to pop up before whiffing Johnny Damon for the final out of the inning. The White Sox later added an insurance run and won the game 5-3 and the swept the series.

2. Scotty Pods' walk-off HR in the World Series Opener. I know some will tell me I'm nuts for not making this the No. 1 moment, but this is *my* list. Podsednik was in his first year with the White Sox in '05. He possessed no history here. He also frustrated Sox fans with his erratic play in the outfield. The little lefty got the job done, however, when it mattered most on this South Side Saturday night. With Houston's Brad Lidge on the bump and the game tied 6-6, Podsednik belted one into the seats in right-center in the bottom of the ninth to give the Sox a 7-6 victory in Game 1.

1. Paul Konerko's World Series Game 1 grand slam. Konerko was the most tenured Sox player on the roster. He had a big year in 2000 when the Sox won the division before being swept by Seattle. He always gave maximum effort and is the type of player who would bust somebody's jaw to win a game. He also doesn't go a day in his life without quoting *Slap Shot*, so that scores extra points with me. Houston was leading the Sox 4-2 in the seventh. Sacks juiced. The 'Stros sent 6-foot-7 Chad Qualls to the mound to challenge Konerko, who had put his signature on every post-season game the Sox had played and was the ALCS MVP. Konerko deposited Qualls' first offering into the seats in left-center field. Grand slam. Sox led 6-4. The ovation was deafening. It was decidedly the most exciting single moment I ever experienced. I was sitting seven rows behind the plate. I was the first guy to stand and extend both clenched fists towards the heavens.

Hawk Harrelson's Five Toughest White Sox

Note: Ken "Hawk" Harrelson has been in the White Sox organization for more than 25 years. The former Red Sox slugger was in the broadcast booth when the Sox won the American League West in '83, and later served as the team's general manager. He returned to the television booth in the early '90s and is beloved by Sox fans because of his no-BS, straightforward approach. We asked him who he thought were the five toughest White Sox since he's been in the organization. These were his thoughts.

5. Ed Farmer. Farmio was a tough sonuvabitch. He'd battle your ass off. At one time, Ed held the Sox record for most saves in a season.

4. Bobby Thigpen. Shit, I've seen him go out there with nothin'—I mean absolutely nothin'—and hang on. That's how you save 57 games in a season. He'd sometimes be at 35, 40 pitches in an inning, and we'd say, "C'mon, Thiggy, try a strike. Throw one of those in there." He was a battler.

3. Jack McDowell. You talk about a guy who would compete, that's Jack McDowell. There were times when it was obvious he didn't have his best stuff. He'd be around the plate, gettin' behind guys, walkin' guys, then you look up at the scoreboard in the 7th inning and we're up 2-1. His hips would be bothering him and he couldn't walk after the game, but he'd battle. Some players just don't connect (with the media and fans) and it's because they don't care to. Jack was one of those guys. He wasn't an asshole, but he didn't play up to the media. Jack and I didn't get along that well off the field, but if I was playing behind Jack McDowell, you can bet I'd be playing my ass off for him. I faced Don Drysdale. I faced Bob Gibson. Jack was right there. He was one competitive sonuvabitch.

2. Bobby Jenks. What he's done, at such an early point in his career, is amazing. Bobby is one of the more impactful players this club's ever had. In '05, we had three closers: Shingo (Takatsu), Dustin Hermanson, whose back was so bad he couldn't walk by the end of the summer, and Bobby. Then, all of a sudden, it was just Bobby. As a rookie, he was just phenomenal. What other manager or GM would allow a rookie to come in, during a pennant race, and take the ball? That shows you the kind of balls that Ozzie (Guillen) has, that Kenny (Williams) has, to say "We're gonna give the ball to the kid." And nobody that year had bigger balls than Bobby. It's been one of the greatest things I've seen in baseball for many years.

1. Jerry Reinsdorf. You start with him. He's gone through guys like [Jay] Mariotti [former columnist who waged war with Reinsdorf]. He withstood it. Behind the scenes, if you would ask anybody who's been here more than 10, 15 years, guys like Ozzie, guys like [hitting coach] Greg Walker, they would tell you he's the toughest. He got off to a bad start with the fans, largely because of that SportsVision thing. That was Eddie's [Einhorn] brainchild. It was the first pay-per-view outlet after people had been getting the games for free on over the air stations. He took a bad rap for the building of that new ballpark. They weren't going to move to St. Petersburg. He wanted a new place. And we needed a new place.

He's gotten terrible publicity and Mariotti exacerbated that. Mariotti took a page out of [New York sports columnist] Mike Lupica's book. Lupica had gone from Boston to New York and his readership was down. So he started ripping the shit out of [George] Steinbrenner. And people read it. But like Mariotti, most of it was lies. Jerry is the most misperceived person I've ever seen in sports. All he's done is bring seven championships to our city. I mean, what the hell? And we're gonna get another one or two in the not-too-distant future. I wouldn't be surprised if he gets 10 world championships before he's done.

The name of poor ol' Steve Bartman has lived in infamy ever since that fateful moment during Game 6 of the 2003 NLCS against Florida. Bartman might have been a convenient scapegoat, but the reality is that many other factors cost the Cubs a trip to the World Series that year. Here are the top ten reasons why the Cubs *really* lost the series.

10. Carlos Zambrano. Big Z was a big zero during the 2003 playoffs. He was staked to a 4-0 lead in the first inning of Game 1 and things looked rosy. Then Zambrano gave up 5 runs in the third and the Cubs went on to lose 9-8 in 11 innings. He also suffered a 4-0 defeat in Game 5. All in all a forgettable playoff for Zambrano.

9. Failing to win Game 5. Speaking of Zambrano, there didn't have to be a Game 6. If the Cubs take care of business in Game 5, Bartman remains just another anonymous Cubs fan. However, with a 3-1 series lead, the Cubs bats come up empty against Josh Beckett. They muster only two hits in a 4-0 defeat. So it's on to Wrigley Field for the supposed clincher.

8. Ivan Rodriguez. The Marlins catcher had a huge series. He hit .321 with two homers and 10 RBI in the seven-game series. He delivered one clutch hit after another, including a single during the 8-run eighth in Game 6, scoring Juan Pierre with the first run of that inning. Rodriguez provided the veteran leadership that was much needed with the young team. Don't discount his contribution.

7. Prior losing his composure. OK, you're the supposed ace of the staff. You've got a 3-0 lead in the eighth with one out and a runner on second. And Luis Castillo just hit a flyball into foul territory in leftfield. The ball could have been caught, but it wasn't. No big deal, right? Instead, Prior snapped. He walked Castillo and ball four was a wild pitch, allowing Pierre to take third. The downfall had begun.

6. Where's the hook, Dusty? Incredibly, Baker must have been chained to the dugout during the eighth inning of the infamous Game 6. How else to explain why he left Prior in so long? Prior clearly lost it mentally after walking Castillo, and he had to be tired physically from what would be a 119-pitch effort. Yet Baker let Prior pitch to three more batters. He finally took him out after Derrek Lee's double tied the game at 3-3.

5. The Cubs bullpen. Perhaps Baker didn't want to lift Prior because he knew what he had in his bullpen. If the Cubs relievers stop the damage with only three runs, perhaps they come back in the eighth and make Bartman a nice footnote to the NLCS clincher. Instead, Kyle Farnsworth and Mike Remlinger threw gasoline on the fire, allowing the Marlins to score five more runs in the inning.

4. Kerry Wood folds. Even after the heartbreaking defeat, the Cubs still had Wood going in Game 7 against Mike Redman, a journeyman at best. The Cubs should have been celebrating, especially when Wood himself hits a three-run homer. But Wood had nothing, giving up seven runs in a 9-6 defeat.

3. Cubs fans panic. Once the Bartman play occurred, the mood in the ballpark changed. All the sudden, a century of doubt and misery overtook the fans. They started to think about the "Goat" and everything else. You know what they say: Bad vibes lead to bad things. The sudden shift in atmosphere in the stands did have an effect on what happened on the field.

2. Alex Gonzalez's error. Gonzalez should be forever grateful to Bartman for letting him off the hook. The Cubs' shortstop butchered a grounder off the bat of Miguel Cabrera for what should have been an inning-ending double play. If you're looking for the real goat, look no further than Gonzalez.

1. Alou never would have caught the ball. It took him five years, but Moises Alou finally admitted he couldn't have caught the Bartman ball. The ball was headed towards the stands, and a fan's natural reaction is to try to catch it. What was Bartman supposed to do? Let the ball hit him in the head? If Alou keeps his cool and returns to his position, who knows what would have happened? Instead, he slammed his mitt on to the ground and the wheels of history began turning against the Cubs again.

Some of Chicago's greatest athletes and coaches had some of the worst fallouts with their teams. In many cases, the split damaged relationships for years. It always made you wonder why, after such a beautiful long run, it had to end so ugly.

8. Frank Thomas. Despite being the team's greatest star, Thomas was never fully embraced by Sox management and fans. After the Sox won the World Series in 2005, allowing an injured Thomas to still get his ring, he was released after the season. Thomas was upset that owner Jerry Reinsdorf never called him personally.

"I've got a lot of respect for Jerry Reinsdorf, I do. But I really thought, the relationship we had over the last 16 years, he would have picked up the phone to say, 'Big guy, we're moving forward. We're going somewhere different. We don't know your situation or what's going to happen.' I can live with that, I really can," Thomas said. "But treating me like some passing-by player, I've got no respect for that."

White Sox General Manager Kenny Williams fired back at Thomas calling him an "idiot." Williams also said, "If he was any kind of a man, he would quit talking about things in the paper and return a phone call or come knock on someone's door. If I had the kind of problems evidently he had with me, I would go knock on his door."

Now that's an ugly ending.

7. Dick Butkus. Long after his playing days were complete, Butkus still remained one of the faces of the Bears. But it didn't end well for Butkus. Despite signing a big contract in 1973, knee injuries forced him to retire after the season. In 1975, Butkus filed suit against the Bears, claiming the team knowingly kept him on the field when he should have had surgery on his knees. He alleged team doctors gave him painkillers so he could play. The rift between Butkus and George Halas lasted for years, although Butkus eventually did return to the fold as a radio analyst.

6. Mike Ditka. Take your choice with Ditka. He had two bitter endings as a Bear. In 1992, GM Michael McCaskey ended Ditka's 11-year run as Bears coach following a 5-11 season. The fact is, the Ditka act had grown old and McCaskey wanted to bring in his own man. Nearly two decades earlier, Ditka and McCaskey's grandfather, Halas, clashed over money. Ditka got off his infamous line about how Halas "throws around nickels like manhole covers." Halas got his revenge by shipping Ditka off to a terrible Philadelphia team.

5. Phil Jackson. Even though Jackson was the glue that held everything together during the Michael Jordan run with the Bulls, the Bulls allowed him to leave the building following the sixth and final title in 1998. The culprit was general manager Jerry Krause, who reportedly was jealous of all the credit Jackson received for the Bulls' success.

There was an indication of things to come in the summer of 1997 when Jackson wasn't invited to the wedding of Krause's stepdaughter. On the invitation list were all the other Bulls coaches and Tim Floyd, Krause's hand-picked successor. Jackson did come back for the 1997-98 season. At that point, Krause said regardless of what happened, it would be Jackson's final year with the Bulls. Sure enough, the Bulls won it all and Jackson was gone.

4. Scottie Pippen. Like Jackson, Pippen also exited after the final championship. Early in his career, he signed a long-term contract that proved to be heavily in the Bulls' favor when he became a star. As a result, Pippen felt underpaid and underappreciated. Pippen also clashed with Krause. When the break-up of the team occurred following the sixth championship, Krause unceremoniously shipped Pippen to Houston.

3. Bobby Hull. Hull always battled with Hawks owner Arthur Wirtz. Still, the notion of him leaving the Hawks was unthinkable. Then it happened. After Hull scored 50 goals for the fifth time in the 1971-72 season, the upstart World Hockey Association offered Hull a contract worth nearly $2 million. Hull jumped, although he insisted he didn't make the move because of the money. "I had been at war with the Blackhawks' management for years," he said. "We hated each other." You would have to be naïve to think it wasn't about the money. However, Hull clearly enjoyed getting his revenge on Wirtz.

2. Sammy Sosa. Sosa's final act with the Cubs was typical of a player known for his me-first approach to the game. On the last day of the 2004 season, Cubs manager Dusty Baker told Sosa he wasn't going to play. However, instead of hanging with his team, Sosa left five minutes after the beginning of the game. Security cameras caught him on video.

Sosa's teammates had enough, and they (probably Kerry Wood) destroyed his signature boom box that had destroyed ears in the Cubs' clubhouse for years. Sosa and his fading act soon were sent to Baltimore.

1. Carlton Fisk. Fisk had been a noble warrior for the Sox. However, at age 46, the years finally caught up to him in 1993. On June 24, 1993, the Sox honored Fisk with his own night as he caught his 2,226th game, breaking the record for most games by a catcher. The good feelings, though, didn't last long. The next day, the Sox released Fisk. It was a huge slap in the face. To make matters even worse, he was denied entry to the Sox locker room when he tried to visit his old teammates during the 1993 playoffs. The messy ending ultimately resulted in Fisk choosing a Boston cap to be placed on his bust at Cooperstown.

The United Center Goes Better with Ice :: DM

I don't question basketball's popularity, especially when compared to hockey. While the Blackhawks have not won a Stanley Cup since 1961, the Bulls reeled off six titles in the '90s, when the United Center was the place to be in Chicago. But give me 1901 W. Madison when the hardwood floor has been removed. Here's why.

10. Hockey sounds. There is no auditory stimulus in sports more exhilarating than a player smashing an opponent into the boards at high speed. The puck crisply hitting the tape of a teammate's stick is music to my ears. The skates shooshing are far more delightful than high tops squeaking in a dead building.

9. The Buzz. Jim Carr, the voice of the Charlestown Chiefs in *Slap Shot*, said it best: "There is an air of expectancy here tonight." It is that way before a hockey game. Fans eagerly anticipate the beauty of the game. At a Bulls game, it is not a prerequisite for attendees to be in their seats before tip—they may be preoccupied by cutting a business deal or discussing what the Dow did earlier in the day. Not so when the puck is about to drop.

8. Less Nonsense. For most of us, the game is the reason to attend a sporting event. It is still that way with hockey games at the United Center. I do enjoy the shapely chick in tight jeans shooting the puck for prizes between the second and third periods, but the game is the attraction. At Bulls games, the sensory overload one experiences during timeouts is dizzying. Too many promotions and not enough action.

7. Introductions. Bulls fans would argue that the starting lineups announcement under the Alan Parsons Project tune "Eye in the Sky" remains one of the most thrilling traditions in Chicago sports. I say it is the most overdone and that it is terribly dated. Give me the three-minute video montage of bone-crushing hits, miraculous saves and breathtaking goals from the Hawks.

6. The Horn. Many cities have tried to replicate the classic horn that screeches when the Blackhawks score, but nothing compares to an original.

5. "Here Come the Hawks." Written by the great Dick Marks, this is by a landslide my favorite Chicago "fight song." "Blades flashin', sticks crashin', trying for the play. And the Blackhawks take control. There's a shot, and a goal." That's songwriting, mister. That really captures the spirit of the thing.

4. The Patrons. Loyal to a fault, Blackhawks fans past and present have a genuine love for the game. They don't attend because it's chic or to be seen. They usually respect each other, best evidenced by the "Wait until the whistle!" directive if any fan tries to scoot past others to his seat while the puck is in play. Nothing in Chicago sends chills down the spine more than a Hawks crowd when the team is playing well.

3. The Anthem. Some say that the cheering from the moment "The Star Spangled Banner" begins is disrespectful. I think it is exactly what Francis Scott Key had in mind when he penned our National Anthem. Before a game against the Red Wings, if you can't feel the hair on the back of your neck stand up during the final moments of The Anthem, you may as well put the other foot in the grave, too.

2. The Indian. The Indian the Blackhawks wear on their "sweaters" is the coolest logo in sports. In the winter of '08, then-head coach Denis Savard said of his players, "You have to commit to the Indian." I have. And the crossing tomahawks that adorn the shoulders on the Hawks jerseys are an awesome accent to the best jersey in sports.

1. It's hockey. If the two sports were drugs, hockey would be amphetamine. Basketball would be Ambien.

For generations, Bears fans worshipped at the altar of Sid Luckman, as in "The Bears haven't had a quarterback since Sid Luckman." Well, just who was Sid Luckman? He was the Bears quarterback from 1939-50. He was enshrined in the NFL Hall of Fame in 1965. After looking at his accomplishments, you'll agree the Bears haven't had another quarterback like him.

8. 73-0. Yes, Luckman was the Bears' quarterback for their famous 73-0 drubbing of Washington in the 1940 NFL title game. But the game got out of hand so early, and Luckman only threw six passes, completing four for 102 yards and a touchdown. In fact, the Bears used four quarterbacks in that game. Of course, everyone remembers Luckman.

7. Running game. Luckman was known for his passing, but his running ability helped the Bears win the 1946 NFL title game against the New York Giants. With the game tied 14-14 at the start of the fourth quarter, Luckman ran 19 yards for the go-ahead touchdown in the Bears' 24-14 victory.

6. T-formation. Remember the line in "Bear Down, Chicago Bears" about "thrilling the nation with your T-Formation"? Well, it probably doesn't happen without Luckman. Luckman proved to be adept in mastering the new complex offense in the 1940s that put more emphasis on the forward pass. Thanks to Luckman, the Bears' T-Formation kept them ahead of the curve during the 1940s, thrilling the nation in the process.

5. Bears loyalty. Luckman had a chance to make a windfall in 1946 when the All-America Football Conference offered him an unthinkable $25,000 to jump to the Chicago Rockets. Luckman declined, saying "How could I quit a club that has done so much for me?" Now *that's* loyalty, Bears fans.

4. Seven Touchdowns. On November 14, 1943, the native of Brooklyn was toasted with "Sid Luckman Appreciation Day" at the Polo Grounds for a Bears-New York Giants game. Luckman definitely appreciated the gesture, throwing for seven touchdown passes in a 56-7 victory over the Giants. The record has been equaled, but never broken.

3. MVP. Luckman had a huge year in 1943. He threw for what was then a league record 28 touchdowns during a 10-game season. His 13.9 percent touchdown rate (he threw 202 passes) remains an NFL record. He capped off the season by throwing five touchdown passes in the Bears' 41-21 victory over Washington in the NFL title game. Little wonder why Luckman was named the NFL's Most Valuable Player.

2. A winner. Luckman guided the Bears to NFL titles in 1940, 1941, 1943 and 1946. It doesn't get much better than that.

1. The record holder. It is a testament not only to Luckman's greatness, but also to the Bears' ineptness at quarterback that after all these years he still holds team records for passing yardage (14,685) and touchdown passes (137). Also keep in mind that Luckman played in an era long before the sophisticated passing offenses of today. He attempted only 1,744 passes for his entire career. That would be about 3½ years' worth of passes for a Peyton Manning. Yes, Luckman was that good. Sadly, we're still waiting for the second coming of Sid Luckman.

The Bears' disasters at quarterback are the stuff of legend. For the purpose of this list, we are examining the quarterbacks who came to the Bears with high expectations—i.e. high draft picks, major trades or free agent signings. Quarterbacks like Vince Evans and Bob Avellini were mid-round selections, and thus don't qualify here. Don't worry, we'll cover them elsewhere.

10. Gary Huff. Huff came to the Bears as a second-round pick in 1973. The Bears had some high hopes for Huff, who had a successful college career at Florida State. But in three years, the Bears won only five of the 22 games Huff started. In 1973, he threw only six touchdown passes and had 17 interceptions. So no, Huff wasn't the answer.

9. Mike Phipps. The Bears paid a high price to land Phipps, trading a first- and fourth-round pick to Cleveland in 1977. What exactly the Bears saw in Phipps isn't clear considering he had only one year with the Browns in which he threw for nine or more touchdowns. Phipps saw only one season of extended playing time with the Bears, when he threw for 1,525 yards in 12 starts. But he didn't do much more, and was waived by the Bears in 1981. Hardly worth the price.

8. Jim Harburgh. The Bears used their No. 1 pick on Harbaugh in 1987. He took over the bulk of the starting duties in 1990 and put up mostly mediocre numbers in four years. Perhaps the most memorable Harbaugh moment occurred when Ditka went ballistic on him during a game against Minnesota. Harbaugh moved on to Indianapolis in 1995 and was a Hail Mary pass away from leading the Colts to the Super Bowl.

7. Erik Kramer. Signed as a free agent from Detroit in 1994, Kramer actually gave the Bears a real quarterback in 1995 when he threw for nearly 4,000 yards and 29 touchdowns. Wow. What was that all about? But it didn't last, as Kramer was injured the following year and never was the same.

6. Jack Concannon. The Bears picked up Concannon from Philadelphia in 1967 in exchange for disgruntled tight end Mike Ditka. He could run a bit, showing some flashes in rushing for 279 yards for the Bears in 1967. But he got hurt in 1968 and never did much of anything for the Bears after that.

5. Kordell Stewart. The Bears thought "Slash" could be the answer when they signed him as a free agent in 2003. Stewart showed he could run and pass during a few up-and-down years with Pittsburgh. He didn't do much of either with the Bears, as they went 2-5 in seven Stewart starts. He didn't get another chance as the Bears slashed "Slash" in 2004.

4. Doug Flutie. He found himself in the center of one of the biggest Bears quarterback storms in team history. With McMahon out for the season in 1986, Ditka brought in Flutie, the former Heisman Trophy winner. The team revolted against the move, and the dissension showed when Flutie failed miserably in an upset loss to Washington in the playoffs. He was traded to New England the following year.

3. Rex Grossman. Few quarterbacks in Bears history have felt the wrath of Bears fans more than Grossman. Drafted in the first round out of Florida in 2003, Grossman was plagued by injury and then by inconsistency. Grossman could be great at times, but mostly was maddeningly terrible. He was the starting quarterback for the Bears in the Super Bowl, making him—along with Miami's David Woodley—perhaps the worst ever to be behind center in the big game.

2. Cade McNown. He came to the Bears with high hopes as a No. 1 pick out of UCLA in 1999. He left as one of the biggest jerks in Bears history, as he was disliked by virtually everybody. Jim McMahon was a jerk too, but at least he could play. McNown couldn't, and he was beyond a disaster in starting 15 games in two years with the team. The Bears finally had enough in 2001, trading him to San Francisco.

1. Rick Mirer. The former Domer was the all-time worst. It still is hard to believe that the Bears gave up a first-round pick (the 11th overall) to Seattle to acquire Mirer in 1997. Then again it was Dave Wannstedt who did the deal. Mirer was dreadful in seven starts, throwing six interceptions and no touchdown passes. Has there ever been a Bears quarterback who looked more lost in guiding the offense? Mirer didn't have a clue, and he was released in 1998.

No book about Chicago sports would be complete without a mention of the "players" who found themselves under center at kickoff and performed with memorable disrepute. When you think of all the nondescript mopes the Bears have trotted out at quarterback since 1980, these are the names that are invariably mentioned. Hard to believe that these guys actually started a game for the Bears.

8. Rusty Lisch. After injuries to Jim McMahon and Steve Fuller in 1984, the Bears were out of quarterbacks for a December game against Green Bay. Ditka had no choice but to start the former Notre Dame quarterback. Lisch, though, was dismal in defeat and Ditka never gave him another chance.

7. Greg Landry. Talk about desperation. After Lisch flopped, Ditka turned to Landry to start the season finale against Detroit in 1984. The former Lions quarterback was decent in his day, but it had been three years since the 38-year-old threw a pass. It didn't matter; with the Bears defense on that day, they pulled out a 30-13 victory.

6. Peter Tom Willis. Ah, yes, here's another wonderful name from the Bears' past. Willis had a decent college career at Florida State, and Bears fans thought he might be a good pro if only given the chance. Willis finally got it when he started two games at the end of the 1992 season. Turned out Peter Tom was a dud, and the Bears sputtered in losing both games.

5. Will Furrer. Furrer was another one of those quarterbacks who looked great in preseason games running the third-team offense against the third-team defense. But when Ditka gave him a chance to start the 1992 season finale, he failed miserably, completing only nine of 25 passes for 89 yards in a loss to Dallas.

4. Steve Stenstrom. Yes, Stenstrom would be the answer. He was endorsed by none other than Bill Walsh, who coached him at Stanford. If he was good enough for Walsh, certainly he would be good enough for the Bears. Alas, he wasn't. Pressed into service, he was 1-6 in seven starts for the Bears in 1998.

3. Moses Moreno. Things got so bad for the Bears in 1998 that coach Dave Wannstedt was forced to start Moreno in a November game against Tampa Bay. The Bears actually hung tough, only trailing 17-14 at the half. But it fell apart in the second half, as Moreno suffered a 31-17 defeat in his only start for the Bears.

2. Henry Burris. With Jim Miller and Chris Chandler out in 2002, coach Dick Jauron had to go with QB Burris to mop up the season. This was almost like using the shortstop to pitch the final two innings in an 18-2 blowout. He was 8 of 22 for 50 yards and a touchdown against Carolina, fumbling twice, and 7 of 19 for 78 yards and four interceptions against Tampa Bay. Those kinds of numbers produced a stunning 10.3 QB rating. Perhaps Jauron should have gone with the strong safety. He couldn't have done any worse.

1. Jonathan Quinn, Craig Krenzel and Chad Hutchinson. These guys have to go in as a combined entry. The situation at quarterback for the Bears never got worse than it did in 2004 when Rex Grossman blew out his knee in third game of the season.

First, the Bears went with Quinn, who hadn't thrown a pass in the two previous seasons. He showed why he rode the bench in losing three starts. Then it was Krenzel's turn. He completed only 45.6 percent of his passes in five starts. Finally, they gave the ball to Hutchinson. He actually excelled in his first game, throwing for three touchdown passes in a victory over Minnesota. But then he revealed his true colors and lost his next four starts. All three quarterbacks deservedly never played in another NFL game after the 2004 season.

Come to think about it, the results might have been the same had Grossman not gotten injured.

Beginning in the late 60s through 1989, the White Sox suffered through more than 20 years of having some of the worst uniforms not only in team history, but in the history of baseball—and quite possibly the history of professional sports, if not the history of uniforms from all walks of life! We are hardly fashion experts, but we know bad when we see it.

6. Losing socks: 1969-70. The Sox downhill uniform slide began in 1969. The team decided to get rid of the pinstripes. Not a good move. They also updated the Old English Sox logo. Then to get really wild, instead of using white sanitary socks, they went with a blue sanitary socks and a white stirrup. The uniforms weren't as bad as the others, but the team went 56-106 in 1970, its worst season ever. So they had to go.

5. The Einhorn cap: 1987-89. The Sox finally ditched the softball-looking uniforms they wore through most of the 80s. However, the new version was eminently dull and highly forgettable. It featured a drab White Sox logo across the front of the uniform and nothing else. However, the hat did cause some controversy. A curly capital "C" actually looked more like a lowercase "e." Some fans thought it stood for co-owner Eddie Einhorn.

4. Red Sox: 1971-75. Sox fans had been used to seeing the team in black or navy blue colors. So imagine the shock when they went to red! The home uniform featured red pinstripes, red stirrup socks, and Adidas three-stripe red shoes. The road unis, meanwhile, were powder blue with all red accents. All this red for a team named the White Sox seemed strangely out of place.

3. Softball: 1982-86. The team's new owners, Jerry Reinsdorf and Eddie Einhorn, wanted to make a splash with glitzy new uniforms. Instead, they concocted a disaster. The end result was the infamous softball uniforms. They featured a pullover shirt and pants with a waistband. Across the front was a red-white-and-blue strip that had S-O-X written on it. It was a shame that such a regal player like Carlton Fisk had to look like he was going out to play beer-league softball instead of professional baseball.

2. PJs: 1976-81. Talk about making a splash only to drown. Owner Bill Veeck really wanted to come up with something unique when he took over the team. Instead, this version of the Sox uniform was among the worst ever seen on a baseball diamond. The unis were derided as resembling pajamas since the shirt wasn't tucked in. They had a floppy collar that looked silly. The throw-back letters to the 1910s wasn't bad, but the all-blue road uniform looked hideous. All in all, a fashion disaster.

1. The shorts: August 8, 1976. Veeck had so many great innovations to liven up baseball. Having players wears short pants wasn't one of them. The Sox actually broke out the shorts for the first game of a doubleheader against Kansas City. They looked completely ridiculous. Really, did we have to see that much of Jim Spencer, the big, beefy first baseman? Thankfully, the Sox wore long pants for the second game. And the shorts never made it out of the closet again.

The Marketing Game :: by John McDonough

Note: John McDonough is unsurpassed in sports when it comes to putting fannies in the stands. Even though the Cubs hadn't won a World Series since the Roosevelt Administration (Theodore, that is), nary an empty seat could be found during McDonough's days at Wrigley Field from 1982 to 2007. The same now holds true at the United Center in his current role as president of the Blackhawks.

Here are McDonough's keys to marketing and being a successful executive in sports.

7. Hiring. The most underrated executive skill is hiring. Great leaders hire great people. They give them guidance and direction, and empower them to do things. That's critical.

6. Understanding the market. One of the advantages I have is that I'm from Chicago. I was born and raised in the city. I am a fan of all the teams. I understand the heartbeat of the fan. The city of Chicago is all about effort. How much effort does the owner put in to succeed? If fans believe you have a plan, they will buy into it.

5. Sell the experience. You have to recognize that every franchise has unique assets. With the Cubs, it was the ballpark; it was Harry Caray, an 80-year-old guy who was revered like Frank Sinatra at Madison Square Garden; it was the bleacher culture. The game is the ultimate social and team sports intersection. That makes every game an event, regardless if it's the Pirates in April or the Cardinals in July. You have to go with the approach that people are coming out for the first time. Make your television broadcast a 3½-hour commercial. Show the experience.

4. Sincerity. The fans have to believe you're sincere with what you're doing. When I took over as president of the Cubs, I said our goal is to win the World Series. I had to hear somebody say that in my lifetime. If the fan base understands what you're trying to achieve, they will be with you. Then—and this is important—you have to back it up.

3. Creativity. I'm not a fan of just thinking out of the box, I don't even want there to be a box. I don't want anybody to come into my office and say, "This is what they did in San Diego, in Philly." I want people to say this is what they did in Chicago. I would spend a lot of time at Wrigley Field on Saturdays in the off-season and challenge myself to come up with different approaches. Then I would say to the staff, "It's open season on me. Tell me why this is a bad idea." My goal is to try to do things that never have been done before.

2. Keep pushing. Never be satisfied for one minute. My own personal mantra is "never enough." You can never win enough championships; you can never draw enough people; your TV ratings can never be high enough; the fan experience can never be good enough. It's tough to expect success if you don't demand success. Inspect what you expect.

1. People. Although we're in the business of sports, ultimately we're all in the "people business." You have to develop strong relationships every day. You have to be engaging. I'm a conversationalist. To generate dialogue, I find it important to ask people about themselves. You can't teach warmth. Personality is going to take you further than anything. If you don't have great people skills, it is going to be difficult to succeed in any business or marketing role.

The most glaring missing tradition is a string of championship banners that stretches from Evanston to Oak Lawn. But, given our seemingly inherent masochistic needs, many other traditions have developed in an effort to "enhance" our sports experience. They are not all good ones. And we need to be cleansed of many of them.

10. "The Chicken Dance." Those of us who attend a lot of Blackhawks games have noticed a marked decrease in the number of spins this silly wedding song ritual gets. I'm including this one, however, so it stays that way. If we never hear "The Chicken Dance" again at a Hawks game, it will be too soon.

9. "Southpaw." I'm not a big fan of mascots anyway, but this fuzzy, non-descript White Sox mascot gives me the creeps. The Sockos do enough to make the park the friendliest in town for young fans. They have the fundamentals deck where kids can burn a little energy. The ballpark has a vast array of delicious treats. On a Sunday get-away matinee, youngsters are allowed to run the bases after the game. The peculiar Southpaw adds nothing to my White Sox experience but bad dreams.

8. Opening Day radio broadcasts in Wrigleyville. Where is it written that every Chicago radio station must broadcast morning and afternoon drive programming near manic Wrigley Field? Even the FM rockers feel the need to put a live microphone in front of intoxicated 22-year-olds at 8:00 in the morning. Lots of woofing. Lots of idiots screaming and predicting great things for a franchise that hasn't sniffed a championship in more than 100 years. I have hosted at least a dozen of these silly affairs in several Clark St. establishments. We could have produced a more quality product broadcasting from a prison riot.

7. "Na Na Na Na . . . Na Na Na Na . . . Hey Hey Hey . . . Goodbye." Many White Sox fans must agree on this one because seldom do they even engage in the taunting anthem chant inspired by a garage band called "Steam." It did very little for me even as a teenage fan. I expect the White Sox lineup to bash in the brains of opposing pitchers. Their dejected walks back to the dugout need no fanfare.

6. The Matadors. If this obnoxious Bulls marketing department gimmick possessed more tenure, it would appear much higher on the list. As if it's not been tough enough on Bulls fans who've endured the post-Jordan era. For several years, timeouts mean Bulls patrons have been treated to hairy, unattractive, fat asses who are willing to jiggle their manmeat in front of 23,000 already disengaged fans. Hideous. Let's hope when the Bulls matter again, somebody in the front office recognizes this is not a positive way to present our awesome city to the world.

5. "And there's a time out." "Where?" "On the field." I have no idea when or why Bears fans began this hideous ritual, but it isn't funny anymore. If it ever was funny. Soldier Field can be an electric, hairs-standing-up-on-the-neck experience, but it doesn't need this audience participation gag to accomplish it. We also can blame the PA announcers who still feel the need to pause between "time out" and "on the field." What's the point?

4. Guest conductors for the 7th Inning Stretch. Anybody who would dispute what Harry Caray did for the boom in popularity of the Cubs, Wrigley Field or the neighborhood in the 80s doesn't know jack shit. "Take Me Out to the Ballgame" meant something when the Mayor of Rush St. did it—a tradition he also employed when he broadcast White Sox games in the early 70s. But the Cubs dropped the ball when they continued the tradition with guest singers after Caray's death in '98. From high school athletes to B-list celebrities to a plethora of intoxicated former Bears and Blackhawks, it's a tradition that needs to go. Unoriginal and predictably mundane.

3. Bulls introductions. It's long past time to deep-six the no-longer-dramatic Alan Parsons Project song "Eye in the Sky." The dimming of the lights, the whirling spotlights, the P.A. man who belts "Aaaand now . . . the starting lineup for YOUR Chicago Bulls!" The only tradition worth keeping is a winning one. When this was a part of the Bulls' 90s run, they were winning. Hoisting the Larry O'Brien trophy was a rite of spring; Grant Park celebrations every June were cool. When the Bulls next appear in the Eastern Conference Finals, they should resurrect the tradition. Until then, I'm tuning in only after tip.

2. Throwing back opponents' home runs. Cubs killer Carlos Lee, in whichever uniform he's wearing this year, will deliver another tater deep into the left field bleachers to give his team the lead. I already hear delirious Wrigleyians cheering in delight after the barley-malted boob who caught the ball fires it back onto the outfield grass. Isn't that kind of tantamount to calling a bully a name after he punches you in the nose?

1. Calling the name of a quarterback or a running back with the first pick in the draft. Clearly this Bears staple has had more to do with the franchise's retardation than any other Bears habit. Cade McNown. Curtis Enis. Rex Grossman. Cedric Benson. Stop it. Let's hope Jay Cutler ends this tradition for the next 10-12 years.

I must begin by noting that Vince Lloyd, the pride and joy of Sioux Falls, S.D., possessed a big voice in the Cubs radio booth and developed a tremendous chemistry with the original "Good Kid," Hall of Famer Lou Boudreau. We all loved Vinnie in the 60s and early 70s. But with five teams in town, the competition is fierce when it comes to this list. So Vince gets an honorable mention. Here are the top 10.

10. Len Kasper, Cubs. Hippest broadcaster ever in Chicago. He speaks music and Christopher Guest movies with the best of them. More importantly, he has warmth and brings out the best in his analyst, Bob Brenly. Kasper wasn't the Cubs' first choice in '05; ESPN's Dave O'Brien was. The network's refusal to let O'Brien out of a deal resulted in a great hire by the Cubs.

9. Joe McConnell, Bears. Great pipes. Crisp, vivid radio descriptions. McConnell's last year in the Bears' booth was '84, when he majestically described Walter Payton breaking Jim Brown's all-time rushing record. McConnell is still at it as the voice of Purdue football.

8. Hawk Harrelson (when flanked by colorman Tom Paciorek), White Sox. Ultimate White Sox fan. Barbecues umpires when they screw the Sox. Great storyteller, especially tales from his Red Sox days in the 60s. A bit too much "mindset of the players" approach, but a great listen and his partnership with Paciorek in the 90s was like peanut butter and jelly.

7. Jim Durham, Bulls. Did both radio and television for the Bulls and was an integral part of the Bulls' culture for almost two decades. His final season was the Bulls' first championship in '91. Unfortunately, J.D. lost perspective and overplayed his hand, via dopey agent Darcy Bozeous, wanting Marv Albert money, and was not renewed, affording Chicago native Tom Dore (tallest announcer in Chi-Town history) his big break.

6. John Rooney, White Sox. "It's a GONER!" Like Durham, Rooney's final season was when the Sox copped the title in '05. Roons possesses a great baseball mind and was adept at extracting the best out of analyst and former Sox closer Ed Farmer. In the World Series clincher in Houston, Rooney invited me to sit down next to him as he described the 8th inning. Farmer slid down to the Sox dugout for immediate postgame reaction. A great thrill for me. Rooney now does St. Louis Cardinals broadcasts.

5. Pat Foley, Blackhawks. As synonymous with the team as any Chicago broadcaster. Foley is the master of the over-excited three-syllable name: "BAAAN-

ERRR-MANNNN!" Pat is as strong in the third period as he is in the first. One of the first things John McDonough did when he was appointed Hawks president in '07 was ensure that Foley returned after stupidly being exiled late in the Bill Wirtz administration. The Michigan State Spartan is sharp at every turn and a great tavernmate.

4. Jack Brickhouse, White Sox, Bears, Cubs. Brick was the first to encourage me to pursue my dream when I was writing him letters (likely in crayon) when I was a kid. The consummate homer. "Any old kind of a run will do it." Legendary party animal. Coined the phrase, "The Friendly Confines" for Wrigley Field. Fantastic storyteller. He lived a full life, but that didn't preclude me from weeping when he passed in August of '98.

3. Lloyd Pettit, Blackhawks. Huge presence. Pettit was Foley's hero when Pat was a kid. He was a hero to many of us, whom he tucked into bed with a transistor radio on Sunday nights in an era when Hawks home games weren't televised locally. Loved his catch phrase: "There's a shot [from the gut] AND A GOAL!" Pettit deservedly was inducted in the hockey Hall of Fame in 1986. A Wisconsin native, he purchased the minor league Milwaukee Admirals following his hallowed days in the Hawks' booth.

2. Wayne Larrivee, Bears, Bulls. The hardest working man in broadcasting. Typical weekend is a Bulls game on a Friday night, then off to Iowa City for a Hawkeyes game on the Big Ten Network, then off to the Packers' Sunday date. Some Bears fans won't forgive Wayne-O for defecting to the enemy in '99. Nobody need apologize for fulfilling a lifelong dream. Delivers more words per minute than any broadcaster in history. Say this in 12 seconds: "Receivers draped to the right and left sides. Now McKinnon comes in motion, near side. I-formation backfield, Suhey the fullback, Payton the tail of the tandem. Give right side to Payton. Bounces off one tackle, veers right side. Now gets tangled up with Stills in the secondary near the Bears sideline and gets rubbed out of bounds in [growling] RUDE FASHION, but enough to pick up the first down just past the 39 yard-line where the Bears will have it first and ten with six minutes and twenty-two seconds left to play in the fourth quarter." Nobody ever painted a better picture on the radio than Larrivee.

1. Harry Caray, White Sox, Cubs. Nobody sold more tickets or more beer, be it Falstaff or Budweiser, than the Mayor of Rush Street. His early 70s work with Jimmy Piersall on Sox TV was brutally honest and invariably entertaining. Caray wasn't the teddy bear everybody thought he was. He could be a mean drunk, but Harry was a man's man (or was it a Bud man?). Never shy about dishing out harsh criticism, but clearly wore the colors of the team for which he broadcast. "I hope we get loaded tonight!" was his declaration when the Cubs post-game show emanated from the visiting clubhouse in Pittsburgh after the Cubs clinched in '84. His stroke in '87 diminished his skills, but nobody cared. He was Harry, a man of the people who preferred broadcasting shirtless from the bleachers. "He might be . . . he could be . . . HE WAS!" the most influential voice, the most well-received voice, in Chicago sports history.

My Least Favorite Announcers and Analysts :: ES

Yes, Chicago has been blessed with some great talent in the booth. But we've also had our share of clunkers too. Here's our list of the not-so-easy listening.

9. Josh Lewin. Lewin is on this list as more of a victim than anything else. The Northwestern grad landed his dream job when the Cubs hired him to call road games in 1997 after Harry Caray had cut back on his travel. It turned out Caray had no use for Lewin, who he viewed as a possible successor for his job. So he froze out Lewin.

In Steve Stone's book, *Where's Harry*, he recounts how Lewin did everything possible to get in Caray's good graces. Once after Lewin's grandmother died, he thanked Caray for giving her so much pleasure from the broadcast booth.

Quoting Stone's book, "With that, Lewin stopped, took a breath and waited for some sort of condolence or acknowledgement. Harry, who to this point hadn't even looked up from his scorebook, stopped writing, threw down his pen, leaned back in his chair and looked out onto the field—without so much as a gaze in Lewin's direction.

"'Yeah, Levine,' Harry said to Lewin, 'all my fans are dying.' Harry went back to filling out his scorebook, and Josh turned around and left the booth."

Little wonder why Lewin lasted only one season with the Cubs.

8. Del Crandell. Crandell was an All-Star catcher for the Milwaukee Braves and one of nicest guys you would ever want to meet. But those traits didn't serve him well in the White Sox radio booth during the mid-80s. He was a dull analyst calling games for a dull team.

7. Chip Caray. During my tenure as the media reporter for the *Tribune*, I got scores of emails complaining about Caray. I actually thought Harry's grandson was passable, especially compared to what you hear in other markets. However, he was following Harry, and he had to be excellent. He wasn't. Chip was woefully prone to making overstatements. He seemed to have a knack for shouting, "Swung on, belted!" for medium flies. Many fans just couldn't handle his act. He made the right career move in leaving town after the 2004 season.

6. Lou Brock. Brock was an exciting, riveting player to watch during a Hall of Fame career with the Cardinals. However, he was terrible during his one season with the Sox in 1981 when he joined Caray and Piersall in the broadcast booth. Traded by the Cubs before he became great, it seems Chicago never got to see or hear the best from Brock.

5. Early Wynn. As was the case with Brock, just because you were a Hall of Famer as a player doesn't mean you'll sound like a Hall of Famer in the booth. Wynn spent two years with Joe McConnell (now there's a name from the past) in the Sox radio booth in 1982-83. "Ole Gus" didn't offer much, and his country twang didn't work in Chicago.

4. Mary Shane. This is one of Bill Veeck's experiments that didn't work. In 1977, Veeck thought the time was right to bring a woman announcer into the booth. He went up to Milwaukee and tabbed Shane, placing her alongside Harry Caray, Jimmy Piersall, and Lorn Brown. Shane was woefully out of place. I have one vintage Caray clip describing the winning run scoring during a Sox victory. In the background, you could hear Shane screaming. It just didn't sound right and the experiment lasted only a year.

3. J.C. Martin. Martin was another country act who had a short stay in Chicago. The former Sox and New York Mets journeyman catcher actually worked the 1975 season with Caray in the Sox television booth. Talk about a mismatch.

2. Gary Bender. It would have been difficult for any announcer to fill the shoes left by Wayne Larrivee when he left in 1998. Bender, though, wasn't even close. Bender was a former network play-by-play man when the Bears hired him. He had no connection to the team. As hard as he tried to do the home-team call, it just wasn't a good fit. Mercifully, he was let go after just two years.

1. Joe Carter. It would be hard to top the dreadful two-year tenure Carter had doing WGN games for the Cubs. He was brought in to replace Steve Stone when he left the Cubs for the first time in 1999. On the surface, it seemed like a good hire. Carter had been a popular and well-spoken star. But he offered nothing in the way of insights as an analyst. Most of the time he just repeated what happened. He also delivered one of the most famous goofs of all time. Carter asked former Bears quarterback Jim McMahon during a Cubs broadcast how his relationship with Pete Rozelle is now. McMahon reminded Carter that Rozelle had been dead for about five years. Ouch.

The Chicago airwaves have been filled with some of the best broadcast teams of all time. Often they were better and more entertaining than the teams they covered on the field. Here are the best of the best.

11. Jeff Joniak-Tom Thayer. I've always been a big fan of Thayer. He offers a clear, concise view of the Bears games on radio. Often, I find myself learning from Thayer, and to me that's the ultimate measure of a true analyst. Joniak also knows the game. You'll be hard-pressed to find another play-by-play voice who spends more time in the film room. Together, they've meshed, giving listeners a complete broadcast.

10. Jack Brickhouse-Lloyd Pettit. Pettit was known more for his work on the Blackhawks, but during the 1960s he teamed with Brickhouse on Cubs and White Sox games on Channel 9. Talk about a play-by-play clinic. Back then, baseball fans were blessed by having two legends in the booth.

9. John Rooney-Ed Farmer. The duo did radio for Sox games for 14 years. The well-prepared Rooney always delivered a solid call. While Farmer could ramble off on strange tangents, there is little doubt about his passion for the Sox. They appeared to be set for an even longer run, but Rooney left the Sox for the Cardinals. However, the pair went out in style, as their last game was the Sox's World Series clincher in 2005.

8. Jim Durham-Johnny Kerr. Kerr had many fine partners during his 30 years behind the microphone with the Bulls, but most would agree his pairing with the superb Durham left the most lasting impression. Perhaps the main reason was they were on the call during the mid-80s when Michael Jordan and the Bulls were becoming more than just another basketball team. Nobody will forget Durham's classic description of Jordan hitting the winner against Cleveland with Kerr going crazy in the background.

7. Pat Foley-Dale Tallon. It was the Pat-and-Dale show for nearly two decades on Blackhawks television and radio. The pair was immensely popular with Hawks fans. Just how big were they? Well, you know you're big when you've got your own bobblehead dolls.

6. Ken Harrelson-Tom Paciorek. "Hawk and Wimpy" were huge during the 1990s for the Sox. They were "homers" in every sense of the word, taking the concept to a new level. While it turned off some casual viewers, if you were a Sox fan, you relished in their enthusiasm. The pairing was split when Paciorek was let go after the 1999 season. To this day, the reasons for Paciorek's ouster remain murky.

5. Pat Hughes-Ron Santo. Not only is Hughes a great play-by-play man, he also is one of the best straight men in the business. He is perfect in bringing out all the good stuff from Santo. It can get goofy at times, and if you're looking for a conventional broadcast, Hughes and Santo aren't for you. However, plenty of Cubs fans like their version.

4. Jack Brickhouse-Irv Kupcinet. For more than two decades, the pair called Bears games on radio. Again, they hardly delivered a classic broadcast. Kupcinet's analysis consisted mostly of "That's right Jack" and sounding like he would fall out of the booth on a winning touchdown. However, as time passes, you seem to forget all the imperfections and recall a simpler time when "Brick and Kup" were it for the Bears.

3. Vince Lloyd-Lou Boudreau. A generation of Cubs fans grew up with Vince and Lou (a.k.a. "the Good Kid") during the 1960s and 70s. Lloyd was a terrific play-by-play man, and Boudreau added the analysis. They were a familiar and comfortable listen, seemingly woven into the fabric of the Cubs.

2. Harry Caray-Steve Stone. They seemed to be an unlikely pair; a fun-loving but aging veteran with a young, recently retired pitcher. But Caray and Stone worked. Stone was adept at playing off Caray and Caray knew how to play the game too. Caray always complained on the air about Stone's cigar smoke in the booth. Off the air, Stone once asked Caray if he really hated his cigars. Caray said no, but he knew it made a great running gag.

1. Harry Caray-Jimmy Piersall. They only were together for five years with Sox from 1977-81, but there never has been a more colorful, boisterous and brutally frank home team announcing duo in sports. Caray was crazy fun and Piersall was off-the-wall. As a result, they delivered a take-no-prisoners broadcast. The pair was too much for new owners Jerry Reinsdorf and Eddie Einhorn, and they were split in 1981. They truly were unique. In this day and age of careful marketing, it's highly unlikely you will see another tandem like Caray and Piersall again.

Dick Allen won't go down as the White Sox's greatest player, but he enjoyed perhaps the greatest season in team history in 1972. Acquired from the Los Angeles Dodgers in an off-season trade, Allen led the league with 37 homers and 113 RBI. Wielding his trademark 40-ounce bat, he was named the American League MVP, rejuvenating the franchise in the process. Here are some of the most memorable moments from the summer of '72.

8. Opening-day blast. A players' strike delayed the opening of the season, and Allen came in completely cold after missing all of spring training. It didn't matter. With the Sox trailing 1-0 in the ninth inning against Kansas City, Allen smashed a dramatic homer to tie the game. Even though the Sox would go on to lose 2-1, a star was born in Chicago.

7. Walk this way. By August, Allen had established himself as the most feared hitter in the league. The Oakland A's weren't about to let Allen beat them. In a riveting 19-inning affair, the A's walked Allen five times in eight at-bats, twice intentionally. The strategy paid off as Oakland pulled out a 5-3 victory.

6. Seeing stars. The California Angels got their fill of Allen during a two-game stretch on May 20 and 21. Allen collected a homer and four RBI in an 8-0 victory and then came back the following night with a homer and three RBI in a 9-8 triumph. It was a stunning display for Sox fans, who were used to seeing a pitter-pat offense for years.

5. Game-ender. Allen's first big homer came on April 26 against Cleveland. He had been held hitless through four at bats, but with a runner on in the 10th, Allen ended the game with a two-run homer to complete a 7-5 victory. It wouldn't be his last dramatic homer during the season.

4. Smokin'. It had been more than five years since a White Sox player appeared on the cover of *Sports Illustrated*, but in June of that year, Allen's torrid play landed him there. However, the photo wasn't an ordinary baseball shot. Instead, it showed Allen in the dugout juggling three balls with a cigarette hanging from his mouth. As always, Allen had to be different.

3. Reaching Caray. On August 23, Harry Caray, who was in his first year in Chicago, ventured out to call a game in the centerfield bleachers at old Comiskey Park. Caray carried his trademark net in the hopes of landing a homer. However, he didn't figure to get any action since it required a cannon to clear the 20-foot wall that was 445 feet away from home plate. Turns out Allen had a cannon in the form of his 40-ounce bat. In the seventh inning against the Yankees, Allen hit a shot off Lindy McDaniel right at Caray. Caray's net just missed snagging the ball. A stunned Caray shouted, "Nobody has ever hit a ball any farther."

2. Watch Dick run. Not only did Allen have breathtaking power, he was something to behold on the bases. Nobody, it seemed, was quicker from first to third. Allen received quite a workout on July 31 in a game at Metropolitan Stadium in Minnesota. Aided by large power alleys and a misplay by Twins centerfielder Bobby Darwin, Allen had not one, but two inside-the-park homers in an 8-1 Sox victory. At the time, he became only the second player in modern history to achieve the feat.

1. A true nightcap. On June 4, the Sox attracted nearly 52,000 fans for a Bat Day doubleheader against the Yankees. After winning the first game, manager Chuck Tanner sat Allen for the second game. Tanner, though, needed him when the Sox trailed 4-2 with two outs and two on in the ninth inning against Sparky Lyle. Allen didn't look like he was ready to play, as he emerged from the dugout without the red t-shirt that he normally wore under his uniform top. It probably is best not to speculate on his condition since he was known to tip a few back in the day.

Regardless, Allen tore into a Lyle pitch and hit a three-run, game-winning blast that has to go down as one of the most memorable homers in team history. Phil Rizzuto, calling the game for Yankees radio, yelled out, "Oh, he creamed one." He certainly did.

Where to begin when it comes to remembering Walter Payton's greatest games? Even when he didn't put up the big numbers, he still did something to make an impact. However, some definitely were better than others. Here's our list.

9. Bears at Pittsburgh, October 19, 1975. Why would we include a game that Payton missed because of an injury? The reason: He never missed another one, and it was because of this game. Bears coach Jack Pardee kept Payton out because of a sore ankle. Payton was livid about it back then, and still was upset over missing the game when he retired. "If you're ready to play and the coach won't let you, is that a missed game?" Payton said later. He lived up to his vow of never missing another game.

8. Bears at Seattle, December 5, 1976. Payton broke out during his second season, and this game proved to be his biggest to date. He rushed for 183 yards on 27 carries in the Bears' 34-7 rout of Seattle. He would go on to lead the NFC in rushing that season with 1,390 yards.

7. New Orleans at Bears, September 14, 1980. Payton only carried the ball 18 times in the Bears' 22-3 victory, which was low for him. However, he made the most of those carries, rushing for 183 yards. The capper came on a 69-yard touchdown run in the fourth quarter.

6. Bears at Dallas, November 26, 1981. Payton put on a Thanksgiving Day show in a losing effort against the Cowboys. He ran for 179 yards on 38 carries. Payton's one-man effort wasn't enough as the Bears went down 10-9. The difference: a missed extra point by the Bears.

5. St. Louis at Bears, December 16, 1979. The Bears came into the game needing to beat St. Louis by 34 points to make the playoffs. Payton almost collected all those points by himself. He scored three touchdowns while rushing for 157 yards. The Bears covered, beating the Cardinals 42-6 to advance to the postseason.

4. Bears at Washington, December 30, 1984. It took Payton 10 seasons to be on a team that won a playoff game, but it finally happened in a 23-19 victory against the Redskins. Payton's versatility was on full display. Not only did he rush for 104 yards, he also threw a 19-yard touchdown pass to tight end Pat Dunsmore. The victory helped set the tone for the Bears' 1985 season.

3. New Orleans at Bears, October 7, 1984. Payton rushed for 154 yards in a Bears victory. However, what made this game significant was his 6-yard run in third quarter to break Jim Brown's rushing record. In Chicago, the game was overshadowed by the Cubs' heartbreaking loss to San Diego in Game 5 of the playoffs. However, Payton received his due when President Ronald Reagan called to congratulate him. "The check's in the mail," Payton joked.

2. Bears at Green Bay, November 3, 1985. I was at this game, and what Payton did against the Packers still is my most vivid memory of him. It was a brutally hard-hitting game, as the Packers decided they were going to try to cheap-shot their way to victory. But it was Payton who landed the crowning blow. He put the team on his back in rushing for 192 yards. He scored the winning touchdown in the fourth quarter when he ran over Packer linebacker Brian Noble. After the 16-10 victory, Mike Ditka said, "I thought Payton's exhibition was maybe as good as I've ever seen a guy with a football under his arm play." Ditka won't get an argument from me.

1. Minnesota at Bears, November 20, 1977. This is the other game fans remember the most about Payton. He torched Minnesota for 275 yards on 40 carries in the Bears' 10-7 victory. Payton's single-game rushing record stood for nearly 23 years. And he did it against the Vikings, which had one of the top defenses in the league. After the game Vikings cornerback Bobby Bryant said, "It's similar to trying to rope a calf. It's hard enough to get your hands on him, and once you do, you wonder if you should have."

After watching film of his performance, Payton said, "I noticed on certain plays I should have got more yardage." Typical Walter.

The Sweetest Bear :: by Dan Jiggetts

Note: Dan Jiggetts spent seven years opening holes for Walter Payton as an offensive lineman for the Bears from 1976-82. Jiggetts lists what made Payton great as a football player, teammate and person.

9. Prankster. That was a big part of his personality. He knew how to lighten up and have some fun, which was most of his life. He would do something at practice to loosen everyone up. He was so much fun to be around.

8. Humility. After his first 1,000-yard rushing season, he bought watches for all the offensive lineman. He knew he couldn't do it without his guys. He understood you were working for him, and that you were making him better. We knew he was definitely making us looking better.

7. Speed. Walter wasn't the fastest guy on the field, but he was fast enough. That's why he developed that little kick step when he got near the end zone. He knew that's where a guy would try to catch you by the knees and ankles. I used to tell him it was because his legs were so short.

6. Improviser. His whole life was an improvisation. That's when he had the most fun, when he was just out there running. Remember the Dallas play [in 1977 when Payton ran around for about 20 seconds for a highlight-reel no-gain]? He would come into the huddle, and he'd be smiling. He was like a kid playing tag, only to the 10th power. It was a blast to watch him.

5. Durability. He only missed one game in his career. People banged on him every game. You'd see him early in the week, and he'd be really stiff. He'd been in a bad mood on Monday or Tuesday, but by Wednesday or Thursday, he'd come around. He'd start messing with people. Then you knew he was going to be available on Sunday.

4. Finisher. Walter would finish off a run. That's where that whole phrase began: finish the run. He would finish it two ways. If you didn't put a hand on him, he would take it the distance. Then if you did lay a hand on him, he was going to make sure he got the best shot. He would explode into a tackler. He always said, "I'm going to hit them harder than they hit me."

3. Work Ethic. He used to run his hill in Arlington Heights, but every now and then he would run a ravine run with us [by the lake front]. You'd do two of those things and you would be ready to throw up. It was like a 45-degree incline. Here comes Walter, and he does about 10 of them. Everyone was like, "Just go home." That exemplified his work ethic. When you'd see him run for 275 yards in a football game, you weren't surprised.

2. Confidence. He was supremely confident. You don't get to be as good as he was without having a high degree of confidence. He wasn't cocky or bragging. He just knew what he could do. He knew his talents, he knew the preparation was there, and that desire definitely was there. It all came together.

1. Heart. We knew his heart would never give out on him. There are some guys who rise up during the difficult times, and become an even better player. Walter was one of them. When it got to be the toughest, that's when he was the best. He was the first one out the door coming after you. He was the entire package.

I don't define "overrated" as something that's flat out bad; it's just an object that garners more love and affection than it really deserves. In Chicago, one of the greatest cities in the world, there is plenty to enjoy. Some of the trademarks here, however, just aren't worthy of the tons of praise that get heaped upon them.

10. Buckingham Fountain. There is no denying that the Northeast side of Grant Park is more aesthetically pleasing because of Buck's presence, but come on. In daylight, the fountain is just a glorified, high-powered lawn sprinkler. Still, hundreds of thousands of Chicagoans consider Buckingham Fountain to be one of the city's most treasured jewels. I say it ain't.

9. WGN Television, the not-so-SuperStation. We all grew up watching it. 'GN used to be home to some of the greatest children's television programming in the world. Programs such as *Ray Raynor*, *Garfield Goose*, and *Family Classics* enriched our young lives, but what has good ol' Channel 9 done for us lately? When Tribune Broadcasting and Warner group sank their teeth into WGN-TV, they communicated the message that the nation is more important than the local audience that made it. Plus, the Channel 9 News is as vanilla as the day is long.

8. Beef sandwiches. Good comfort food, no doubt. I like mine covered with hot giardiniera. And I have a favorite joint, which may defeat my argument that the beef sammy is overrated. That would be Mr. Beef on Orleans St. Once every year or two I run down there for this little treat. Upon arrival, it invariably occurs to me, "This is good, but it's just a beef sandwich."

7. Lincoln Park Zoo. Can't hold a candle to Brookfield Zoo. I suppose for city kids it's a place to go see what a polar bear or a monkey looks like when it isn't on television. To me, it's a humane society on steroids.

6. The Picasso sculpture. Maybe I'm just not one with an appreciation for art because to me, it looks like something we could have created at my fantasy football draft. Even with the qualifier, it is incomprehensible how the Picasso is slapped on postcards designed to define a great city. Show a stalled 'El' train or a chubby copper in mid-donut. That's Chicago.

5. Wrigley Field. See page 163.

4. One Magnificent Mile. Gucci. Louis Vuitton. All of the world's most renown designers camp out on the North end of Michigan Ave. in Chicago's so-called "Gold Coast." The only thing magnificent I experience there is slipping out the door after avoiding dropping three grand on a handbag for my wife.

3. Navy Pier. It looks cool on television, especially all lit up at night. It plays host to the 4th of July and New Year's Eve fireworks spectaculars, and everybody likes an air show. Fact is, almost nobody I know actually uses Navy Pier, which has a smattering of shops and restaurants and a small convention center. But if somebody asks you where they can catch a spin on a Ferris wheel, tell 'em Navy Pier is their spot.

2. Deep Dish Pizza. I don't know who is responsible for attempting to turn pizza into lasagna, but it wasn't a good idea. The Giordano's stuffed special is the most appealing of this mutated species, primarily because it holds together well enough to eat like pizza was supposed to be eaten—with your hands.

1. Taste of Chicago. An annual near-4th of July pig fuck. "The Taste" creates terrible traffic problems around Grant Park. There are a few cheesy amusement park rides, but you can catch those when the carnies hit a suburban church parking lot every summer. The bands usually are not top shelf. Still, hundreds of thousands come every year to stand in long lines in steamy weather to get an over-priced barbequed turkey leg. We have great restaurants in Chicago. Call me crazy, but I think the best place to enjoy a fine restaurant is inside of it.

Because Chicago is such an international city, it is easy to take for granted the things we use or see every day. In some cases, there is so much to do here, nobody talks much about some of these relatively undiscovered gems.

10. United Center neighborhood. When I first started driving to the Chicago Stadium, it was understood that the doors be locked and you keep your head on a swivel. Nothing but hookers, purse-snatchers and other deviants used to work Madison Street. Shortly after the United Center replaced the Stadium, however, renovations took place everywhere. Now, there are classy townhouses and condos that surround the West Side and there are many restaurants and bars where Bulls and Blackhawks fans can go to get a good bite to eat and a pre- or post-game beverage.

9. John G. Shedd Aquarium. I'm a long-time fresh and salt water aquarium enthusiast. And I've been to many of these facilities around the country. The Shedd is a great place to kill a day. It features thousands of species, a coral reef with several diver feedings each day and a Sea World-quality dolphin show. It also is most reasonably priced for a family and there is ample parking. This decidedly beats a day at the Museum of Science and Industry or the Planetarium.

8. Greek Town. Get me in a cab and drop me at Halsted and Madison now! Rodititys, the Parthenon and the Greek Islands restaurants are my favorites. All feature huge portions of delicious Greek food and all are fairly priced. I can smell the souvlaki plate just thinking about it.

7. Northwestern football experience. Because the Bears are so big, Northwestern football doesn't get much play in our town. Ryan Field, however, offers outstanding tailgating space (my favorite is on the far north end, adjacent to the baseball field). The stadium is small by Big 10 standards, which means there isn't a bad seat in the house. And tickets are easily accessible at a modest price. Plus, since '95 the Wildcats have produced damn good football teams.

6. Edison Park neighborhood. Located in the upper reaches of Chicago's northwest side, Edison Park offers several fine restaurants and bars in what is arguably the safest neighborhood in town. Many city employees—like cops—live there and intend to keep it that way.

5. Lake Michigan fishing. If you haven't seen the skyline from a mile out on Lake Michigan, you're missing out on one of the finest scenic delights Chicago has to offer. There are outstanding, easily accessible harbors off Belmont Ave. and downtown at Monroe and Burnham. Charter boat service is available from early spring to late fall and the king salmon fishing on the lake has been spectacular for the past dozen years or so. Perch fishing in the harbors also is popular and makes for an inexpensive and tasty meal opportunity.

4. Aurelio's Pizza. Those of us who grew up south of Chicago proper grew up on Aurelio's. The original store was in Homewood and that south suburb still boasts the Mother of All Aurelio's. It's pizza the way it was meant to be: thin crust, pure pork sausage, a snappy tomato sauce and tantalizing sweet green peppers. Strangely, Aurelio's has only one downtown location. I bet they felt it just wouldn't be fair to the other pizzerias if they infiltrated the city. Get an Aurelio's pie soon. "Tell 'em Joe sent ya."

3. Tap water. Ever take a drink from your hotel sink in Phoenix? Brutal. Big towns like New York, Boston or Houston are no bargain, either. We're very lucky in Chicago to have the best damn tap water in the nation. Clear and clean. Best when served chilled.

2. The expressway system. I hear people complaining all the time about the CTA. The only public transportation I use has wings. We have an awesome express-way system in Chicago and there are alternative routes one can explore in the event of construction or accident congestion. I love blasting in-bound on the Stevenson to the city after playing one of my favorite west-suburban golf courses. The new 355 is amaz-ing asphalt, connecting people from as far south as Route 80 near Joliet to Woodfield Mall in Schaumburg. From downtown, I can sail to the casinos in Northwest Indiana on the Chicago Skyway in just minutes.

1. Public golf courses. It's odd to me we don't get many PGA events here and when we do, they seem to be at the snobbish private clubs. Nothing against the good people at Olympia Fields, where Jim Furyk won the '03 U.S. Open, but Seven Bridges in Woodridge is as nice a track as you will find anywhere without an ocean. Bolingbrook Golf Club is exceptional and boasts one of the largest, most beautiful clubhouses in the country. From Milwaukee to Merrillville, Chicagoland is blessed with some of the best public golf courses in the nation.

If there's one thing Chicago owners have shown over the years, it is their ability to pinch a penny. As a result, many big-name athletes left town because ownership wouldn't ante up to keep them.

9. Jeremy Roenick. Roenick was a star almost from the minute he joined the Hawks in 1988. He had back-to-back 50-goal seasons in 1991-92 and 1992-93. He was the focal point of the franchise. However, faced with the prospect of losing him to free agency, the Hawks dealt the center to Phoenix after the 1996 season. They received Alexei Zhamnov, who was a bust.

8. Bill Madlock. Madlock looked to be the Cubs third baseman for years to come when they acquired him from Texas. He won two straight batting titles in 1975 and 1976. However, the Cubs wanted no part in paying him what he was worth. Said owner P.K. Wrigley: "When these players are impossible to deal with, I'd rather let somebody else have them." So the Cubs shipped the batting champ to San Francisco, getting an aging Bobby Murcer in return. Madlock would go on to win two more batting titles for Pittsburgh.

7. Richie Zisk. The Sox acquired Zisk from Pittsburgh after the 1976 season for Rich Gossage and Terry Forster. Zisk delivered, as he hit 30 homers to help power the "South Side Hitmen" to a memorable season in 1977. However, owner Bill Veeck was going with his "Rent-A-Player" approach back then and Zisk went on to sign a free agent contract with Texas.

6. Bucky Dent and Oscar Gamble. These two players are twinned. Dent was an All-Star shortstop with the Sox, but after the 1976 season, Veeck knew he wouldn't be able to sign him once he became a free agent. So the Sox sent Dent to the Yankees for a package that included Gamble. Gamble had a huge year for the Sox in 1977, hitting 31 homers. But like Zisk, he and his Afro were gone after the season. Gamble signed with San Diego.

5. Wilber Marshall. With his speed and power, Marshall was a game-changing linebacker for the Bears. Even as rookie, he was a key component in their 1985 Super Bowl team. After the 1987 season, Marshall decided to test the free agent waters. Back then, there wasn't much movement because teams had to pay a high price to sign a free agent. Washington, though, grabbed Marshall, giving the Bears the first-round picks in the next two drafts. The draft picks didn't compensate for losing Marshall. His departure marked a missing piece in the erosion of that great defense.

4. Horace Grant. Horace Grant was a vital cog in the Bulls' first three title runs. He was a strong rebounder and defender. After Jordan "retired" in 1993, Grant received some of the spotlight, earning an All-Star selection in 1994. But the Bulls decided against rewarding Grant for all his hard work. He was allowed to become a free agent after that season, eventually signing with Orlando.

3. Bruce Sutter. Sutter emerged as the best reliever in baseball with the Cubs. He won the Cy Young Award in 1979 and led the league in saves in 1980. Obviously, he was a valuable commodity for the Cubs. So what did the Cubs do? Instead of signing him to a big contract, they dealt him to St. Louis for Leon Durham and Ken Reitz. Sutter's plaque in Cooperstown depicts him wearing a Cardinals hat. It should have been a Cubs hat.

2. Bobby Hull. Hull was the town's biggest star in the 60s and early 70s. However, he never felt he was paid his true worth by the Hawks. When the new World Hockey Association started in 1972, they went after Hull. He eventually jumped for what was then an astounding $1.75 million. It was unthinkable that he ever would leave the Hawks, but he did.

1. Greg Maddux. Maddux won the Cy Young Award in 1992. Even though he was a free agent after the season, he wanted to stay with the Cubs. He even agreed to a 5-year, $25-million deal. However, the Cubs pulled it off the table after Tribune Company chairman Stanton Cook decided to get involved in the negotiations. Incredible. Things bogged down from there, and Maddux eventually signed with Atlanta. The pitching-starved Cubs then watched Maddux win three more Cy Young Awards with the Braves. The botched contract easily goes down as one of the low moments in Cubs history.

Note: Most people think Len Kasper has a dream job as the TV play-by-play voice of the Chicago Cubs. You know, he does. However, Kasper's other dream would be banging away in a rock band. Kasper is a well-known music buff, something he often talks about on the telecasts. Here are his favorite bands.

10. The Figgs. A very underrated rock band from New York. They've toured as Graham Parker's backing band and feature many Stones-inspired rockers. Plus, they're big baseball fans, which counts a lot with me.

9. The Dirtbombs. The name says it all. Mick Collins' Detroit-based band features two drummers, a bass player and a fuzz guitarist, giving the bottom end a booming sound. Collins plays guitar and sings lead in a band best described as garage rock meets Motown soul. Oh, and if you catch them live, don't leave early or you might miss one of the best encore covers ever, INXS's "Need You Tonight."

8. Secret Machines. I've never heard a power trio make as much noise as Secret Machines. I stumbled upon them at Lollapalooza a couple years ago and have been hooked since. Hard to pin down what they sound like, but there's some Led Zeppelin, Echo & The Bunnymen and Black Sabbath somewhere in there.

7. The Byrds. I could easily have put The Beatles and Stones on my list, but the one 60s band that still finds its way onto my iPod playlists to this day is The Byrds. They no doubt influenced most, if not all, the power pop bands I've grown to love. If for no other reason than that incredible, jangly 12-string Rickenbacker sound made famous by Roger McGuinn, I have to put them on the list.

6. Superdrag. Led by the ultra-talented John Davis, Superdrag made a splash in the mid-90s, then kind of faded away in the early part of this decade. But they reunited in 2007 and performed one of the most rocking shows I've ever witnessed at Metro in 2007. I'm counting the days until their new record comes out in the spring of 2009.

5. The Romantics. I've seen them live more than any other band. I've caught them in clubs, street festivals, a zoo, a greyhound racetrack, in front of a hotel pool in Florida, you name it. Why? Because in my opinion, they're the tightest and bluesiest rock band of the last 30 years.

4. DM3. Singer/guitarist Dom Mariani has been cranking out garage rock gems since the 1980s with bands like The Stems, Someloves and my favorite of his groups, DM3. Aside from Tommy Keene (#2 on my list), Mariani's song-crafting and guitar-playing skills are as consistently stellar as any power popper I've heard.

3. Wilco. I jumped on the Wilco bandwagon pretty late in the game, but the more I listen to them, the more layered and amazing their songs become. They've mellowed out a bit over their last couple records, which I really like, leading me to believe I'm getting old.

2. Tommy Keene. Tommy has been criminally overlooked throughout his long career. All he's done is write dozens of perfect rock songs for the past 20 years or so. Because of a mutual friend, Matt Hickey, I've been able to hang out with Tommy on a couple of occasions, which has honestly been as thrilling to me as meeting any baseball star.

1. The Replacements. The one regret in my life is not seeing them on their final tour. I was at Summerfest in Milwaukee and I really wanted to catch Roger McGuinn. I'm glad I saw McGuinn, but when it's all said and done, The Replacements' music has had a far greater impact on my life. They were just the coolest guys in the world. If I could be anyone else for a day, I'd love to be Paul Westerberg on stage.

Linebacker 101 :: by Dick Butkus

Note: Perhaps no other player personified his position more than Dick Butkus. The top college linebacker wins, what else, the "Butkus Award." The Bears legend played with such ferocity that players he battered still talk of being hit by him as if it were a badge of honor. Butkus offers his insights into what it takes to be a great linebacker. Listen up; he's only going to do this once.

6. Speed. Speed, of course, is important. But if speed is going to help you get out of the way then I don't think it's that important. Sometimes people use their speed to get out of the way instead of making the tackle. They chicken out. If you use speed the right way, it is a tremendous attribute. You've got to have speed.

5. Leadership. The linebacker needs to be a good leader. He's the quarterback of the defense. He is the one calling the signals. He is reading what the offense is doing. The other players have to be convinced that the guy knows what he's doing and that he's got his act together. They have to believe: "Hey, I'm going to follow that guy."

4. Instinct. This comes from the desire to put in the extra time to work at the game. So much time is needed to prepare. That's what makes your instincts better when you're out on the field. You have to watch hours of film and players to try to find a link to them telegraphing what the play is going to be. I don't know of any great player who didn't put in the amount of time that's necessary. I don't think anybody is physically that dominating that they could go into it cold.

3. Intelligence. There has to be some intelligence in there to go with instinct. Certain things are done on offense. You've got to be able to figure out why in order to help you with your instinct. You have to know all the situations. I studied a lot film. Back then, it was 16 mm. I still have the camera. I ripped it off from the Bears.

2. Toughness. You need the ability to continue with the drive and desire to get it done under difficult circumstances. You might be playing some big and better people, but the true greats don't quit. The regular guy will find a way to slough off. And indeed they do.

1. Desire. This is what it's all about. At linebacker, you need the desire to make the plays more so than any other position. You have to take the attitude that you've got to make the tackle. In order to do that, you have to have the desire to overcome a lot of things to make that happen. The desire to go beyond what normal people would do is where it's at.

While the Bears have struggled at quarterback, they have cornered the market at linebacker. It has been the defining position for the franchise, with one top linebacker following another, including the best who ever played the game. Here are the best of the best.

11. Lance Briggs. He doesn't always get his due because he works next to a superstar in Brian Urlacher. Opponents, though, are well aware of his presence. Working from sideline to sideline, Briggs always seems to be in on the stop. He had a season high 176 tackles for the Bears' 2006 Super Bowl team.

10. Larry Morris. He was one of the stalwarts of the Bears' 1963 NFL championship. Morris saved the best for last that year, being named the MVP of the title game against the New York Giants. His long interception return off of Hall of Famer Y.A. Title set up the Bears' first touchdown.

9. Otis Wilson. Known as "Mama's Boy," Wilson came into his own in 1985. Wilson was unleashed in the 46 defense, compiling 10.5 sacks that year and many other hurries. Opposing quarterbacks saw plenty of Wilson, and it wasn't a pretty picture.

8. Doug Buffone. He was overshadowed by playing on the same field with Dick Butkus, but Buffone was a solid performer in his own right. He holds the Bears' record with 24 career interceptions. He was a rock for 14 seasons, playing in 186 games—the third most in Bears history.

7. Clyde "Bulldog" Turner. Turner gained entry into the Hall of Fame largely because of his play at center. But he was also a top linebacker. A smart player with halfback speed for a big man, Turner led the league with eight interceptions in 1942. He also had an interception return for a touchdown in the 73-0 slaughter over Washington in 1940.

6. Joe Fortunato. He was also overshadowed in his day, playing on the same field as Bill George. Fortunato, though, was named to five Pro Bowls as a vicious hitter. He also had a knack for being around the football, as he recovered 22 fumbles.

5. George Connor. Connor started his career as a defensive tackle before he eventually made his mark at linebacker. Big, fast, and mobile, the former Notre Dame great had the ability to make all the plays. In the 1952 Pro Bowl, he had four straight plays in which he made a tackle for a loss; had a solo tackle; recorded a sack; and batted down a fourth-down pass. As usual, Connor was everywhere, including Canton, where he was inducted into the Hall of Fame in 1975.

4. Brian Urlacher. A safety in college, Urlacher was switched to middle linebacker in the pros. However, with his amazing speed for his size, he covers the ground like a safety. Few players in history have ever been able to close on a ball carrier like Urlacher. When his time comes, he will join the other Bears linebackers in the Hall of Fame.

3. Mike Singletary. Putting Singletary third gives you an indication of the strength of this list. A three-time defensive player of the year, "Samurai" was the leader of that great Bears defense in the 80s. The lasting image is of his eyes, virtually exploding out of his face as they darted around to survey the scene. The eyes personified Singletary's intensity, his greatest strength and ticket to the Hall of Fame.

2. Bill George. All George did was create the middle linebacker position, paving the way for Butkus, Singletary and Urlacher. George started his career as a middle guard on the line, but he eventually stepped back on passing situations. Then he just stayed there, becoming a dominating force at middle linebacker. *Sports Illustrated* once called him "the meanest Bear ever." Of course, that was before the No. 1 player on this list broke into the NFL.

1. Dick Butkus. He was big, fast, tough, mean, and perhaps even dirty. Butkus was all that and more as the best middle linebacker of all time. Green Bay running back Macarthur Lane once said, "I would prefer to go one-on-one with a grizzly bear." Butkus inflicted his share of punishment during his all-too-short nine-year career. He had a simple goal: "When they say All-Pro middle linebacker, I want them to say Butkus." They sure did.

Our city is steeped in a rich tradition of outstanding broadcast journalists, many of whom have gained national acclaim. As the mode by which people consume news has evolved, it's fun to reflect on those who presented news like pros long before the Internet was born.

5. Ron Magers. For more than a decade, Magers has been the top dog at WLS-TV, Channel 7. He filled a big chair in '98, succeeding the veteran John Drury. Magers' resignation from WMAQ-TV, Channel 5 followed that of co-anchor, Carol Marin. The tandem objected to the hiring of Jerry Springer as a news commentator. Their defections shifted the balance of power in the ratings for the 10 p.m. news. Magers and Marin owned the ratings between '81 and '97 and Channel 5 forever should regret allowing their departures. Magers, whose passion is raising horses (and betting on them) is a bit smug, but when he "looks at you" every weeknight, you buy whatever he's selling. He is decidedly the most credible broadcast journalist in Chicago today.

4. John Drury. Drury was as solid off the air as he was on it. In 1983, he was named Illinois Father of the Year. Lost his battle with ALS in November of '07. Drury's Chicago reign began on WBBM-TV, Channel 2, in '62. He was the great Fahey Flynn's first co-anchor when they teamed on Channel 7 between '67 and '70. The smooth, yet self-deprecating style of Drury moved to WGN-TV, Channel 9 in the early 70s, before he returned to WLS. In '96, John was enshrined in the Chicago Journalism Hall of Fame. He was named Illinois Broadcaster of the Year in '02. John was a terrific reporter and created an "every man's man" approach. A very comfortable watch.

3. Floyd Kalber. "The Big Tuna" began his broadcast career in his hometown of Omaha, NE, before joining WBBM, Channel 2 in the early 60s. Like most television or radio talents, his tour included many stops. He also worked for WLS, Channel 7, before '60 finding a bigger opportunity at NBC-owned WMAQ. Between '76 and '81, the smooth Kalber hosted *NBC Today* with Tom Brokaw and Jane Pauley. His cherry on the sundae was his return to Channel 7, where he enjoyed a long run ('84-'98) as lead anchor on the 6:00 p.m. news. Kalber passed in May, '04 at the age of 79.

2. Fahey Flynn. This is a guy who won six Emmys. He was the man to whom Chicagoans looked most for their news for more than 40 years. On Channel 7, Flynn and co-anchor Joel Daly were the city's most watched, most credible 1-2 punch. Ever. Flynn was 67 and still working when he fell ill and died in August of '83. Said *Sun-Times* veteran media critic Robert Feder: "Flynn was an avuncular Irishman with a jaunty bow tie and a twinkle in his eye." The bow tie was a Flynn signature. That and "How do you do, ladies and gentlemen? I'm Fahey Flynn." A Michigan native, Flynn arrived in Chicago in the early television news era of the late 50s.

1. Bill Kurtis. Born to read the teleprompter. Booming, rich voice. Handsome. Smooth as a gravy sandwich. Tremendous presence. Kurtis graduated from the University of Kansas in '62, then went on to pass the bar exam, but chose journalism over law. It was a good move. He joined WBBM-TV Channel 2 as a reporter in '66, but Kurtis quickly ascended up the ladder. In '82, he was plucked by the network to anchor *The CBS Morning News*. Kurtis now has the freedom (and capital) to pick and choose his assignments. He hosts and narrates for A&E's *Cold Case Files* and *American Justice*. Kurtis has invested in raising and harvesting grass-fed beef in his native Kansas. When the producers and director went looking for a credible, polarizing voice to narrate the movie *Anchorman*, they found the right guy in Kurtis. Just like Will Ferrell's character, Ron Burgundy, Bill Kurtis "was the balls."

The country's third-largest television market always has been well stocked with attractive women with brains. All of our news babes here are well educated and have won Emmys. But you don't care about that. Be honest. When you're alone at home for the 10:00 news, your mind wanders from deadly fires, City Council decisions and elections. When these kittens purr before the teleprompter, you're somewhere else. Chances are excellent our bevy of beauties were in your thoughts when you first discovered your penchant for self-service.

5. Joan Esposito. Likely would compete in the Senior Division if we were to bracket a Chicago news "Babe Off" in '09. The Joan was an early-to-mid-80s darling before her mysterious departure from WLS-TV, Channel 7. She hasn't surfaced on local television in years. Her reputation as a "free spirit" escalated as her career evolved. Joan's second husband's death in 1994 was an alleged suicide at the couple's Michigan vacation home, though rumors of foul play swirled. Originally a WGN-TV Channel 9 reporter before stopping at WMAQ-TV Channel 9, the dark-eyed, dark-haired, playful Esposito was regarded as a solid health beat/medical reporter. She played herself in the awful '91 Chicago-produced film *Backdraft* and made a similar cameo in *Cheaters* in '00.

4. Deborah Norville. Also starring today on the Senior Circuit, Norville was every young man's dream in the early-to-late 80s on Channel 5. She had a girl-next-door presence. Fair complected with deep blue eyes and plump, rosy red lips. Born a Georgia Peach in '58, Delightful Deb graduated summa cum laude from UG. Chicago couldn't hang onto her, however, and the blonde bombshell split for the network when NBC's *Today* show fingered her as Jane Pauley's successor in the fall of '89. Oddly, ratings sank and Norville was blamed. I'm saying the smug Bryant Gumbel was most responsible. Deb later worked national gigs such as *CBS Evening News*, *Street Stories* and *Inside Edition*.

3. Allison Payne. Allie has been on the mend after a series of mini-strokes in January of '08 sidelined her from the WGN 9 o'clock news. All of us are rooting for her healthy, happy return on a full-time basis. She's a sweet person, not to mention much easier on the eyes than the slightly fleshy Micah Materre. The angular, slinky Payne was born in Richmond, Va., but was reared in Detroit. She graduated magna cum laude from the University of Detroit before earning her Masters from Bowling Green in Ohio. Payne, 45, joined Channel 9 in '90, following stops in Saginaw and Toledo. Allie is a light-skinned African American who possesses striking facial features, with classically high cheek bones, meticulously well-buffed eyebrows and supple lips that accent her million dollar smile. Come back, girl!

2. Anna Davlantes. Oopa! The slender-but-busty Davlantes looks better in a baseball cap than any girl you ever have seen. Brains before beauty, however. Lovely Anna was educated at Oxford and graduated from Northwestern's Medill School of Journalism. Colloquially, some media refer to said grads as "Medilldos." Anna has to be the hottest Medilldo ever. Despite Davlantes' enormous appeal among men, Channel 5 hasn't green-lighted her graduation to the 10 o'clock anchor chair. Instead, the sweet matriarch Alison Rosati rides the venerable Warner Saunders' sidecar. Perhaps that's the biggest reason NBC5 still can't make a run at ABC7 in the battle for evening ratings. In '05, the sassy Greek tantalized viewers in what is believed to be the first underwater live shot in primetime news history. Davlantes slipped into a wet suit at the Shedd Aquarium in a story called "Swimming with Sharks." We all would like to see more of that.

1. Marion Brooks. Brooks is the bomb. Has been since she joined our city's NBC affiliate in '98 after doing Atlanta—as in former Atlanta mayor Bill Campbell. While the smoking Brooks and hubby Ruye Harkins were expecting the arrival of their first child, word broke of Campbell's scandalous activities. Included was a steamy, four-year affair with Brooks, who had "covered" the mayor for WSB-TV. Brooks took time off and Channel 5 gave her a mulligan for the indiscretion. Oh, did I forget to mention Miss Marion attended Spelman College and got a degree in English? She did. Because of her tight, light skin, many are unaware she is African American and is heavily involved with meaningful endeavors in the black community. Brooksy has an athletic build, streamlined by great legs. She sports a sassy smile and has soft, silky hair and kind of an exotic, girl-next-door appeal. I forgot to mention she's Canadian! Never imagined Canada could give the world something so beautiful that is unrelated to hockey or walleye fishing. Marion was born in Vancouver, but grew up in Portland, OR. Had she gone to Oregon State, she would have been one popular Beaver.

The Sutter Brothers :: ES

The Sutter brothers were hockey's most prolific family, as six of them played in the NHL. Five Sutters found their way to the Blackhawks at one point in their careers, and two served as head coach. Only Ron Sutter somehow managed to avoid making a stopover in Chicago during his 19 seasons. Perhaps Ron will still wind up here as a coach.

Here is a rundown of the Sutter brothers.

5. Rich Sutter. The right winger was journeyman, playing mostly for Philadelphia, Vancouver and St. Louis. He only played one full season for the Hawks, scoring 12 goals in 1993-94. He played in 15 games for the Hawks the following year before moving on to Tampa Bay.

4. Duane Sutter. Duane enjoyed his biggest years with the New York Islanders, winning four Stanley Cups. He was nicknamed "Dog" because he barked before and during games. However, his bark was mostly gone by the time the Hawks acquired him in 1987-88. He played his last three seasons with the Hawks, never scoring more than 7 goals.

3. Brian Sutter. Brian never laced up the skates for the Hawks. He played his entire career with St. Louis, scoring a career-high 46 goals in 1982-83. Brian, though, did work behind the Hawks' bench, serving three seasons as their coach. He had a big opening season with the Hawks in 2001-2002, guiding them to 41 victories and 96 points. But Brian's former team, the Blues, knocked out the Hawks in the first round. Brian missed the playoffs the next two years, and Dale Tallon fired him after the 2003-04 season.

2. Brent Sutter. Like brother Duane, he had his best years with the Islanders dynasty, recording 102 points in 1984-85. However, unlike Duane, he still had some gas left when he arrived with the Hawks. He scored 50 points on the Hawks team that went to the Stanley Cup Finals in 1991-92 and then followed it up with a 20-goal effort the next year. He played seven seasons with the Hawks.

1. Darryl Sutter. Darryl made his impact felt as a player and coach for the Blackhawks. The hardworking left-winger scored 161 goals in seven full seasons with some of the exciting Hawks teams in the 1980s. He had a career-high 40 goals in 1980-81. Then Darryl became coach in 1992-93. In his first season, the Hawks won 47 games, but they were knocked out in the first round. Darryl's team also departed after the first round the next year. Then midway through 1994-95, he stepped down with a 24-19-5 record to spend my time with his son Christopher, who had Down's Syndrome. Of all the Sutters, Darryl gave his best for Chicago.

Let's start in the early 90s because that's when sports radio mushroomed in Chicago. Chet Coppock (on the AM Loop) and Chuck Swirsky (on WGN) were drawing good audiences then and I was an original cast member of the Score (AM 820) when it launched on January 2, 1992. As a host, I've doubled over in pain from the regular battle cries about which listeners have flapped their gums in the last 20 years. As a consumer, I've broken four fingers (the same one twice) punching the button because of tired topics. I know that one of the most important functions of sports radio is giving Joe Fan a place to vent, but the redundancy—and sometimes lunacy—pains the ass far more than one can tolerate.

10. Move Zorich to linebacker. This has been dead for many years, but its legend lives whenever a host or a caller, in woofing Bears superfans voice, utters the question "Why don't da Bears move Zorich tuh linebaaaker?" Drafted by the Bill Tobin-Mike Ditka administration in '90, Chicago native Chris Zorich was an undersized, overachieving defensive tackle out of Notre Dame. He was a powerful man, but not an NFL difference maker on the nose. Because this town loved him, many thought he would be more productive as a "linebaaaker" than as a DT.

9. Pete Rose and the Baseball Hall of Fame. Thankfully, this debate largely has disappeared as we've moved into the 21st century. It isn't possible another point can be made that hasn't been made already. Yes, he deserves to be in Cooperstown because he is among baseball's best 10 players of all time. Anybody who would debate that is an idiot. And yes, he disgraced the game. He bet and he bet often. There were rules against it. He also lied about it. Nothing more needs to be said.

8. Reinsdorf bashing. One of a few good things that resulted from Jay Mariotti's resignation from the *Sun-Times* in the summer of '08 was that his irrelevant-to-the-topic swipes at Reinsdorf went away. Reinsdorf isn't warm. He isn't always honest. He created his share of the angst during his perceived break-up of the championship Bulls. Under his regime, however, the Bulls copped six NBA titles. The White Sox won a World Series. He was influential in building two great stadiums. He has been fiscally responsible. There are negatives, too, but often those who do the hammering of the chairman—be they media or spiteful fans—don't have a clue about what they're writing or saying.

7. 1985 Bears drama. I was an intern producer on the Bears flagship (WGN) when they were the Rolling Stones in shoulder pads. I can speak to their significance from experience. They galvanized Chicago more than any team ever did. It never will be eclipsed. But the nonsense that surrounds them—the in-fighting, their bitterness over winning just one championship, their basking in yesteryear by taking gigs in the media—enough already. It made for good radio when Mike Ditka and Dave Duerson berated each other over union/player pension issues on my ESPN show in the summer of '07, but the '85 Bears, in many ways, have gone about their post-'85 Bears lives like a bunch of jealous, petulant, gossipy old ladies. And this town's continuing need to use the '85 Bears as a reference point on how everything should be done also makes many of us want to put our heads in the oven.

6. No college football playoffs. There are only a few dissenting voices on the stupidity of the absence of a legitimate college football postseason. One is the *Tribune's* Teddy Greenstein, an otherwise bright and thoughtful college football scribe. The most prevailing wisdom is that the lack of a playoff system is just plain dumb. That's because it is. No debate where 99% of the opinion is on one side is a debate worth having in a public forum. We in sports radio might as well open it up for phone calls on topics like: "Should scientists continue to try to find a cure for cancer?" or "Do you oppose child abuse?"

5. "Cubs fans don't know baseball." The flipside of this one would be "Sox fans all live in trailer parks or in their parents' basements." Sweeping generalizations designed to inflict pain on the other side. Fan on Fan crime. It's repugnant. Who cares if casual fans, or maybe not even baseball fans at all, go to Wrigley Field to have a beer in the sun and look at girls? And because the Cell is on the South side, many ill-informed Cubs enthusiasts equate Sox fans to the poverty-stricken or "white trash." This discussion really vexes me. There are many upsides to life in a two-team city. Promulgating these stereotypes is not among them.

4. "Fire and passion." Many who follow sports confuse emotion for accomplishment. Testosterone needs to be blasting through the sky for many fans. These are the types who believe the Bears were World Champs in '85 because Mike Ditka wore his emotions on his sleeves. Fire-breathing, cursing, snot-bubbling athletes—not necessarily successful ones—are the only acceptable ones for this contingent of meatballs. I'd prefer Lovie Smith-speak on the Bears sideline. He may be the only coach in NFL history to go an entire game without speaking to an assistant coach or a player. But Smith wouldn't be any more effective if he whipped gum at fans or tore into media the way Iron Mike did. I only can hope Mike Singletary—who proved that Bears "woof woof" is still in his DNA in his first game as 49ers head coach—doesn't succeed too much in '09 because the mindless "fire and passion" callers will be taking over the airwaves.

3. Ron Santo and the Baseball Hall of Fame. I don't care to share with you my opinion on it and I don't care about yours. The Cubs have three members of the '69 chokesters (Ernie Banks, Billy Williams and Fergie Jenkins) already in the Hall. That's ample for a team that never made a postseason appearance. How about we make *that*—a World Series title—more an integral part of sports radio and barroom conversation on the Cubs? And why haven't Cubs fans, those who prefer the team's radio broadcast in English, make more of a fuss about Santo's inability to be a credible analyst? If you've seen Dick Clark on New Year's Eve the past handful of years, you've wanted to pull the covers up over your head like I have. At home, we have that luxury. We don't while driving down the highway listening to Santo sputter through e-mails from adoring listeners or not know the players on the field.

2. "The Cubs get more coverage than the White Sox." Whiny White Sox fans sound this battle cry every year. I even know of one green-with-envy Sox fan who literally takes out a pica ruler and measures the volume of ink devoted to the two clubs in all the papers. The truth is this: media reflect interest, they don't attempt to create it. If the White Sox are playing well or are interesting off the field, they will receive coverage. When the White Sox captured the championship in '05, this red-headed-stepchild syndrome should have disappeared because the Sox were everywhere. And the *Tribune*, which owned the Cubs at the time, covered the Sox with the same zeal as the *Sun-Times* or the periphery papers. I want as big an audience as possible in my afternoon drive slot. The topics discussed will be chosen based on the level of interest at that time. I assume my colleagues are smart enough to approach their content similarly.

1. White Sox attendance. You can count on a fraction of Cubs fans to roll this one out anytime the Sox are good. "Yeah, the Sox won their seventh in a row last night, but how come there were so many empty seats?" North side fans seem to revel in their annual "attendance trophy." Debate over the safety in the neighborhood (hideous), the lack of restaurants around the park (you can tailgate in the lots) and the park not being as nice as Wrigley wear out my ass. The neighborhood isn't a ghetto. The food inside is ter-rific. And they do serve alcohol inside the Cell. Should the Sox draw three million fans when they're a playoff team? Sure. But they don't. Maybe it's because Chicagoland just prefers the Wrigleyville neighborhood to Bridgeport. Enough said, already.

I recognize that athletes, coaches and front-office types are not actors or stand up comics. I get that. A little warmth and willingness, however, go a long way. It doesn't seem like too tall an order. Here are 10 guys who I hope never are on the other end of the phone when I'm on the radio.

10. Steve Larmer. "Gramps" was as consistent a performer as the Blackhawks ever had. Consistently mumbly and stumbly, however. The guy who holds the Hawks' record for consecutive games played also holds the high standard for dull.

9. Ryne Sandberg. Ryno pulled up a chair on my radio show right after two big things happened in his life: he was inducted into baseball's Hall of Fame and the Cubs announced they were retiring his jersey no. 23. The '84 N.L. MVP was, for the first time I can recall, engaging, warm, honest and even a little provocative. It will never get any better than that and I hope I never feel the need to have him on again. He finally appears comfortable in his own skin, but that doesn't excuse the more than 20 years of painfully mundane, monotone responses to very simple questions.

8. Jim Hendry. The Cubs general manager is accessible, but he invariably sounds like there is no place he'd rather be less than on the air. His quick, defensive responses to any reasonable questions make me want to put ice picks in my ears.

7. Jim McMahon. If the topics include hockey, golf, fishing or the joys of making art while sitting on the toilet, the punky QB is your guy. When the conversation moves to football, however, McMahon is as indifferent and withdrawn as the day is long. I can't wait to see him in a saloon or on a golf course soon. If he's on the radio or on television, however, it's time to run for the hills.

6. Ben Gordon. If you can understand him, you're a step up on me. Gordon is, perhaps as much as any local sports figure I've interviewed, the most indifferent. It's amazing to me that a player who has flirted with superstar status is so willing to present himself as such a stiff. He simply doesn't care how he's perceived.

5. Derrek Lee. The former N.L. batting champ and perennial Gold Glove first baseman seems like a decent guy. He is a very charitable sort. And those things add to the frustration of interviewing him. He's not a dumb guy, but as an interviewee, he is monotone and dull. Keep it.

4. Devin Hester. As exciting as Hester was during his first two years in a Bears uniform in '06 and '07, he is equally as uninteresting off the field. I don't suspect there's a guy who ever played for the Bears who struggles to make speech as much as Hester. Mercy.

3. Greg Maddux. His more than 300 wins do not translate into excitement when he speaks publicly. It's baffling to me how such a student of the game and seemingly bright guy can make for such dead weight whenever asked to discuss his craft. Maddux has what it takes to be a good interview, but chooses the alternative.

2. Jerry Reinsdorf. The chairman of the White Sox and Bulls is bright and has a sense of humor. You would never know that if you heard him on the radio. There, Reinsdorf is disengaged, defensive and evasive. He once told my colleagues on ESPN 1000, "You'll never get another bite of this apple," after they asked him a few questions about the Bulls when it was Opening Day at the Cell. I don't dislike Jerry Reinsdorf. I just don't want any conversations I may have with him to go public.

1. Lovie Smith. I did the obligatory welcome-to-Chicago interview with the Bears head coach shortly after he arrived. He was sitting right across from my showmates and I at a charity golf outing. Normally, face time enhances the chances at a connection. Before Smith removed his headset, I promised myself that no matter how many Super Bowls this guy may win, this would be the last time I tried to pull sentences out of his mouth. He is the most boring man who's ever been a ring leader in Chicago.

Several big-name players have swung through Chicago at the end of their careers. In most cases, we didn't get to see them at the height of their greatness.

13. George Gervin. The "Iceman" melted by the time he arrived to the Bulls for the 1985-86 season. A career 26.2 points per game scorer in the NBA, he averaged only 16.2 points per game for the Bulls. At age 33, it proved to be his final season.

12. Dizzy Dean. Ol' Diz pitched for the Cubs in 1938. Even though he had a sore arm, owner P.K. Wrigley paid $185,000, a huge sum back then, to acquire Dean from the Cardinals. Dean somehow managed to go 7-1 starts in helping the Cubs to the pennant. But he had nothing left, winning only 10 more games in the next three years with the Cubs.

11. Ralph Kiner. Kiner was one of the great sluggers in his era. However, embroiled in a salary dispute, Pittsburgh traded Kiner to the Cubs in June, 1953. Pirates general manager Branch Rickey got off when one of the all-time parting shots when he said to Kiner, "We finished last with you. We can finish last without you." Kiner didn't help the Cubs' fortunes in 1½ years with the Cubs and was shipped to Cleveland in 1955.

10. Bo Jackson. The Sox took a chance on Jackson and his artificial hip and had some positive results. He hit a dramatic opening day homer in his first at bat in 1993 and then clubbed a mile-hit blast in the division clincher that September. However, he was a bust in the playoffs, going 0 for 10. The Sox let him go after the season.

9. Jose Canseco. Canseco closed his career with the White Sox in 2001. He actually had decent numbers with 16 homers and 49 RBI in 76 games. The question: Was he on steroids while with the Sox? Who would be willing to bet against it?

8. Robert Parish. The Hall of Famer actually picked up a fourth championship ring with the Bulls during the 1996-97 season. But unlike the three previous titles he won with Boston, Parish, at age 43, played an insignificant role, appearing in only 43 regular-season games and two games in the playoffs.

7. Nate Thurmond. The Bulls thought Thurmond would be the center they needed to put them over the top when they acquired him from Golden State for the 1974-75 season. However at 33, he was on the downside of the hill, averaging only 7.9 points per game. The Bulls wound up losing to Golden State in the playoffs. Among the players who shined for the Warriors was Clifford Ray, the player the Bulls traded for Thurmond.

6. Rich Gossage. The White Sox got the Hall of Famer on the front end of his career, while the Cubs caught him on the back side. Gossage showed his vast potential with the Sox, making the American League All-Star team as a reliever in 1975. However, for some reason, they converted him into a starter in 1976 and he went 9-17. They traded him the following year to Pittsburgh, and he began his Hall of Fame run. By the time he returned to Chicago in 1988, he was 36 years old and past his prime. He managed only 13 saves that season and was let go by the Cubs in the spring of 1989.

5. Ken Griffey Jr. The slugger came to Chicago during mid-season in 2008 in search of that elusive World Series. He didn't find it here. Just a shadow of his former self, he hit only 3 homers during the last two months of the season.

4. Alan Page. Page was one of the great defensive players in history during an 11-year run with Minnesota. He still had a little left when he arrived with the Bears in 1978, registering 40 sacks during a four-year run. But he hardly was the same dominating player.

3. Steve Carlton. After being released by Philadelphia and San Francisco in 1986, Carlton, then 41, was so desperate to pitch, he hooked up with a team going nowhere in the Sox. Pitching mostly on fumes, he went 4-3 with a 4.35 earned run average. However, the player who never talked actually held a news conference when he joined the Sox. But that was it. He kept his mouth shut during the rest of his short stay.

2. Bobby Orr. Orr was one of the most exciting players to play in Chicago Stadium, or any arena. However, his knees were gone when the Hawks signed him as a free agent in 1976. He played in only 26 games during the next three seasons. However, he showed what kind of person he is by never cashing a check from the Hawks. He said he wouldn't accept a salary if he didn't play. A class act.

1. Tom Seaver. The Sox stunned the Mets when they claimed the 39-year-old Seaver in a free agent compensation draft in 1984. The Sox felt he would be the perfect addition to a high-powered rotation that won the American League West in 1983. While the plan didn't work out that way, Seaver did his part, winning 15 games in 1984 and 16 in 1985. His Sox highlight came with his 300th victory, a complete game against the Yankees in 1985.

Chicago has had its share of great players who never got a chance to achieve true stardom here. Be warned: It could a little depressing when you think of the talent that went elsewhere. Here's the rundown.

10. Rafael Palmeiro. Palmeiro looked to be only a good average hitter during his three-year stay with the Cubs. He hit only 6 homers. Thinking "Who needs a singles hitter?" the Cubs dealt him to Texas in 1989 in the trade that brought reliever Mitch Williams to Chicago. Palmeiro eventually found some power (did anybody say steroids?) and wound up hitting 569 career homers.

9. Denny McLain. McLain actually was on the White Sox 40-man roster in 1963. However, they failed to protect him and eventually Detroit eventually selected McLain in the waiver draft. McLain went on to win 31 games in 1968 and two Cy Young Awards for the Tigers. And here's a good trivia question: Who did the Sox protect? None other than pitcher Dave DeBusshere, who went on to be a star in basketball.

8. Bobby Bonilla. Bonilla actually made his Major League debut for the Sox in 1986. He had great size and definitely had the look of a power hitter. However, he hit only two homers in 75 games. In mid-season, then-general manager Ken Harrelson shipped Bonilla to Pittsburgh for pitcher Jose DeLeon. Bonilla went on to become a big star, joining Barry Bonds to form the 1-2 punch that led the Pirates to three straight National League East titles.

7. Norm Cash. Cash was a rookie first baseman for the Sox in 1959. After failing to win the World Series against the Dodgers, the Sox wanted to go for veterans in 1960. Cash was dealt to Cleveland in a deal that brought Minnie Minoso back to the Sox. A year later, Cash hit .361 for Detroit and wound up with 377 career homers.

6. Johnny Callison. See Cash above for the same reason on why the Sox got rid of Callison after the 1959 season. He hit only .173 as a 20-year-old for the Sox. So he was sent to Philadelphia for third baseman Gene Freese. Callison would go to be a four-time All-Star for the Phillies.

5. Joe Carter. Carter was a budding prospect for the Cubs in 1984. However, Cubs GM Dallas Green thought he needed to acquire a pitcher to put them over the top. So he shipped Carter in a package to Cleveland for Rick Sutcliffe. Sutcliffe delivered big time for the Cubs, winning the Cy Young Award in 1984, so there wasn't true buyer's remorse. But Carter did go to have a stellar career, hitting 396 career homers and driving in more than 100 runs in a season 10 times.

4. George Blanda. Blanda was a mediocre quarterback for the Bears during the 50s. In fact, he had only season in which he threw more than 300 passes with the Bears. The Bears didn't have any qualms when Blanda, at the age of 33, jumped to the Houston Oilers in the new American Football League in 1960. All he did was light it up for the Oilers and then the Raiders en route to a spot in the Hall of Fame.

3. Dominik Hasek. Hasek began his career with the Blackhawks in 1990. But he was stuck behind Ed Belfour and played in only 25 games in two years. In 1992, the Hawks traded Hasek to Buffalo, getting little in return. As a result, they watched Hasek become "The Dominator" for somebody else.

2. Phil Esposito. Esposito was a decent young player in three seasons with the Blackhawks. He scored 27 goals in the 1965-66 season. The Hawks, though, wanted to shake things up and traded Esposito, along with Ken Hodge and Fred Stanfield, to Boston in 1967. All Esposito did for the Bruins was camp out in front of the net and score goal after goal. In 1970-71, he put 76 pucks in the net, as he truly became one of the NHL's most dominant players.

1. Lou Brock. The all-time big one that got away from Chicago. Brock never hit higher than .263 in two-plus seasons with the Cubs. So they shipped him off to St. Louis in a mid-season trade for sore-armed pitcher Ernie Broglio in 1964. Brock would go on to hit .348 during the remainder of the 1964 season and never stop running for another 15 years. Brock-for-Broglio became a trade that would go down in Cubs infamy.

Supreme Fan :: by U.S. Supreme Court Justice John Paul Stevens

The Cubs have fans in high places, but few sit on a higher perch than longtime Supreme Court Justice John Paul Stevens. The native of Chicago shares his favorite memories of following the Cubs, which includes being on hand to witness Babe Ruth's famous "Called Shot." He also recalls representing legendary owner Charlie Finley as an attorney.

8. Radio waves. I grew up on the South Side [in the 1920s], but I became a Cubs fan. The Cubs were the really good team at the time, and the Sox were not. Obviously, there wasn't TV back then, so I listened on the radio to every game. Three stations carried the Cubs back then. I listened to Hal Totten on WMAQ. I got hooked.

7. Favorite early players. I guess I worshipped all of them. Kiki Cuyler was one of my heroes. Somebody told me I was a 19th cousin to him. He was fast. He stole a lot of bases. Riggs Stephenson was the most reliable hitter. Hack Wilson hit a lot of homers. That was a good team. That team went to [four World Series in a 10-year span], but they never won it all. Very disappointing. A tragedy.

6. First time. The first game I went to was Game 1 of the 1929 World Series [when Stevens was nine years old]. The Cubs played the Philadelphia Athletics. We had really good seats behind home plate. The Athletics had Lefty Grove and [George] Earnshaw, but [manager Connie] Mack started Howard Ehmke. He was thought to be a has-been. He threw a nothing ball up there. He struck out 13. My heroes struck out one after another. It was the saddest day of my life.

5. Charlie O. I represented Charlie Finley in connection with the A's move from Kansas City to Oakland. He was a character. A very interesting guy. He was totally honest. He had a bad temper and he did some dumb things from time to time. But his word was absolutely good. When he would tell somebody he was going to do something, he would do it. There were difficulties from time to time, but I enjoyed working with him.

4. Wrigley Field. It's a beautiful field. I always remembered the ivy being there. Basically, the ballpark looks the same. I could see how players could concentrate on the game and not have the crowd in mind. There's a universe you're concerned with, and it's that ball field.

3. Throwing out the first ball at a Cubs game in 2005. That was one of the major events of my life, I have to confess. I have a lot of grandchildren in Chicago. On that day, I was really a hero. When they suggested it to me, I went out to throw a little with my daughter. My arm was totally useless. I couldn't believe it. I realized had to throw it as if I was in right field trying to get somebody at the plate. I pitched it high and outside, but I got it there.

2. The "Called Shot." You wonder what really happened or is it the memory of your memories? I do have a clear recollection. We had good seats behind third base.

That was not Ruth's first homer that day. During the game, [Cubs pitcher] Guy Bush was razzing him. He and Ruth were in some kind of discussion back and forth. I do remember Bush came out of the dugout and engaging in a colloquy with him.

When Ruth was at the plate, my interpretation was that he was responding to what Bush was saying. He definitely took the bat in his hand and pointed it towards centerfield. My interpretation always was, "I'm going to knock you to the moon." That was a kid's reaction. He pointed and then hit the ball over the centerfield scoreboard. I don't know what his motivation was, but he definitely pointed. It was something.

There are a million people who say they were at that game. But I was definitely there. It's part of history.

1. On being a Cubs fan. My law clerks gave me [a Cubs bow tie] and I wore it at the Chicago Bar Association meeting. I'm very proud of it. The funny thing is, most of the people I shook hands with were Sox fans. But there were enough Cubs fans too.

Some years I haven't followed them closely. But I've followed them closely lately. I watch the games on WGN. It would be great to see them win the World Series after all these years.

Perhaps the biggest day of the football season is draft day. Score big with your selections in the spring and chances are you're on your way to victories in the fall. The Bears have had several strong draft classes, laying the foundations for their top teams. Here is a ranking of their best drafts dating back to 1965.

8. 2006. The Bears didn't have a first-round selection, but plenty of teams would have traded a No. 1 pick for the player they took in the second round: Devin Hester. The Bears' gamble on taking a return specialist paid off when Hester became their top weapon during a Super Bowl run. The Bears also scored with their fifth-round pick, Mark Anderson, who turned into an effective pass rusher as a rookie.

7. 2000. The top two picks gave the Bears the cornerstones of their defense for the next decade. They used their top choice on Brian Urlacher and their second-round pick on safety Mike Brown. Both players quickly became forces for the Bears. Too bad in Brown's case that he couldn't have stayed healthier.

6. 1985. There's little question that a series of solid drafts formed the core of the 1985 Super Bowl team. This class provided the finishing touch with the selection of No. 1 pick William Perry. The Super Bowl Shuffle wouldn't have been the same without "Fridge." The draft also produced the Bears best-ever kicker in Kevin Butler, a fourth-round pick, and a future starter, linebacker Jim Morrissey, who was taken in the 11th round.

5. 1984. The Bears lucked out when linebacker Wilber Marshall slipped to 11 in the first round. The Bears grabbed him, and by 1985 he was one of most lethal forces in the NFL. The draft also netted the Bears linebacker and future defensive coordinator Ron Rivera in the second round, and a bargain in safety Shaun Gayle, who was taken with a 10th-round pick.

4. 1981. The Bears' first two picks provided them with two key components to their Super Bowl team. They used their first-round selection on huge Keith Van Horne, who went on to become an anchor on the offensive line. However, they really scored with their second-round pick: a smallish linebacker from Baylor named Mike Singletary. All he would do was go to the Hall of Fame. The draft also produced all-pro safety Todd Bell with the fourth-round pick and safety and future Tennessee Titans coach Jeff Fisher in the seventh round.

3. 1983. You could make the argument that this was the Bears' greatest draft. It produced seven starters on the Bears' Super Bowl team two years later. The Bears had two first-round picks, selecting offensive tackle Jimbo Covert, who would have been a Hall of Famer with better health, and receiver Willie Gault. Starting cornerback Mike Richardson was taken in the second round, and safety Dave Duerson came the Bears' way in the third round. Offensive guard Tom Thayer was picked up in the fourth guard. Then there was the bonanza in the eighth round with the choices of defensive end Richard Dent, the 1985 Super Bowl MVP, and offensive guard Mark Bortz. Now that is a draft to remember.

2. 1975. Any draft that begins with taking Walter Payton with the fourth pick in the first round is a Grand Slam, even if you struck out with everyone else. However, this draft was deep in both quality and quantity. While Payton was taken with the No. 1 pick, the Bears found his longtime backfield mate with their 17th-round pick, Roland Harper. Sandwiched in between, the Bears landed starters in defensive tackle Mike Hartenstine (second round), defensive back Virgil Livers (third), offensive lineman Revie Sorey (fifth), quarterback Bob Avellini (sixth), and hard-hitting safety Doug Plank (12th).

1. 1965. With the third pick in the first round, the Bears selected Dick Butkus. Then they immediately grabbed Gale Sayers with the fourth pick. The Bears got two Hall of Fame, once-in-a-lifetime players at their positions in back-to-back picks. It has to be the best draft combo by one team in NFL history. This draft also produced receiver Dick Gordon in the seventh round. But it was the selections of Butkus and Sayers in the first round that made this draft one for the ages.

I was scanning a history of the Bears draft picks and was astounded to see an incredible litany of terrible Bears No. 1 drafts picks since 1991. Little wonder why Bears fans had so much anxiety over the draft in recent years. More often than not, the top pick ended in disaster. Here are the worst of the worst.

9. Rashaan Salaam. The Bears selected Salaam with the 21st pick in the 1995 draft. The Heisman Trophy winner actually had a decent rookie season, rushing for 1,074 and 10 touchdowns in 1995. Salaam, though, had trouble holding on to the ball and then was plagued by injury problems. Later, he admitted he was a habitual marijuana smoker during his three hazy years with the Bears. Gee, just what the Bears needed: a pot-smoking, fumbling, injury-prone running back.

8. Michael Haynes. The Bears used the 14th pick to select Haynes in the 2003 draft. The defensive end from Penn State obviously came in with high expectations. Trouble is, he couldn't get on the field. He simply wasn't good enough, making him the classic definition of a first-round bust. The Bears cut Haynes after the 2005 season.

7. John Thierry. The Bears took Thierry with the 11th pick in the 1994 draft. Thierry was a small-college linebacker that Coach Dave Wannstedt envisioned turning into a Charles Haley-like defensive end. Turns out it wasn't that easy. He had little impact, barely ever reaching the quarterback. After the 1998 season, the Bears thought so little of Thierry they let him go to Cleveland in the expansion draft.

6. David Terrell. The Bears used the eighth pick in the 2001 draft to take the wide receiver from Michigan. Like most receivers, Terrell liked to talk about his talents. Too bad Terrell never backed it up on the field. He was wildly inconsistent, as he managed to score only nine touchdowns in four years. The Bears decided they had enough, waiving him after the 2004 season.

5. Alonzo Spellman. The Bears drafted Spellman with the 22nd pick in the 1992 draft. Spellman actually had some bright spots, recording 23½ sacks during a three-year span. However, it all deteriorated after a shoulder injury forced him to miss the last nine games of the 1997 season. It turns out Spellman was diagnosed as being bipolar following a bizarre incident in the winter of 1998. The Bears released him shortly thereafter. A sad story.

4. Cedric Benson. The Bears selected Benson with the fourth pick in the 2005 draft, their highest selection since 1979 when they took Dan Hampton. The Bears hit the jackpot with Hampton. Not so much with Benson. On the field, Benson had injury problems and never flashed evidence that he would be a special back. Off the field, Benson got arrested twice during the spring of 2008. The Bears had enough and said bye-bye, permanently sealing the fate of another draft bust.

3. Curtis Enis. Randy Moss was on the draft board when the Bears selected Enis with the fifth pick in the 1998 draft. To be fair, plenty of other teams passed on Moss because of character issues. Well, it turns out Enis had his own character issues. He was a dog from the beginning, holding out of training camp. Then he reported out of shape. He blew out his ACL during the ninth game of the 1998 season and was out of football after the 2001 season at the age of 24.

2. Stan Thomas. The Bears selected the big offensive tackle from Texas with the 22nd pick in the 1991 draft over the objections of Mike Ditka. "I wanted nothing to do with Stan Thomas but the owner wanted him, and that's the way it was," Ditka said. The coach had questions about Thomas' character and work ethic. Turns out Ditka was right, as Thomas was pathetic, lasting only two years with the Bears.

1. Cade McNown. The Bears thought they were getting another Jim McMahon when they selected McNown with the 12th pick in the 1999 draft. McNown only resembled McMahon in that he was a jerk. Unfortunately, he didn't have a fraction of McMahon's talent. After holding out in training camp, McNown looked clueless when he finally got on the field. He went 1-6 as a starter in 1999. Things got worse from there, and McNown was shipped out of town after the 2000 season.

Because of our city's over-the-top affection for the Monsters of the Midway, it's difficult to imagine fielding a team of players who were underrated, but you could. Here are some guys who never gained the attention they deserved.

10. Mike Hartenstine, Defensive End. Overshadowed by the more-popular Wally Chambers, Hartenstine was a versatile defensive end. A second-round pick out of Penn State in '75, Hart was stout against the run and possessed above-average pass rushing skills. He was an integral part of the Bears defense that became the NFL's best in the mid-80s. Because of all the flashy, commercially successful Bears (William Perry comes to mind immediately), few even remember Hartenstine was a mainstay on the Bears' defensive line during the Super Bowl run.

9. Revie Sorey, Guard. One of the biggest falsehoods in Bears lore is that Walter Payton did it all on his own until "The Black and Bruise Brothers" arrived in the early- to mid-80s. Sorey was the best of the group that called itself "The Cosmic Rays." The fifth-round pick out of Illinois in '75 was terrific when he pulled and led the sweep. Sorey also has been one of the most community-oriented Bears of his era and remains active making life better for Chicagoland kids.

8. Mark Bortz, Guard. "Bortzilla" was an eighth-round selection in '83, from the same draft class that produced tackle Jimbo Covert, wide receiver Willie Gault, safety Dave Duerson and Super Bowl XX MVP Richard Dent. Bears personnel chief Bill Tobin saw Bortz when he was an Iowa Hawkeye defensive tackle and thought the Pardeeville, WI native would make a fine guard at the next level. Tobin was right.

7. Jim Morrissey, Linebacker. Affectionately referred to as "Judge Smails" by his teammates, Morrissey was an undersized 'backer who was a specialist covering backs in the flat. The 11th-round selection out of Michigan State struggled to keep his weight above 220, so he employed instincts and speed to earn an NFL check. Though he was recognized as the "Frito Lays Unsung Hero" of '85, Morrissey never garnered a fraction of the attention fellow LBs Mike Singletary, Otis Wilson and Wilber Marshall did. Holds the Bears record for longest INT return in Super Bowl play (47 yards). Also solid on special teams.

6. Wendell Davis, Wide Receiver. The second of a pair of first-round picks in '88, Davis was clutch on third down. Despite his scrawny physique, Davis wasn't shy about going inside to make the big play when the Bears offense needed it. The former LSU Tiger had his career truncated when he blew out both patella tendons on the crappy artificial turf in Philadelphia's Veterans Stadium, stretching for a pass that was overthrown by quarterback Jim Harbaugh.

5. Todd Berger, Guard. There were few highlights during the Dave Wannstedt Era. Under Wanny's direction, the Bears did win a playoff game on the road when they popped the Vikings on New Year's Day of '95. Raymont Harris had a big day for the Bears, whose offensive line was anchored by the feisty Berger, a likeable flake out of Penn State. Berg was as tough as nails and it was a mistake when the Bears let him get away. Biggest calves in Bears history.

4. Dennis McKinnon, Wide Receiver/Punt Returner. "Silky D." Authored the most exciting punt return in Bears history when he took one 94 yards for a score in the Monday Night Football season lid-lifter against the defending champion Giants in '87. McKinnon's 127 career returns are the most in team history. Gault was the deep threat on the Super Bowl Bears; McKinnon was the football player. Silky D was as interested in planting a defensive back down field as he was making catches. The Florida State alum arguably was, pound-for-pound, the Bears' toughest player in the modern era.

3. Donnell Woolford, Cornerback. The first-round pick out of Clemson was thrown right into the fire as a rookie in '89, a nightmarish 6-10 season that followed an NFC title game appearance the previous January. "Woody" was vertically challenged at 5'9" or so, but was a tremendous open-field tackler. Woolford screwed himself a few times from an image standpoint, like the time he tried to bribe a police officer with Bears tickets after being pulled over on suspicion for DUI, but Woolford was a gritty player who never got the recognition he deserved.

2. Walt Harris, Cornerback. Football fans regularly forget the best DBs are assigned to the best WRs. And in the NFL, big-time receivers make plays. Harris, for whom the Bears traded up in the first round in the '96 draft, was a scrappy, lanky cover corner with good closing speed and excellent jumping ability. He got beat for big plays sometimes, but that happens in pro football. My question for Bears fans who regularly bashed Harris is this: If he were so God awful, how is it he's still earning an NFL payday 13 seasons after the Bears drafted him out of Mississippi State?

1. Neal Anderson, Running Back. Biggest mistake: following Payton. A first-rounder out of Florida in '86, Anderson proved he was tough by busting his ass on special teams as a rookie. More than any Bear, Anderson never got the credit he deserved. The guy went to four Pro Bowls. He rushed for more than 6,100 yards and scored 71 TDs in his injury-abbreviated NFL career. The shelf life for a pro running back is a short one and Anderson probably should have quit sooner than he did. At the end, he was looking for a place to fall down and some of us remember Wannstedt's ill-fated idea to make Anderson a wideout. The other side of that coin is that Mike Ditka probably should have gone to Anderson earlier in his career because Payton was just hanging on in '86 and, more noticeably, in '87. Neal Anderson was a monster. Bears fans should pay homage to him more appropriately.

In Chicago, outstanding disc jockeys always have been plentiful. I must note that this collection of air talent is exclusively for those whose primary focus is, or was, the music. Steve Dahl, Johnny B. and many others have played songs, but the success of their shows was predicated on their personalities. These are the air talents whose personal touch added to the music, not got in the way of it.

Most Honorably Mentioned, Dick Biondi. Born in Endicott, N.Y. in '39, Biondi is the old war horse of Windy City jocks. His 21-year run on oldies format WJMK is a testament to both his talent and popularity. When 'JMK scrapped its format in '05, he split for "True Oldies" WZZN. Biondi's energy, passion and charitable endeavors were the recipe for his induction into the Radio Hall of Fame in '98. Biondi is believed to be the first disc jockey to play the Beatles on American radio, when he spun "Please, Please Me" in '63. He first hit the air in Chicago in '60 on WLS, before splitting for Los Angeles. Biondi returned in '67 and was a staple at "Super 'CFL" until '73.

5. John "Records" Landecker. Records joined the very popular Top 40 WLS AM 890 in '72. The Michigan State alumnus enjoyed a nice run there, unleashing popular segments "Boogie Check" and "Americana Panorama." After a short stint in Toronto, Landecker returned to Chicago in '84 for a stop at The Loop, 97.9 FM, before circling back to 'LS. A very approachable guy with an encyclopedia-like mind for music, Landecker enjoyed a long, successful run doing morning drive on WJMK between '93 and '03. He now hosts "Into the Seventies," a nationally syndicated weekend program.

4. Frank E. Lee. It's rare when station management and talent find a way to co-exist for as long as Lee's marriage has lasted with WXRT, 93.1 FM. He's been there so long the 'XRT website doesn't really track his bio—he's been with them since he cut his broadcast teeth in El Paso in the early 80s. In case you didn't know, it's Frank "E with a period" Lee. For decades, Chicagoans eagerly have awaited his show's commencement, when "The Lee-ettes" proclaim, "One, two, three. Here comes Mr. Lee." Frank is an awesome guy whose cool approach complements the music. Example, backselling one of my favorite reggae songs like this: "Bob Marley and the Wailers asking the musical question 'Is this love?'"

3. Patti Haze. "The First Lady of Rock and Roll." Patti has been a role model for female disc jockeys across the country for decades. Her husky, sultry voice (okay, cigarettes may have been involved) was her calling card. The Haze did stints at WMET, The Loop and WCKG before taking her show on the road and moving to Florida several years ago. She always smelled nice.

2. Bobby Skafish. Rob S. was as responsible as anybody for helping put a willing-to-go-non-mainstream WXRT on the map in the late 70s and early 80s. Bobby did two stints on the Belmont Avenue station, with a long run at The Loop ('83-'93) in between. Today, you can hear Skafish in afternoons on WDRV, 97.1 FM. He is a fellow Northwest Indiana kid, who attended Gavit High School before Indiana University. Bobby is just cool. Whether it's a "Daddy-O" or a "Thank Jah it's Friday," you just feel hipper after listening to the cat. And he always knows the temperature at the Baby Doll Polka Club in East Chicago.

1. Larry Lujack. I know. This was supposed to be more about the guys who presented music. But it is my opinion that Larry Lujack did that and talk as well as anybody in history. Lujack was the precursor to "Shock Jock" radio. He began his Chicago career in '67 on WCFL, but his ship came in when Uncle Lar teamed with Tommy Edwards (Li'l Tommy) on WLS in the 70s. It was there where the tandem unleashed "Animal Stories" and "Klunk Letter of the Day." Born Larry Blankenburg (not a real good ring to it) in '40 in Iowa, The Superjock owned Chicago. It was the only era I remember when consumers could find pop music and entertainment on the same AM-banded station. Lujack left the city in '89, moving to New Mexico, but he has resurfaced a time or two via ISDN. He was inducted in the Radio Hall of Fame in '04.

Like his good friend Michael Jordan, Tiger Woods also has enjoyed plenty of good times in Chicago. Through 2008, he won six PGA Tour events here, including two majors. Here is a review of some of the magical moments.

9. 1995 Western Open. Even for Woods, merely making the cut in a pro tournament once was a big accomplishment. Beginning with his debut at the age of 16, he missed the cut in his first eight tournaments. However, he finally broke through at Cog Hill in 1995. Still an amateur at 19, he made the cut and finished tied for 57th. A final round 69 was a sign of big things to come.

8. 1994 Western Amateur. After winning three straight U.S. Junior Amateur titles, Woods was primed to take on the highest level of amateur competitor. The 1994 Western Am at nearby Benton Harbor, Mich. provided the springboard. First, Woods had to survive a 20-hole victory in the semifinal over Chris Tidland. Then he got past future Ryder Cup teammate Chris Riley 2 and 1 in the finals. A few weeks later, he would go to win the first of three straight U.S. Amateur titles.

7. 1999 Western Open. Woods put it on cruise control. He seized the lead with opening rounds of 68, 66, 68, allowing him to coast home with a three-shot victory over Mike Weir. The victory set the tone for a blazing finish to 1999, in which he won seven of his last nine events.

6. 2003 Western Open. Thanks to Woods, the tournament was over almost from the moment he stepped on to the first tee. Woods tied the Cog Hill course record with an opening-round 63. He then shot a 65 on Saturday. The final day was a no-brainer, as he registered a five-shot victory over Rich Beem.

5. 2006 Western Open. For once, Woods didn't win. However, he helped put on quite a show, pushing Trevor Immelman to the limit before losing by two shots. This would be the last Western Open, as the tournament changed its name to the BMW Championship the following year.

4. 2007 BMW Championship. Fittingly, it was Woods who would claim the first BMW Championship en route to winning the first Fed Ex Cup trophy. How good was Woods? He shot 65 and 63 over the weekend. Now that's pretty good.

3. 2007 PGA Championship. Medinah is supposed to be a brutally tough course, right? The never-ending series of trees seemingly feed on the damaged psyches of beleaguered golfers, right? Well, not for Woods. In an amazing performance,

Woods shot four straight rounds in the 60s, including a 65 on Saturday. His 18-under score was good enough for a five-shot victory.

2. 1997 Western Open. Woods' first Western victory always will be his most memorable at Cog Hill. He recorded a three-shot triumph over Frank Nobilo, but that was only part of the story. Tiger Mania enveloped Cog Hill, as the galleries went wild over the new star. Then it erupted on the 18th hole on Sunday. As Woods walked to the green, the fans burst past the ropes and filled the fairways behind him, much like what you would see at a British Open. It will be a picture for the ages for golf in Chicago.

1. 1999 PGA Championship. The tournament at Medinah was an all-timer. Woods looked like he would win easily, but 19-year-old Sergio Garcia put a charge in the well-served crowd by making a run at Woods on the back nine. At one point, "El Niño" hit a miraculous shot from the base of a tree. Woods, though, managed to hang on. He made a key 8-footer to save par on 17, enabling him to take a one-shot victory. Great stuff in a tournament we'll never forget.

When it comes to public golf, all the golf experts agree: Chicago ranks second to none. The collection of public golf courses in the area helps counterbalance the bad weather we have to endure here. I've always said you could play 30 different public courses in 30 days and have a great experience in Chicago. Here are Ed's top 10.

10. Thunderhawk. The Robert Trent Jones Jr. course always eats me up, so I can't say it is one of my favorites. However, for a public facility, it is hard to beat the Lake County course that meanders through wetlands and woods, and features several visually inspiring holes. It is a first-class experience. Too bad I never seem to bring my "A" game out there.

9. Balmoral Woods. It might seem like you have driven halfway to Champaign given its remote location in Crete, but it definitely is worth the haul. It has a variety of top-notch holes, rolling terrain and fast, interesting greens. Also, given its location, you won't have to pay a premium price to play a premium course. A favorite course for Danny Mac.

8. Cog Hill No. 2. It gets lost in the shadow of big brother, the No. 4 course. But No. 2 is a top course in its own right. The course has some of the most interesting terrain in the area. There's a par 4 that goes straight uphill and a par 5 and par 3 that winds through ravines. No. 2 won't beat you up as much as No. 4, but you still have to play good golf to post a score.

7. Harborside. Whoever thought a garbage dump could produce two quality golf courses? Making something out of nothing, the courses are link-style with plenty of hazards to keep you interested. And on a clear day, you have a nice view of the Chicago skyline, an added bonus.

6. George Dunne National. The Oak Forest course always has been one of my favorites. Designer Dick Nugent's layout gets it: Wide fairways allow us hackers to keep the ball in play, but you still need to hit decent approach shots into the greens. The conditioning sagged big time during the 90s, but new management has brought up the standards considerably.

5. Village Links. The Chicago area has many top village courses, but the Glen Ellyn course probably rates as the best. This course is for serious players. It was one of the first facilities to institute a "Keep Pace" program in an effort to eliminate the five-hour rounds. That in itself is worthy of our vote.

4. Cantigny. The Wheaton facility has 27 holes, with three different nines: Woodside, Lakeside and Hillside. So there's plenty of variety to go around. Also, Cantigny features a bunker shaped like Dick Tracy. How can you not want to play a course that has a Dick Tracy bunker?

3. The Glen Club. This is one of hybrid public-private courses. If you want to play as a public golfer, you will have to pay a $150-plus rate that might feel like an initiation fee. But money aside, the course is highly enjoyable. Designer Tom Fazio took what had been a flatter than flatter landing strip (the former Glenview Naval Air Station) and created mounds, ravine, creeks and a couple of lakes. The course is playable for us hackers, but can be ratcheted up to challenge best of the best in pro tournaments. That's the sign of a good layout.

2. Pine Meadow. This is probably the premium public course I play the most. I just love the layout and feel of the place. The holes are challenging, but not killers. If you're on one hole, you rarely can see another hole. That gives you the feeling of having the course to yourself. And if there's slow play, the pace police will be right on top of it. They keep things moving.

1. Cog Hill No. 4. If it is good enough for Tiger Woods, it should be good enough for you. There aren't many PGA Tour courses that are available to the public. Playing it gives you a chance to see how good those guys really are. When you're having trouble breaking 100 from the front tees, just keep in mind that they break 70 from the back, back tees. Rees Jones' redesign should have "Dubsdread" in the hunt for a U.S. Open. It's a major upgrade to what was already an excellent course.

I have played most of the top private courses in the area, but not all of them. So this is a list of the clubs where I have actually chunked a shot or topped a drive. If you don't see your course in these rankings, give me an invite. I could be persuaded to change my mind.

14. Merit Club. The Libertyville course has it all: wetlands, lakes and a few trees. It also has three excellent "practice" holes to get you warmed up for the match. When in town, Michael Jordan plays a lot of golf here. So there's a chance you could run into him at Merit.

13. Olympia Fields South. When you have a U.S. Open course as your neighbor (the North course), you tend to get overlooked. But the South course clearly is one of the best in the area. A recent redesign just made it better. In fact, many people prefer to play the South over the North. For the average player, it is more fun.

12. Medinah No. 1. See Olympia Fields above. Again, the same situation holds true. The No. 1 course gets dwarfed by No. 3. The No. 1 course, though, is a terrific layout in its own right. It also offers weary Medinah members a respite after they get beat up on No. 3.

11. Beverly Country Club. This course is a gem on the South Side. The club took out some of the trees, but not all of them. So you still can count on rattling a few balls off the branches.

10. Black Sheep Golf Club. A relatively new men's club in Sugar Grove, it features 27-holes of high quality links-style golf. And it's all golf here. The smallish clubhouse doesn't even have a grill, offering deli-style sandwiches instead. They don't want you to waste time eating. They want you out there playing.

9. Old Elm Golf Club. The all-male club tries its best to be invisible. The club doesn't even have a sign at the entrance. In other words, if you weren't invited, they don't want you here. If you do get invited, you will be in for a treat. The course was designed by Donald Ross. While the holes are relatively short, they do feature Ross' signature greens. They have all sorts of breaks on contours. Lots of fun.

8. Skokie Country Club. This is another example of a classic tree-lined course. The Glencoe club also was the site of Gene Sarazan's U.S. Open victory in 1922. You can experience some history by playing there.

7. Rich Harvest Farms. This course is the creation of the appropriately named Jerry Rich. Rich started building a few holes on his property back in the 90s. Soon one thing led to another, and he had an 18-hole course that was worthy of hosting the Solheim Cup. The thing you should know is that Rich is a good player. As a result, he designed a difficult course. That means you better have your A game when you play at Rich Harvest.

6. Conway Farms. I always look forward to a round at this Lake Forest club. It is a walking-only course, which is fine with me since I love to walk. The Tom Fazio-design has several great holes and it has a nice variety of short and long par 4s. A good place for pure golf.

5. Shoreacres. The Lake Bluff club is another exclusive venue. The course cuts through a series of ravines that produces a memorable layout. Again, if you get an invite, throw the clubs in the car and head to Lake Bluff.

4. Olympia Fields North. It didn't get rave reviews in hosting the 2003 U.S. Open, which was won by Jim Furyk. The critics didn't think it was interesting enough to warrant an Open. Compared to other Open venues, they might be right. Still, the North course is a top layout, featuring several holes into elevated greens. It is plenty interesting for me.

3. Medinah No. 3. I love going to Medinah and hanging out in the spectacular clubhouse. However, I can't say I would want a heavy dose of No. 3. The holes are too long and there are too many trees. I always feel like I've been in a fight when I'm done. And of course, I've lost. However, once or twice a year, it is worth playing what has evolved as Chicago area's major tournament venue.

2. Butler National. Guess I have a thing for all-men clubs, because this is one the third one on my list. However, I do hope that Butler will eventually allow women members because I think the course is good enough to host a U.S. Open. It already beat up the pros back when it was the site of the Western Open in the 70s and 80s. Since then Tom Fazio has updated his original design, making it even better.

1. Chicago Golf. Designed by the legendary Charles Blair McDonald in the 1890s and updated in the 1920s by Seth Raynor, Chicago Golf usually rates highest in the national rankings among local courses. With good reason. With few trees, the layout is defined by its use of natural grasses along with McDonald's bunkers. The first holes are about as tough as you'd ever want. The rest of the course is wonderfully unpredictable and intriguing.

Danny Mac's Top 10 Steakhouses :: DM

It was almost impossible paring this list to 10. What else would you expect from a city made famous by the stockyards? Chicago is a world class restaurant town for any fare from around the globe. When it comes to meeting the needs of the carnivore, these are my best recommendations.

10. Japonais. 600 W. Chicago Ave. I know what you're thinking: he's beginning a list of great steakhouses by going to the Pacific Rim? You would be making a mistake if you didn't give it a whirl. While its signature dishes are fish offerings, the Kobe beef is exceptional and must be sampled by any self-respecting meat lover.

9. Sabatino's. 4441 W. Irving Park. Delightfully, classic Italian. Very romantic. Enzo and Angelo would have it no other way. Every steak on the menu is carefully prepared. The pastas are the best in the city. Wednesday night is lobster night. Many desserts are prepared tableside and the oysters on the half shell are fresh and abundant.

8. Morton's on Wacker. 65 E. Wacker. Yes, you can eat at a Morton's in almost any city. This particular venue makes my list because of its convenient location, consistently solid service and always reliable prime beef. If you searched the world over for the perfect blue cheese olive, this is where you would find it. I dunk mine in a Ketel One martini before the bacon-wrapped scallop appetizer arrives.

7. Keith's Bar and Grill. Indianapolis Blvd. and 119th, Whiting, Indiana. Merely a 15-minute drive down the Chicago Skyway. Dr. Keith's establishment features a warmth that's very difficult to accomplish in city limits. And he's always there, sipping his favorite Zin behind the bar. Steaks, ribs and lamb are the stars of this movie. Oh, and plenty of roasted garlic. Best apps are the spicy shrimp with slivered almonds and the sautéed mushrooms.

6. N9NE. 440 W. Randolph. General Manager Tim Griffin and Chef Michael are exceedingly proud of their broiler, which tops out at more than 1,100 degrees. Perfect temp for the perfect sear. N9NE offers an awesome, huge bar on the main level and a wide variety of awesome entrees. The appetizers not only are presented like works of art, they tantalize the taste buds. The seared ahi is a must. Great food in a casual, non-pretentious downtown location.

5. Gamba. 455 E. 84th Dr. Merrillville, Indiana. A bit of a hike from downtown, it's worth every minute of windshield time. Benito Gamba is the host with the most. Elegant dining. The veal scallopini is the best I've ever had. The bone-in rib-eye, pastas and salads also are top notch. A relaxed atmosphere in the adjacent bar where smoking is allowed. If you're planning a wedding or a banquet and great food is important, check it out.

4. Sullivan's. 415 N. Dearborn. Great steaks. I mean amazing. And before Illinois went California and banned all smoking, the lounge upstairs was a sanctuary for unwinding. It still is, just don't light up a Honduran. The servers are as easy on the eyes as the presentation of the fare. That's because Ray K. insists on it.

3. Gibsons. 1028 N. Rush. In the heart of the infamous Viagra triangle, Gibsons is more than a place to hook up. The prime beef is a mouth-watering experience. If lobster bisque is your thing, you have to go to Gibsons. Cocktails and appetizers rock at this Chicago landmark. Service is amazing for an establishment this busy.

2. Harry Caray's. 33 W. Kinzie. Dinner at the bar, with HD monitors in every direction, is recommended. HC's is not merely a sports bar, however, as its name might imply. The Kansas City strip and lamb chops oreganato are among my favorite entrees in the world. Plus, you may bump into the always affable Dutchie Caray. And if you're counting calories, the Dutchie salad is a nutritious, savory option.

1. Chicago Chop House. 60 W. Ontario. I cannot dismiss the 15+ years I have been a customer at the Chop House, but I list it as No.1 with trepidation. The restaurant was sold in the fall of '08 and with it comes new ideas, new approaches. No more "Johnny the Gent" Pontarelli, whose managerial and people skills helped make the Chop House a Chicago landmark. The Gent always was the host with the most. The Chop House features a variety of prime beef options, including their signature dish, the slow-roasted, then fire-grilled, bone-in prime rib. The potato pancake is a must. The Chop House also offers a variety of outstanding seafood items, my favorite being the swordfish. The cold shellfish appetizer platter is a must for larger parties. There is no more expansive wine list in the city than that offered by the Chicago Chop House. I prefer dinner downstairs, which features a piano player and a classic, old-style horseshoe bar and friendly, fast barkeeps. The walls are adorned by photos and descriptions of Chicago's most notorious gangsters and the city's Mayors and founding fathers. My recommendation to the current proprietors is to change nothing. Don't quarrel with success.

White Sox-Yankees Battles :: by Bob Vanderberg

Note: Bob Vanderberg spent his early years as a White Sox fan watching the Sox engage in a futile battle against the Yankees during the 50s and early 60s. Four times during that span, the Sox finished second to the Yankees. Only once did they prevail, winning the pennant in 1959. Still, it was an exciting era for the Sox. Vanderberg chronicled it in his book, *Minnie and The Mick: The Go-Go-White Sox Challenge the Fabled Yankee Dynasty, 1951-64*. Here are Vandy's most memorable Sox vs. Yankees moments from the 50s and 60s:

10. May 18, 1951. In the first game of a lengthy Eastern road trip, Eddie Stewart's grand slam at Yankee Stadium snaps seventh-inning tie. The Sox go 11-0 on trip, and eventually stretch the win streak to 14. They move into first place, recapture the attention of a city that had lost interest, and begin a string of 17 successive winning seasons.

9. July 17, 1959. Before 42,020 at Yankee Stadium, Early Wynn takes a one-hitter into the ninth, the Yankees' Ralph Terry a no-hitter. Jim McAnany breaks up the no-no with a single, and Jim Landis delivers a two-run single. Wynn finishes off the two-hit, 2-0 victory that keeps Sox a game up on Cleveland in the pennant chase.

8. June 22, 1964. After winning the first three games of a Comiskey Park series 1-0 in 11 innings, 2-0 in regulation and 2-1 in 17, the Yankees give Mickey Mantle, Elston Howard and Tony Kubek the night off. And still, the Yanks beat the Sox 6-5 to sweep the series and run their season record against Chicago to 10-0. Sox end the season one game behind first-place New York.

7. June 13, 1957. Yankee pitcher Art Ditmar ignites a 20-minute Comiskey Park brawl by throwing at Larry Doby's head. Doby takes offense and decks Ditmar, and the fight is on. Main bouts are Doby vs. Billy Martin and Walt Dropo vs. Enos Slaughter, a decisive loser. "Best baseball fight I ever saw," Jack Brickhouse always said. New York loses the fight, but after order is restored, the Yanks win the game 4-3 to cut Chicago's lead to four games.

6. September 10, 1955. After host Yankees KO Billy Pierce and build 6-1 lead after two, Sox rally and take lead on Walt Dropo's two-out bases-loaded single in ninth. Then they watch the Yanks tie it when Minnie Minoso drops a two-out fly ball. However, the Sox win 9-8 in 10th on an error by ex-Sox first baseman Eddie Robinson. Thrilling victory (which employed 41 players) keeps Sox pennant hopes alive.

5. August 20, 1964. Sox KO Whitey Ford early—he had thrown 43 straight scoreless innings against Chicago entering this game—and Johnny Buzhardt goes on to blank the Yankees 5-0. The triumph, before a Comiskey Park weekday crowd of 36,677, completes a four-game sweep and lifts the Sox into first place, a half-game ahead of Baltimore and 4½ ahead of the Yankees. It also raised Buzhardt's lifetime record vs. the Yankees to 5-0.

4. June 27, 1959. The Yankees, after having beaten the Sox the previous night to tie them in the standings (both teams 36-32, in third place, two games out), lead 2-1 with two out in the eighth inning before Bob Turley yields a single and two walks to load the bases for the well-traveled outfielder Harry "Suitcase" Simpson. Simpson hits Turley's first pitch off the facing of the upper deck in right-center for a grand slam. The Sox hold on to win 5-4 and then sweep a doubleheader from New York the next day. In fact, after Simpson's slam, Sox win 44 of their next 61 games to take command of AL race.

3. July 14, 1957. The Sox win Game 1 of a Sunday doubleheader before 48,244 at Comiskey Park to close to within two games of the Yankees and take a 4-0 lead into the ninth inning of Game 2. Bob Elson intones, "And the White Sox are going to sweep a doubleheader from the world champion New York Yankees." But Dick Donovan surrenders a run and leaves a bases-loaded, one-out jam to Jim Wilson, whose first pitch to pinch-hitter and native Chicagoan Bill Skowron is belted into the left-field upper deck for a game-winning grand slam.

2. May 16, 1953. The Sox trail Yankee ace Vic Raschi 3-0 in the ninth at Yankee Stadium before the visitors push a run across and load the bases with two out. Casey Stengel calls in sidearming right-hander Ewell Blackwell to face Vern Stephens, who has 10 career grand slams. Sox manager Paul Richards, however, calls to his bench for Tommy Byrne, a former Yankee pitcher and a sometimes-dangerous left-handed hitter. Byrne runs the count to 2-2 and then smokes a line drive into the bleachers in right for a grand slam that beats the Yankees and remains a classic White Sox moment.

1. June 22-24, 1956. The wildest Comiskey Park weekend of the decade. First, on Friday night, before 48,346, Dick Donovan pitches no-hit ball into the eighth. The Yankees, though, go up 4-2 in the 11th before the Sox tie it on rookie Sammy Esposito's two-out two-run pinch double and then win it in the 12th on Esposito's bases-loaded single. On Saturday, Jim Wilson beats the Yanks 2-0 to trim their AL lead to three games. Then, on Sunday, before 47,255 fans—several hundred of whom will eventually be celebrating on the field—Larry Doby hits a three-run homer in the first inning of both games as the Sox sweep, 14-2 and 6-3, and find themselves a game out of first place.

Good Sammy, Bad Sammy :: by Paul Sullivan

Note: Longtime *Chicago Tribune* baseball writer Paul Sullivan rode the rollercoaster that came with covering Sammy Sosa during his career. Sosa provided many memorable moments, both good and bad. Sully offers his best and worst of Sammy.

FIVE BEST MOMENTS

5. June 21, 1989. In his sixth major league game with Texas, Sosa homers off Boston ace Roger Clemens in the fifth inning, the first of his major league career. He'd wind up with 609 homers, trailing only Barry Bonds, Hank Aaron and Ken Griffey Jr. on the all-time list. Ironically, Sosa and Clemens would later be linked as two of the most prominent players whose careers were sullied by rumors of steroid use. During congressional hearings on the steroids controversy on March 17, 2005, Sosa claimed he didn't understand the questions because of his limited command of the English language.

4. September 27, 2001. After the '01 season is postponed by the terrorist attacks of September 11th, Sosa homers in the first game back at Wrigley Field. He's handed a small American flag by first base coach Billy Williams and waves it while rounding the basepaths, providing the Cubs with an iconic moment to obscure an otherwise forgettable finish.

3. June 20, 2007. After returning from a one-year absence and playing in Texas, Sosa hits his 600th career home run off Cubs pitcher Jason Marquis, who took Sosa's uniform number (21) when he signed in the off-season.

2. October 7, 2003. Trailing 8-6 with two outs in the bottom of the ninth in the opener of the National League Championship Series, Sosa hits a two-run homer onto Waveland Avenue off Florida closer Ugueth Urbina to tie the game and send it into extra innings. It was the first career postseason homer for Sosa, but the Cubs went on to lose 9-8 in 11 innings.

1. September 13, 1998. On his way to his first and only MVP award, Sosa hit his 61st and 62nd home run onto Waveland Avenue in an 11-10 win over Milwaukee, tying Roger Maris' old record with his first homer, and tying Mark McGwire for the league lead with his second—a game-tying, two-run shot in the ninth. "I always cry, but I was crying inside today," Sosa said.

FIVE WORST MOMENTS

5. July 2002. While being interviewed by *Sports Illustrated* columnist Rick Reilly, Sosa is asked if he would be first in line for testing if Major League Baseball decided to administer tests for steroids. After Sosa replied "yes," Reilly handed him a business card directing him to a steroid-testing lab in the Chicago area. Sosa called Reilly a profane name and immediately ended the interview.

4. 1998-2004. Sosa's ubiquitous boom box first appeared in 1998 and provided the soundtrack to the Cubs clubhouse through the 2004 season, when it was smashed to pieces by an unknown player (or players) upset about his final game walkout. The mystery over who really smashed Sammy's boom box has never been solved, and Kerry Wood denied any involvement after a radio report singled him out.

3. May 17, 2004. Before a Cubs-Padres game at Petco Park, Sosa sneezes at his locker and suffers back spasms, sending him to the disabled list. The sneeze would go down in history as one of the strangest Cubs injuries of all time. "It would have been better if I had hit off the wall or we have a fight or something," Sosa said. "But this . . . you know what I mean? What can you do? Some things in life you cannot control. This is strange that it happened."

2. June 3, 2003. In the most infamous game of his career, Sosa is ejected in the first inning when his corked bat explodes on contact in a game against Tampa Bay at Wrigley Field. Sosa insisted he mistakenly chose a bat he used for batting practice, and that he didn't have any other corked bats. MLB tested 76 bats and found no evidence of corking. Sosa would eventually serve a seven-game suspension for the illegal bat.

1. October 3, 2004. In what turns out to be an ugly exit from the Cubs organization, Sosa walks out on his team in the first inning of the season finale at Wrigley Field, then lies about it in an interview with the *Sun-Times*, insisting he left in the seventh. The Cubs later announce that videotaped evidence from the players' parking lot proves Sosa left at the start of the game, greasing the skids to an off-season trade to Baltimore.

The Best of Chicago High School Basketball :: by David Kaplan

Chicago always has been a fertile ground for basketball excellence. David Kaplan has seen the best of the best as a former college coach, NBA scout, and operator of a high school basketball recruiting service. The host of *Sports Central* on WGN Radio and *Chicago Tribune Live* on Comcast Sports Net, Kaplan looks at the best high school players from the Chicago area since 1970.

Just missing the list: Teddy Grubbs, Ben Wilson, Glen Grunwald, Jon Scheyer, and Jamie Brandon.

12. Glenn "Doc" Rivers. A star at Proviso East who broke DePaul's heart when he chose rival Marquette. He had a solid but unspectacular collegiate career. Rivers then enjoyed a 13-year NBA career and went on to hit the jackpot as a coach with Boston.

11. Maurice Cheeks. Even though he was a star as DuSable High School, he was not heavily recruited. He attended West Texas State. He then played 15 years in the NBA and was a four-time All-Star.

10. Michael Finley. He was the third wheel on a Proviso East team behind more heralded names like Sherrill Ford and Donnie Boyce. Finley became a star at Wisconsin and is enjoying a long and productive NBA career.

9. Juwan Howard. He was part of Michigan's Fab Five after a sensation prep career at CVS. He had a long career in the NBA.

8. Dwayne Wade. He wasn't a huge star at Richards compared to some other players on this list, but he blossomed at Marquette, taking his team to the Final Four. Then he became a superstar in leading Miami to an NBA title.

7. Eddie Johnson. The Westinghouse star was a tremendous high school scorer, who starred at Illinois before playing an astounding 17 seasons in the NBA.

6. Quinn Buckner. The Thornridge guard was one of only three players in history to have won titles at every level: high school, college, pro and an Olympic gold medal.

5. Jim Brewer. The Proviso East star was the first dominant big man to come out of the Chicago area. He played for Minnesota in college and was the No. 2 pick by Cleveland in the 1973 NBA draft.

4. Mark Aguirre. He went from a pudgy but prolific scorer at Westinghouse to the national college player of the year, as he helped resurrect DePaul's program. A long and productive NBA career solidifies his ranking.

3. Derrick Rose. The Simeon product was the best point guard out of the talent-rich Chicago area since Isiah Thomas. His legend only will continue to grow as he stars for the Bulls.

2. Kevin Garnett. Perhaps the most talented player in the history of the Windy City. A sure-fire Hall of Famer. However, because he only played one season of high school ball in Chicago, he finishes No. 2 to Isiah.

1. Isiah Thomas. The best point guard in the history of the Chicago area. Thomas broke hearts when he didn't go to DePaul, but he gave "The General" a national title at Indiana. Not bad in the pros either.

Top High School Basketball Coaches :: by Barry Temkin

Note: Barry Temkin wrote a popular high school sports column for more than 20 years for the *Tribune*. During that time, he got an up-close look at the top basketball coaches and their teams in the area. Here is his look at the best of the best.

10. tie, Dave Weber, Glenbrook North, and Bob Williams, Schaumburg. Jon Scheyer had a lot to do with Glenbrook North's 2005 Class AA state title, 2003 third-place finish and 2006 quarterfinal berth, but the Spartans would not have achieved that without Weber's solid defense and precise motion offense. Schaumburg produced one of the great upsets of Illinois state championship game history when it shocked Eddy Curry-led Thornwood 66-54 in 2001. Williams, a strong defensive coach, also grabbed a fourth-place trophy in 1999 and reached the quarterfinals in 2006.

9. Rocky Hill, Thornton, Julian, Crete-Monee. Thornton had a 93-4 run from 1995 through 1997 under Hill but had the bad luck to run into Peoria Manual, which won the AA state title all three years. The teams had epic battles each season, with Thornton finishing second the first two years and third in 1997. Still, Hill helped pull off one of the big upsets of Elite Eight history when his team, led by Tai Streets, shocked a Farragut team led by Kevin Garnett and Ronnie Fields 46-43 in the 1995 quarterfinals.

8. Roy Condotti, Westinghouse, Homewood-Flossmoor. Condotti thrived in vastly different environments, first on Chicago's West Side and then in the far south suburbs. He led Westinghouse to the Class AA Sweet Sixteen from 1990 through 1994, finishing third in 1992. He got H-F to the Sweet Sixteen in 1996, 2004 and 2005, finishing second in 2004 with Julian Wright. He retired as head coach in 2005.

7. Robert Smith, Simeon. Smith succeeded his mentor, Bob Hambric, and won Class AA state titles in 2006 and 2007, his second and third years as head coach. With Derrick Rose, Tim Flowers & Co., the low-key Smith had the best team both years, but he belied his inexperience by helping his players cope with the pressure of great expectations and stay focused on team goals. With Rose and Flowers gone in 2008, Smith led Simeon to second place in the new Class 3A.

6. Bill Hitt, Proviso East. Hitt coached the "Three Amigos" 1991 AA state championship team led by Michael Finley, Sherell Ford and Donnie Boyce. He rebuilt and won the 1992 crown behind Kenny Davis, Jamal Robinson and Ray Gay. Proviso East went 65-1 those two years, then reached the state quarterfinals in 1993 before Hitt retired from coaching with an average record of 24-6 over his 10 years as a head coach.

5. Mike Flaherty, Mendel Catholic, Thornridge, Mt. Carmel.
Flaherty is one of the best coaches not to have won a state title, though he finished second in Class AA with now-closed Mendel in 1982. No coach gets more from his talent, largely because his teams play with great discipline. Flaherty had only one losing season in 22 years at Thornridge—which included a AA state quarterfinal berth in 1989. His Mt. Carmel team upset powerhouse Young in 2008 before losing to Evanston in the Class 4A quarterfinals.

4. Gordon Kerkman, West Aurora. West's head coach since 1976, Kerkman won a AA state title in 2000 to go along with a runner-up trophy in 1997 and third-place finishes in 1980, 1984 and 2004. Kerkman's best teams, including those in 1997 and 2000, often lacked dominant stars, a tribute to his stress on fundamentals and team play. The 2000 squad is the only team from hoops-crazed Aurora to win a state basketball title.

3. Luther Bedford, Marshall. Bedford gained his greatest fame as Arthur Agee's coach in the acclaimed documentary film *Hoop Dreams* but he thrived in the rugged Chicago Public League and reached the state semifinals three times, including a third-place Class AA finish in 1991, Agee's senior year. A great teacher and man, he refused to recruit 8th graders, and though he never won a state title, he often stopped teams with better talent from doing it. Bedford, who died in 2006, was regarded as the "Godfather of Public League basketball" but was respected statewide as well.

2. Landon Cox, King. "Sonny" Cox was the rare high school coach who had a national reputation, the result of rosters packed with talent, an .850 winning percentage, a larger-than-life personality and a knack for controversy, much of it tied to recruiting allegations. King games were theater as much as athletic events, with overflow crowds and Cox scowling his way to victory. He had so much talent—including guard Jamie Brandon on his 1990 Class AA state championship team and center Rashard Griffith on that team and King's 1993 champ—that many refused to concede he could coach. And while it's true some of his teams underachieved and he was no Xs and Os genius, Cox knew how to handle and use talent. He also won a state title in 1986 and had three second- or third-place finishes before retiring from coaching in 2001.

1. Gene Pingatore, St. Joseph. Pingatore, St. Joseph's coach for almost 40 years, has demonstrated almost unparalleled longevity and consistency, keeping the Chargers among Illinois' hoops elite since leading them (and guard Isiah Thomas) to a Class AA runner-up finish in 1978. He has added trophies for first, third and fourth place, winning the state title in 1999 with a team not considered among his best when it came to pure talent. Still one of the most demonstrative coaches around, Pingatore joined the 800-victory club during the 2007-08 season.

October 16, 2008 looked to be a slow day on the sports front in Chicago. Then out of nowhere, the Blackhawks announced they had fired Denis Savard only four games into the season. It wasn't the first time an unexpected upper management change rocked the town. Here's the complete list.

8. Eddie Collins. Collins was one of the Sox's all-time greats. The second baseman became player-manager at the end of the 1924 season and then guided the overachieving Sox to respectable 79-75 and 81-72 finishes in 1925 and 1926. However, when Collins retired as a player after the 1926 season, owner Charles Comiskey decided he no longer needed Collins as a manager. In an incredible act of disrespect, Comiskey never personally informed Collins of his dismissal. Instead, he put the future Hall of Famer on waivers.

7. Charlie Grimm. The old Cub always seemed to be popping up as manager. In 1960, he was given his third shot at the helm. However, after opening the season with a 6-11 record, he was ousted. Here comes the good part. Owner P.K. Wrigley decided Grimm and Cubs radio analyst Lou Boudreau should switch jobs. So Boudreau went to the dugout to manage the team. Grimm went up to the booth and watched Boudreau compile a 54-83 record the rest of the way.

6. Jeff Torborg. Torborg wasn't technically fired, but that was because he jumped before getting pushed. After taking over as manager of a talent-starved Sox team in 1989, Torborg led the resurgence with 94 victories in 1990 and 87 in 1991. However, new general manager Ron Schueler wasn't a fan of Torborg. When the Mets came calling after the 1991 season, Schueler told Torborg to grab the first flight to New York.

5. Larry Himes. Himes was the man who hired Torborg. The Sox General Manager also drafted Frank Thomas, Jack McDowell, Alex Fernandez, and Robin Ventura and acquired other key players. The sudden infusion of talent had the Sox soaring during their last year in Comiskey Park in 1990. Himes, though, never got to finish out the season. Owner Jerry Reinsdorf fired him on September 15th of that year. Reinsdorf said Himes had "a personality problem," and that he couldn't get along with people. That may have been the case, but he definitely knew talent.

4. Jerry Vainisi. Vainisi was immensely popular as the general manager of the Bears' 1985 Super Bowl team. However, after the Bears lost to Washington in the 1986 playoffs, team president Michael McCaskey abruptly fired Vainisi. Reportedly, the McCaskey family didn't entirely trust Vainisi. Bears coach Mike Ditka did, and he cried at the press conference. So did other Bears fans, as many people point to Vainisi's dismissal as the beginning of the end for that team.

3. Doug Collins. Collins had a young Bulls team on the rise in 1988-89. Thanks to Michael Jordan's buzz-beater, the Bulls defeated Cleveland in five games. They played eventual NBA champion Detroit tough in a six-game series. Then stunningly, the Bulls whacked him. To this day, there never was a satisfactory reason given. Rumors circulated that Collins' personal life led to his dismissal. Whatever the case, Collins was out, and his assistant, Phil Jackson, was in.

2. Denis Savard. All the pieces seemed to be place. The Hawks were creating a buzz in town at the start of the 2008-09 season. Despite losing the first three games, the Hawks bounced back with an impressive 4-1 victory over Phoenix in Game 4. However, when Savard showed up to practice the following morning, GM Dale Tallon told him he was gone. Hawks fans were in an uproar. How could the team treat one of their greats that way? All in all, it wasn't one of the Hawks' best days, but it wasn't their worst. See below.

1. Billy Reay. Reay is the winningest coach in Hawks history with 516 victories and three trips to the Stanley Cup Finals. He was a faithful soldier in 13 years as coach. So how was he rewarded? On Christmas Eve, 1976, legend has it that the Hawks slipped a note under his door telling him he was fired. Merry Christmas, Billy, and get out. Sort of makes Mr. Scrooge, not to mention Mr. Comiskey, look good by comparison.

A show of hands for all those people who can recall watching Terry Dischinger win the NBA's Rookie of the Year Award for the Chicago Zephyrs in 1962. OK, how about a show of hands for those people who can even remember the Zephyrs. OK, not too many there. Dischinger's exploits may have been cast to oblivion, but other Chicago players have produced memorable rookie seasons, with a couple ranking among the all-time best in sports. Here's the list.

13. Elton Brand. The Bulls used the No. 1 pick in the draft to select this big forward out of Duke in 1999. Brand didn't disappoint, averaging 20.1 points per game in joining Michael Jordan as the franchise's only other ROY winner up to that point. He looked to be a fixture on the Bulls for years, but two years later, GM Jerry Krause made the ill-fated trade sending Brand to the Los Angeles Clippers for Tyson Chandler. The Bulls then spent most of the decade trying to find a power forward to replace Brand.

12. Patrick Kane. Kane immediately justified the Hawks' decision to take him with the No. 1 overall selection in the 2007 draft. Only 18, he came in to record 21 goals and 51 assists in winning the 2008 ROY honors. His arrival also helped spark a revival in the Hawks, as local fans rediscovered hockey again in this town.

11. Ozzie Guillen. Sox fans had their first introduction to Guillen when he was a rookie in 1985. He was skinny and looked to have a weak arm, hardly the kind of player who would seem to be the centerpiece in a deal that saw the Sox trade 1983 Cy Young Award winner LaMarr Hoyt to San Diego. Turns out Guillen had plenty of heart and some talent too as a shortstop. He was named the American League's Rookie of the Year. It was just the start for Guillen with the Sox.

10. Jerome Walton. Walton burst on to the scene for the Cubs in 1989. He ignited the lineup at lead-off, hitting .293 and playing solid centerfield as a vital part of the Cubs' run to the NL East title. Named National League Rookie of the Year, it looked to be the start of solid career for Walton with the Cubs. Alas, Walton petered out quickly, as 1989 was his high water mark.

9. Luis Aparicio. "Little Looey" had the difficult task of taking over for another Venezuelan shortstop, Chico Carresquel, in 1956. Aparicio didn't miss a beat, displaying his incredible skills at shortstop in being named Rookie of the Year. It was his speed that provided the extra dimension, as he led the league with 21 stolen bases. It was a great start to a Hall of Fame career.

8. Brian Urlacher. Urlacher's rookie season actually started slowly in 2000. Early on, he lost his starting job to Rosevelt Colvin. However, an injury to Barry Minter gave Urlacher the starting job at middle linebacker. He had a big showing against the New York Giants in Game 3 and didn't stop hitting people for the rest of the season. He went on to be named the NFL's Defensive Rookie of the Year and made his first Pro Bowl. A new era had begun in Chicago.

7. Beattie Feathers. This list wouldn't be complete without Beattie Feathers, right? All he did as a rookie in 1934 for the Bears was become the first NFL player to rush for 1,000 yards in a season. He averaged a record 8.4 yards per carry in running for 1,004 yards. Feathers, though, proved to be a one-year wonder, as injuries plagued him during the rest of his career.

6. Ron Kittle. The 1983 season was straight out of a storybook for Kittle. The outgoing native of Gary took the town by storm by launching several massive rooftop homers. All told, he hit 35 homers with 100 RBI, represented the Sox in the All-Star game at Comiskey Park and was named ROY. Pitchers figured out how get him out in 1984 and beyond. But that one season made Kittle a folk hero on the South Side forever.

5. Kerry Wood. It took only one game for Wood to become an institution for the Cubs. In only his fifth career start in 1998, Woods posted 20 strikeouts in a 1-0 victory over Houston. Arguably, it was the most dominating one-game performance ever by a Cubs pitcher. Wood went on to record 13 victories and 233 strikeouts in 166 innings en route to being named ROY. Wood, though, suffered from arm problems at the end of the year, beginning a long-running soap opera about his health.

4. Michael Jordan. It's hard to believe Jordan would be fourth on this list because by some measures his first season should be first. Everybody thought Jordan would be good in 1984-85, but nobody thought he would be this good! He put on a highlight show every night with a flurry of dunks and explosive moves, averaging 28 points per game. Naturally, he was named the NBA's Rookie of the Year, and a case could have been made that he was the player of the year. However, the Bulls were eliminated in four games by Milwaukee in the playoffs. That drops Jordan down to fourth.

3. Devin Hester. Hester's presence in the return game completely transformed the Bears during his rookie season in 2006. He recorded six return touchdowns. Included in the list was a stunning fourth-quarter punt return to beat Arizona and a 108-yard return off a missed field goal in a victory over the New York Giants. Teams kicked to Hester at their own risk, and more often not, they didn't, giving the Bears excellent field position. Hester then made history in the Super Bowl, becoming the first player to return the opening kickoff for a touchdown.

2. Tony Esposito. Few rookies have ever had a bigger impact than Esposito did with the Blackhawks in 1969-70. An off-season pick-up from Montreal, Esposito recorded an NHL record 15 shutouts and a 2.17 goals against average. He was named the NHL's ROY and was runner-up in MVP voting to Bobby Orr. Esposito truly lived up to his nickname, "Tony-O."

1. Gale Sayers. Sayers' feats as a rookie in 1965 are staggering. He posted a record 22 touchdowns with 2,272 total yards. Back then, those were records in 14-game seasons. Sayers scored from anywhere on the field. Years later, you watch the old clips and wonder if the film had been doctored. No way does a human make those moves. Sayers saved his best for last, scoring six touchdowns in the season finale against San Francisco. It definitely was a rookie season for the ages.

Best Concerts :: DM

I am a rocker. Born in '61, I grew up listening to the Rolling Stones, the Doors and the Who. Most of us late baby boomers favor any music that was loud and proud. I don't dislike all of today's music, but I don't get the over-the-top attraction to acts such as the Dave Matthews Band, 311 or Linkin Park. To each his own, however. These are my own. These are the 10 best rock shows I've seen in Chicagoland since I first held a Bic lighter in the air in the winter of '77.

10. Nazareth, Aragon Ballroom, Spring of '79. These goofballs from Scotland were not the most talented musicians ever to produce records and tour the world, but I love 'em. This particular Naz Fest was in the antiquated, general admission-seating "Brawlroom" on Lawrence Ave. The capacity crowd warmly received the shrieking Dan McCafferty and the boys. And why wouldn't they? If you can't stand on your chair and pump your fist to "Razamanazz," you may as well put the other foot in the casket, too.

9. Any Pretenders show. I've seen the band a number of times, between '83 and '02, and have never been disappointed in this band. I think my favorite Pretenders show was at the UIC Pavillion in '86 or '87. Iggy Pop was the warm-up act that night. Drummer Martin Chambers is perhaps the most underrated skinsman in rock and roll in the past 30 years or so. And when Chrissie Hynde sings a sad song like "Back on the Chain Gang" (written for the departed guitarist James Honeyman Scott and bassist Pete Farndon), "Stop Your Sobbing" or "2000 Years," my heart aches.

8. UFO, Hammond Civic Center, Spring of '79. The rock 'n' roll gods never shined on this talented act. They had a few tunes that got radio airplay, such as "Lights Out," "Love to Love," and "Doctor, Doctor," but these guys never garnered the attention they richly deserved. Michael Shenker was one of the more explosive lead guitarists in his era, but never got the attention he richly deserved, either. Chicago had a love affair with the band, fortunately, and the *Strangers in the Night* live album was recorded primarily at the International Amphitheatre on Halsted. Glad I spent a few nights with these troubled but talented ear benders.

7. Roxy Music, the UIC Pavillion, Spring of '83. I was on spring break and came home because a buddy suggested I'd love Bryan Ferry's band. And I did. All I knew from RM was "Love Is the Drug." They didn't have a lot of radio tunes. I don't think I ever enjoyed a concert more when going in so totally unfamiliar with a band's library. Roxy had just released its *Avalon* album and I walked away from the show itching to get to the record store to load up on my newly-found friends. Roxy broke up shortly after this tour. Glad I got to be a part of it before they did.

6. Lynyrd Skynyrd, Soldier Field, Summer of '77. This would be Skynyrd's last Chicago appearance. A few months later, the band's small aircraft went down and claimed the lives of three band members, including front man Ronnie Van Zant. Skynyrd was second on the bill at one of those "Super Bowl of Rock" shows. Ted Nugent headlined this one. I always loved Skynyrd and to this day I believe if they would have marketed themselves as something other than a Confederate flag waving, redneck act from Florida, they would have gained more mass appeal. How many bands that really rock out do it with the presence of a piano? I feel lucky I got to see them. I still listen to Skynyrd when I have a lot of windshield time in front of me.

5. Rush, Hammond Civic Center, Winter of '78. This was the "Farewell to Kings" tour and my second of five or six evenings I'd spend with the Canadian power trio. I still am amazed how much quality noise Geddy Lee, Neil Peart and Alex Lifeson produced. A very talented band and in the early days (before the 80s) an act that produced honest raunch and roll. *Fly by Night* and *2112* were fabulous albums. The need for acceptance on a broader scale grabbed Rush, unfortunately, and the band found greater success with commercial crap like "Free Will" and "Tom Sawyer." Any band that is five albums deep, however, is a success, and Rush's first six albums were rockers. I'm glad I was on board long before they sold out.

4. Alice Cooper, International Amphitheatre, August 27, 1977. How do I remember the exact date? Easy. It was my 16th birthday. Cooper had hits like "Eighteen," "School's Out," and "No More Mr. Nice Guy," but I don't believe there is a more misunderstood act in rock history. Given credit primarily as one of the first "shock rockers," Cooper's writing was brilliant and the band was produced deftly by the great Bob Ezrin. This particular show was after the release of the *Lace and Whiskey* album, which was not one of Coop's best. The *Welcome to My Nightmare* tour was still fresh, however, and they performed a good amount from it. I've seen Alice perform at least a half dozen times and I've interviewed him as well. Always will be one of my favorites.

3. Page and Plant, the United Center, Winter of '95. "Close the door, turn out the light. We won't be coming home tonight." I loved Led Zeppelin. Still do. Always will. And I always will regret that I wasn't on-board more as a teenager when I had a chance to see the hardest hitter ever, Mr. John Henry Bonham, pound the skins. Page and Plant did the UC in consecutive years in the mid-90s and I saw both shows. Jimmy Page is the most versatile, most talented guitar player ever. There is nothing Pagey can't do with the guitar. Accompanied by the Chicago Symphonic Orchestra, the performance of "Kashmir" put tingles up the spines of the 20,000 attendees that night. It was an unbelievable experience and I hope to have another crack at it again some day.

2. AC/DC, Tinley Park, August of '00. Some critics believe AC/DC is a cartoon. An overrated act that lacks soul and substance. That's cool. I won't be picking those people up en route to the next AC/DC show I attend. On this sticky, summer night, the loud and proud Aussies delivered a two-hour, foot stomping, fist pumping, in-your-face rock show. They had just released *Stiff Upper Lip* and played a couple

from it, but the band was smart enough to know why we were there. "Highway to Hell," "You Shook Me All Night Long," and "Thunderstruck" all rocked the house. AC/DC is neither pretty nor pretentious. AC/DC is powerful. You don't sit down at an AC/DC concert. That's why I never miss them when they hit Chicago.

1. The Rolling Stones, Soldier Field, July of '78. You never forget your first. This was my first of many Stones' shows and it was one of the greatest days in my young life. My ragged buddies and I camped out all night outside Soldier Field to get the best position possible for this general admission show. We were about 10 or 12 rows back, close enough to get baptized by Jagger's firehose when he drenched the crowd during the encore presentation of "Satisfaction." The Stones had just released *Some Girls*, and "Shattered" quickly became a favorite in my crowd. I recall the late Peter Tosh also being on the bill that day and he joined Jagger for an awesome duet of "Walk and Don't Look Back." Keith Richards, by landslide, is the coolest man alive. I remember after the show, we were thinking, "Man, good thing we got to see 'em before they're all dead." More than 30 years later, they're still making music and delighting millions with their glitzy, amazing live performances. Keep 'em coming, boys.

I believe the cliché is "never judge a book by its cover." Looking good when stepping off the team bus clearly doesn't ensure success on the playing field. Here's a quick look at five physical specimens who underachieved. I only can give an honorable mention to Blackhawks forward Eric Daze. At 6-foot-6, 255 pounds, Daze never was a physical front-liner, much to the chagrin of Hawks fans who marveled at his presence. Back injuries, including three disc surgeries, entitle Daze to only a mention. Eric "The Daisy" did score 30 goals in his rookie season in '96 and was an '02 All Star.

5. James "Robocop" Thornton, Bears. The Bears drafted the 6'4", 245-pound Thornton in the 4th round in '88, but he spent only four seasons in Chicago. The Cal product earned the nickname "Robocop" for his uncanny facial resemblance to the 80s film star Peter Weller. That's where the comparisons to the effective, indestructible character ended. Robobust's only productive season (and that's being generous) was '89, when he caught 24 passes for 392 yards and 3 TDs.

4. Daryl Boston, White Sox. A 1st-round pick in '81, Boston was an athletic 6'3", 205-pound, smooth, left-handed outfielder who couldn't hit a bull in the ass with a snow shovel. When I first saw Boston gracefully stride to centerfield at old Comiskey Park, I thought the Sockos had found the next Willie Mays. Something about his best year in '88, when he belted 15 HRs with 31 RBI but hit only .217, convinced me my early returns were wrong.

3. Kyle Farnsworth, Cubs. Farnsworth now is best known for a solid form tackle he laid on Reds pitcher Paul Wilson after Wilson objected to an inside pitch in a game in Cincinnati in '03. He also beat the crap out of an electric fan in the Cubs dugout after a crummy outing against Astros the next year, which led to his departure. At 6'4", 220, Farnsworth was the prototype closer, a role he flirted with but never earned, as evidenced by his four career saves in a Cubs uniform. He struck out 107 batters with just 29 walks in '01, but the guy with the thick, long hamstrings always will be known in Wrigleyville as a colossal disappointment.

2. Marcus Fizer, Bulls. After his junior year at Iowa State, where he led the Big 12 in scoring twice and was a consensus All American, Fizer bolted for the NBA. He was 6'8" and 265 pounds and was a lock to put the Bulls back on the map after they drafted him with the 4th pick overall in '00. Oops. Fizer made just 35 starts in his 289-game NBA career, averaging a scant 9.6 ppg and 4.6 rbp. Knee injuries riddled his career, and he was so underwhelming, the expansion Charlotte Bobcats couldn't find a place for him on their roster in their inaugural season of '04. Finished with Milwaukee, though it's doubtful anybody outside of Beertown recalls that.

1. Alonzo Spellman, Bears. If you were choosing guys for your side in a brawl in an alley, you'd chose Spellman and like your chances. Nobody ever looked more ferocious than Spellman, who was a starter in all three of his years at Ohio State. The Bears picked the defensive end in the 1st round (22nd overall) in '92. He was ripped and stood 6'4" and weighed 250 pounds. His arms dangled seemingly to his toes. One problem: Spellman sucked. He was Velcroed to offensive tackles and wasn't stout against the run, either. Diagnosed as bipolar, Spellman's problems weren't limited to the football field. He was arrested for disrupting a flight from Cincinnati to Philadelphia in '02, a couple of years after an infamous episode in a north suburban Chicago. Former teammate Mike Singletary assisted a S.W.A.T. team arrest after Spellman had threatened rampage and suicide and was considered armed and dangerous. On the field, he was only armed.

John Jurkovic's Favorite Chicago Athletes

Note: "Jurko" (pronounced "Yer'-ko") grew up in Calumet City dreaming of someday playing for the Bears. The jolly "Good Kid" would have to settle for playing against them. And for five years ('91-'95) it was in the uniform of the hated Green Bay Packers. We asked the popular ESPN Radio host to give us his 10 favorite Chicago athletes.

10. Doug Wilson, Blackhawks. No helmet on his head, Willie was one of the last of a dying breed. He was the thinking man's defenseman. Skilled at both ends. Big slapshot.

9. Reggie Theus, Bulls. Before Michael Jordan arrived, Theus was the only reason to watch the Bulls. He was a smooth shooter. Loved watching Theus play.

8. Ron Kittle & Greg Walker, White Sox. Both came up in the early 80s and they remain best friends so I'm counting them as one. They were the first autographs I got when I was a kid.

7. Jeremy Roenick, Blackhawks. The best No. 27 in Chicago sports history. Skinny, gritty little bastage who helped propel the Hawks to the '91 Stanley Cup Finals.

6. Dave Kingman, Cubs. Treated the media like the vermin they were. When he came to the plate, I stopped and watched. Everybody did.

5. Jim McMahon, Bears. The punky QB is the only legitimate QB the Bears have had in my lifetime.

4. Doug Plank, Bears. The only reason the Bears of the 70s and early 80s were worth watching. He used to murder Tampa Bay tight end Jimmie Giles.

3. Dick Butkus, Bears. Tenacious and ferocious. Even though he was a jerk when I met him, I loved the way he played.

2. Bill Buckner, Cubs. My favorite Cub of all time. Black bat and bushy mustache and a noticeable limp from ankle surgery puts this grinder at the top. '86 World Series be damned.

1. Walter Payton, Bears. The best and hardest-working running back ever. Better than Gale Sayers. Always punished the tackler and fought for the extra yard every time he carried the ball.

The Zen Master :: by Bill Wennington

Note: Bill Wennington got a firsthand look at Phil Jackson's unique coaching style. The 7-foot center spent six years with the Bulls, picking up three championship rings during the second half of the team's dynasty. Of Jackson, Wennington said, "It's not what you know basketball-wise. Every coach knows the game. Phil showed there's more than one way to skin a cat."

Wennington ranks Jackson's best traits.

7. Rodman. He said, "Dennis, these are the team rules. You're subject to all those rules. What you do off the court is your business." Dennis appreciated that. There weren't special Dennis rules. The rules were for everyone.

6. Body reader. He had a knack of reading body language and understanding when players were upset. He knew when he needed to treat a player with kid gloves or whether to apply more pressure. It's very important to be able to do that because the players aren't the same and everyone responds to different stimuli.

5. Practice as you play. When we played five-on-five in practice, Steve Kerr and I never started off on the floor. We always were sitting down. It was like, "We're not in the first 10 guys?" Finally, Steve said, "We want to play." Phil said, "What do you do in a game? Come off the bench, right? I want you guys to know what it's like to come off the bench." He did it that way to even further prepare our minds. All of the sudden, it clicked.

4. Game coach. No matter what happened, he maintained a good demeanor. It was rare that he would lose it. You also were able to play through a lot of mistakes. As long as you were playing well, he would let you play through a bad quarter, even a half. A lot of coaches would pull you out right away, but Phil would allow guys to play through the mistakes, get their rhythm, and they would eventually respond.

3. On edge. He didn't let anyone get comfortable. Nobody could ever say, "This is who I am and it's going to stay that way." We had a lot of good players on that team and we all wanted to play. He used us to motivate each other.

2. Native American. When he would talk about Native Americans, it was a way for him to break down the barriers of all the players, and relate to all of us as one. When he would bring up something, it wasn't just one or two guys going, 'What's he talking about?' It was all 12 of us. He then would explain it to us as an Indian tribe going into battle and relate it to us going into a game. When he did it that way, he got everyone's attention.

1. Team. He got everyone to buy into the team concept. He got Michael to buy into the system. He made us believe that every link is important to the team—it's not just one guy scoring 30 points per game. Obviously, some links are bigger than others and we needed Michael. But Michael also understood it was important for Bill Wennington to do what he did, for Steve Kerr to do what he did. He convinced everyone that we all were fighting for the common good.

Some of the biggest moments in sports history involving some of the biggest names took place in Chicago. They served to further enhance this town's sports heritage.

9. Match race. Horseracing fever gripped the nation on August 31, 1955 when Nashua met Swaps in a match race at Washington Park. Swaps won the Kentucky Derby, but Nashua came back to win the Preakness and Belmont. A crowd of 35,262 fans watched two legendary jockeys, Eddie Arcaro on Nashua and Willie Shoemaker on Swaps, go to battle. Arcaro had Nashua break fast early in messy conditions, and the horse held on for victory, avenging the loss in the Kentucky Derby.

8. 1994 World Cup. Soccer hardly moves the needle in this town. However, for one day, the eyes of the rest of the world were on Soldier Field on June 17, 1994. A match between Germany and Bolivia kicked off the 1994 World Cup, the first time ever the event was held in the United States. The world took note of Germany's 1-0 victory. Chicago fans, meanwhile, were more concerned about the Sox and Cubs.

7. 1922 U.S. Open. Two of the all-time greats, Gene Sarazan and Bobby Jones, went to battle at Skokie Country Club in Glencoe. Jones, still in the early stages of his career, had his eyes on winning his first major title with the third-round lead. But an upstart, 20-year-old Sarazan, had a blazing final round, beating the great Jones by one shot. It would be the first of many memorable battles between the stars during the 20s.

6. 1999 PGA Championship. Woods had gone more than two years in search of his second major when he arrived at Medinah in August, 1999. He finally broke through, but not without surviving a memorable battle with Sergio Garcia. The 19-year-old Garcia won the crowd with his youthful antics, but Woods bagged his second major, winning by a shot.

5. Feller's gem. There's only been one opening day no-hitter in baseball history, and it belongs to Bob Feller. On April 16, 1940, the Cleveland right-hander was untouchable in shutting down the White Sox 1-0 at Comiskey Park.

4. Joe Louis wins. Louis met Jim Braddock in a heavyweight title fight at Comiskey Park on June 22, 1937. Louis only was 23 years old at the time, but he knocked out Braddock in the eighth round to become the youngest heavyweight champion in history. He would go on to hold the title for 12 years.

3. Stars. With the World Fair being held in Chicago, *Chicago Tribune* sports editor Arch Ward came up with the idea of hosting an exhibition game between the best players from the National League against the best from the American League. The end result was the first All-Star game on July 6, 1933 at Comiskey Park. The game was a huge success, as fittingly Babe Ruth hit the first All-Star homer in the AL's 4-2 victory. A tradition was born.

2. The Called Shot. Speaking of Ruth, his signature moment occurred at Wrigley Field during Game 3 of the World Series on October 1, 1932. The debate remains: Did he point to the centerfield flagpole before going deep with a massive homer off the Cubs' Charlie Root? Or was he gesturing to the Cubs dugout? Ruth had been arguing with the Cubs bench. Root never thought Ruth called his shot. "If he had pointed to the stands, he'd have gone down on his fanny."

1. The Long Count. Just like Ruth's "Called Shot," "The Long Count" fight between Jack Dempsey and Gene Tunney has been the subject of debate for generations. With more than 100,000 fans watching at Soldier Field (how did anyone see the ring?), Dempsey knocked down Tunney in the seventh round. It was the first time he ever hit the canvas.

Dempsey, though, didn't immediately move to his corner, and referee Dave Barry delayed starting the count. As a result, Tunney had 13 seconds to get back on his feet and resume the fight. The extra time allowed Tunney to recover and go on to win on points. It still remains the most controversial fight in boxing history.

Cubs Collapse in 1969 :: ES

No matter how many World Series titles the Cubs win in the 21st Century, they never will take away the pain inflicted on Cubs fans in 1969. The Cubs were in first place for 155 days in that magical summer. The players were rock stars and the win-starved fans couldn't get enough. Then it all came apart. Here are some of the reasons.

7. Don Young's blunder. The rookie centerfielder earned his place in Cubs infamy by dropping two fly balls in a tough 4-3 loss to the Mets in July at Shea Stadium. Ron Santo lost his composure, and yelled at Young after the game. Not a sound veteran move. The Cubs still were solidly ahead at the time, but the cracks were beginning to show.

6. The Vulture. Phil Regan, a.k.a, "The Vulture," didn't feast down the stretch. He was the culprit in one of the season's back-breaking moments. Willie Stargell hit a booming two-out, ninth inning homer off of him to tie a Cubs-Pittsburgh game in September. The Pirates would go on to win in extra innings. It was the Cubs' fourth straight loss in a fatal eight-game losing streak. Who knows what would have happened if Regan retired Stargell?

5. Lost focus. Perhaps being treated like rock stars wasn't a good thing. The constant flow of endorsements and people visiting the clubhouse now appears to be a distraction. For whatever reason, the players took their eyes off the ball.

4. The heat. Playing day baseball in the summer has been blamed for wearing down the veteran team. Manager Leo Durocher failed to adjust, putting the same guys out there every day. He rarely changed his lineup to give some players a much-needed day off. Catcher Randy Hundley appeared in 151 games. Santo played in 160 games. Billy Williams, the Iron Man, was out there for all 163 games. Mr. Cubs, Ernie Banks, played in 155 games at the age of 38. It is hard to quantify fatigue, but clearly it might have played a factor. Banks hit only 1 homer and batted .186 in September.

3. The Miracles. Even though the Cubs only were 31-33 after the All-Star break, they still won 92 games for the season. In some years, that would have been good enough to win. The "Miracle Mets" caught fire, going 41-15 down the stretch to rack up 100 victories. Led by the young pitching staff of Tom Seaver and Jerry Koosman, they were unstoppable. Even if the Cubs had won 99 games, it still wouldn't have been enough.

2. The black cat. A fitting metaphor for the season occurred on September 9th of that year. During a crucial series with the Mets at Shea, a black cat suddenly appeared on the field and circled Ron Santo as he stood in the on-deck circle. Talk about receiving a dose of bad luck. The Cubs would go on to lose the game and fall out of first place, never to return.

1. The goat. Forget about the cat. At the time, the "Billy Goat Curse" was only 24 years old. It still had many, many more years to haunt the Cubs.

The Cubs have had an incredible knack for inventing new and unique ways of ripping out the hearts of their fans through the years. Just when you think you've seen everything, they come up with yet another way to choke. Here are the Cubs' biggest flops during the regular season and postseason.

8. 1977. This season doesn't often make many of these lists, but it should. The Cubs shocked everyone in 1977 by getting off to a sizzling start. They hit their high-water mark with a 47-22 record on June 28th, good enough for an 8½ game lead in the National League East. They were in first place for 62 days that summer. But it wasn't to be, as the Cubs sank in the second half. Incredibly, they only finished with an 81-81 record.

7. 1929. This crew, which included Hall of Famers Rogers Hornsby, Gabby Hartnett, Hack Wilson and Kiki Cuyler, was a hitting machine, posting a "team" batting average of .303 for the season. However, against the Philadelphia Athletics, they hit only .249 in the World Series. They suffered two gut-wrenching losses in that five-game series, blowing an 8-0 lead in the seventh inning of Game 4 and a 2-0 edge in the ninth inning of Game 5.

6. 1945. The Cubs won a dramatic 8-7 victory in Game 6 to send the World Series to a seventh game against Detroit. With the momentum on their side and playing in Wrigley Field, the Cubs looked prime to celebrate their first title since 1908. But it wasn't meant to be, as Detroit scored five in the first inning and never looked back in a 9-3 victory.

5. 1906. Led by the famous double play combination of "Tinkers-to-Evers-to-Chance," this team compiled a 116-36 regular-season record, still the highest winning percentage (.763) in baseball history. All they had to do in the World Series was beat the Crosstown White Sox, an uninspiring bunch dubbed "The Hitless Wonders" because of their .228 batting average. However, it was the Cubs who looked futile in the World Series, losing in six games.

4. 1969. This is the season that seems destined to describe Cubs heartbreak forever. You know the story. Up 8½ games in August, the Cubs suffer a mighty collapse. They lost 11 or 12 games at one point in September, watching the "Miracle Mets" whiz by them. As *Chicago Tribune* writer Paul Sullivan wrote, "This is the season you learned a valuable lesson about being a Cubs fan—the more you put your heart into the team, the deeper the scar from the inevitable heartbreak."

3. 2008. You could make an argument that this was the Cubs' most stunning collapse. The Cubs won 97 games, the best regular-season record in the National League. They seemed more than primed to end their 100-year title drought. Then they go out and lose three straight games to decidedly inferior Los Angeles Dodgers team in the division series. They couldn't hit, couldn't field, and couldn't pitch. They lost the first two games at home by a combined score of 17-5. It was an incredible display of feebleness. Even Sox fans had to have some sympathy at watching the Cubs fans' hearts get shattered again.

2. 2003. You really can't make up this stuff. The Cubs are five outs away from going to the World Series when a fan interferes with Moises Alou's attempt to catch a foul ball down the leftfield line. Everything disintegrates from there, as the Cubs go on to lose Game 6 and then Game 7 against Florida in a meltdown of epic proportions. The poor fan, Steve Bartman, becomes part of Cubs legend.

1. 1984. You could make some arguments over which heartbreak was the worst, but this one still is the all-timer. After rocking San Diego in the first two games of the NLCS at home, the Cubs, needing just one victory to go to their first World Series since 1945, couldn't get it done. They lose three in a row against the Padres.

On a personal note, I was a young reporter then. With the Cubs on the verge of winning, I was assigned to go to the "Ultimate Sports Bar" in Lincoln Park to ask Cubs fans about the team's chances in the upcoming World Series against Detroit. I went there for three straight nights and never got to ask my questions.

As a college football enthusiast, the Windy City's apathy regarding college athletics pains my ass. Collectively, we just don't embrace college sports as much as we should. One would think that the "me-first" nature of pro jockos in the 21st century would open the door for an increase in interest in college sports, both locally and nationally, but it hasn't. Here are the reasons why.

10. Loyola basketball is dead. Ask any local old timer about college basketball and he will tell you how Loyola captured the national championship in 1963. Ask any late-teens or 20-somethings about Loyola and they couldn't tell you the team nickname is the Ramblers. I suspect college hoops would be much more compelling if Loyola had continued to excel.

9. No great venues. When you think of great places to watch college football—whether you've been there or not—you think of the Big House in Ann Arbor, MI. The Horseshoe in Columbus, OH. The Swamp in Gainesville, FL. While Ryan Field in Evanston offers a fine place to tailgate and a decent view of a Northwestern game, it isn't what you would call "center ring." And Memorial Stadium in Champaign is a 70,000-seat dinosaur. The same problem exists with the basketball facilities. All State Arena is a decent place, but it isn't on campus and has no buzz for DePaul games. Northwestern's Welsh-Ryan Arena is a high school gym. The Assembly Hall at Illinois wins the tallest midget award for best local college basketball arena. Still, the folks at North Carolina, Duke or Kansas aren't losing sleep over being leapfrogged for atmosphere anytime soon.

8. Jay Berwanger played a long time ago. Want to win a drink at your neighborhood tavern? Ask the guy sitting next to you who won the first Heisman Trophy in '35. The answer is Berwanger, a University of Chicago running back, who also was the first player selected in the NFL's first college entry draft (Philadelphia Eagles). They don't play football in Hyde Park anymore and most don't know they ever did. Berwanger died in June of '02, long after the Maroons football program passed.

7. Notre Dame is no longer considered a Chicago school. The Fighting Irish fancy themselves as an international institution of higher learning. Had Notre Dame accepted one of several invitations to join the Big Ten, there might be a more visceral connection with the locals and ND. The days of Moose Krause, an outstanding hooper in the 30s, and '53 Heisman winner Johnny Lattner (still a legend at Fenwick High School) are well in the rear-view mirror. Yeah, the Irish had other Chicago kids who broke a sweat before Touchdown Jesus (Mt. Carmel's Tony Furjanik and Chicago Vocational's Chris Zorich come to mind), but ND is not a Chicago school anymore.

6. Northwestern men's basketball sucks. Let me get this straight. Schools with high academic standards such as Stanford, Duke and Texas compete for national championships regularly, but Northwestern never has been to the NCAA tournament? How can this be? In hoops, you need two or three terrific players and a decent supporting cast. That's it. If Northwestern can field a competitive football program, one would think they also could achieve that on the hardwood. Plausible arguments can be made that Northwestern never having been to the NCAA tournament is the most embarrassing reality in Chicago sports. By accident, they should have a 20-win season and a trip to The Dance every now and again.

5. Lack of national championships. The Fighting Illini have come close in men's hoops, but close isn't enough. Nobody walked away from the 75-70 loss to North Carolina in the '05 championship game thinking "We are the next Carolina!" or "Move over Duke!" And to add insult, rival Indiana has won five national championships and got to a title game in a "down year" in '02. On the gridiron, nobody even thinks about a trip to the BCS title game by a local entrant. Big Ten championships are ample satisfaction when they arrive every blue moon.

4. DePaul basketball doesn't matter anymore. In the 70s and 80s, Blue Demon basketball was as synonymous to a Chicago winter as a snow shovel. The late Ray Meyer didn't win a national title, but DePaul won a lot of games under his direction and the Demons generated a buzz before Michael Jordan made the Bulls viable. Mark Aguire. Terry Cummings. Dave Corzine. Some terrific players have spent time on Belden Avenue. These days, DePaul is a punching bag in the Big East and anybody who agrees to coach this outfit is a glutton for self abuse.

3. Illinois can't handle prosperity in football. Almost every year the Fighting Illini do something meaningful on the gridiron, they encore it by laying an egg. It would stand to reason that success would breed more success and recruits would be lining up to wear the orange and blue. They don't. And because the Bears regularly underwhelm, a football crazed town like ours would love to have a consistent winner. Mike White. John Mackovic. Ron Turner. Ron Zook. Doesn't seem to matter who's wearing the headset. Have a great season and piss the bed the following year.

2. Neighboring schools win more consistently. This speaks to points just made regarding Illinois football. Barry Alvarez resurrected the Wisconsin program in the 90s and Brett Bilemma has kept the standard high since Alvy took over as Badgers A.D. Wisconsin is always in the hunt. In a so-so year, Kirk Ferentz's Iowa Hawkeyes play on New Year's Day. Illinois, and to a lesser extent, Northwestern, can't seem to stay on target. In basketball, Purdue is almost always in the hunt. Gene Keady reeled off three straight conference championships in the 90s and that included one after Big Dog Glen Robinson was gone. Indiana has been a factor in the Big Ten for the better part of 35 years, while Illinois regularly changes coaches. Even Wisconsin, under Bo Ryan's direction, has performed more consistently than Illinois.

1. This is a pro town. Jordan helped ensure this reality. No blame cast in his direction for his enormous success, but everything else was exceedingly peripheral to the Bulls' six titles in an eight-year stretch between '91 and '98. And then there's the Bears factor. Chances are excellent that because you are reading this fine publication, you are at least 25 pounds overweight, have a cholesterol count of more than 250 and look forward to your pile of sausages before the next rivalry renewal with the hated Packers. Say it with me: Da Bearsss.

The Best Summer Job—Ballpark Vendor :: ES

I literally grew up at Comiskey Park and Wrigley Field. I became a vendor during my senior year in high school. I kept the job through college. Being a vendor was a Sherman family tradition. My father did it and so did both of my brothers. Unfortunately, I never got to sell beer because I retired before I turned 21. Still, I couldn't think of a better way to spend the summer than at the ballpark. Here are my favorite memories.

7. Frosty Malts. Getting assigned to Frosty Malts on a hot day at Wrigley Field was easy money. Well, perhaps easy isn't the word. You had to carry the Malts with a big slab of dry ice. Then to really score, you had to drag a double load to the upper deck. So you were hauling 50-60 pounds up those ramps. But once you got up there, you practically sold out in 30 seconds. Loved those Frosty Malts.

6. Upper deck peanuts. This was another prime assignment for the under 21-set. There weren't many vendors in the upper deck at Comiskey Park. However, there still were plenty of fans up in the upper regions. You had the place to yourself, enabling you to make a big score.

5. Elmer. At the end of each game, we had to stand in line to check out. At Comiskey Park, that meant dealing with Elmer. Elmer was a large older man who never said more than a grunt. He was supposed to deduct taxes from our payout. However, that didn't happen with Elmer. All of us would push a quarter in his direction and say the magic words, "Go easy, Elmer." Presto, no deductions for Federal and State taxes. All for a quarter. Needless to say I have fond memories of Elmer.

4. Batting practice. Being a vendor meant getting to the ballpark three or four hours early to wait in line to get our assignment. Then we had some time to kill before the gates opened. Usually, we would sit in the outfield and watch batting practice. We had the place to ourselves, making it easy to collect balls that landed in the stands. Alas, they cracked down on us at some point and made us throw back the balls.

3. Super Bowl of Rock concerts. During the summer, Soldier Field would host these big concerts with Ted Nugent, Lynyrd Skynyrd, Bob Seger, etc. Needless to say, there was a certain smell in the air. You could get high just by walking around. However, we never made it outside. I sold Coke, the drinking variety. It was so hot that people would converge on our stations and grab the Cokes before we even got out the door. Here's the bonus. Most of them were so buzzed, they would throw $5 at you for a 75 cent Coke and walk away without getting their change. Needless to say, those Super Bowl of Rock concerts were profitable experiences.

2. Southside Hitmen. My first summer vending was in 1977. The Sox came out of nowhere that year to emerge as a surprise contender. With Richie Zisk and Oscar Gamble, the balls were flying out of Comiskey Park. The place rocked every night. Every other minute the scoreboard seemed to be going off. I was having so much fun, I almost was sad when I had to leave for my freshman year of college.

1. The competition. Back then, we earned money on a 20 percent commission. The more we sold, the more we made. As a result, we rarely watched the game. We were out there humping, trying to sell our loads as fast as possible. It truly was an art, and a competition developed to see who could sell the most. You had to be quick and map out a good strategy, figuring out what sections were hot at a particular time. The race added more motivation to keep selling. And it was fun. I can't say I was the best, but I held my own in the top 10-15 percent. Even more important, the lessons I learned in that job when it came to hustling carried over into my career as a journalist.

William Petersen's Fondest Childhood Sports Memory :: DM

I met *CSI: Crime Scene Investigation* star William Petersen in the mid 90s. Unbeknownst to me, he was back in Chicago and had become a listener of the radio show I was doing with Terry Boers on "The Score." He called to discuss whatever it was we were debating as "Bill from Evanston." And that's really who he is, just a regular guy who loves Chicago sports. Billy P. and I became fast friends and started tailgating together at Northwestern football games. Despite his enormous success in television, film and the theatre, Bill remains an extremely grounded guy and comes back home a couple times a year to see his friends and go to Cubs games. I have had no luck convincing him to come over to the "dark side" and take in a White Sox game, even though his wife, Gina, is a Sox fan. A few years back, he told me about his favorite sports memory from his youth, so I called and asked him to elaborate on it.

DM: You said something about Cubs shortstop Don Kessinger hitting a foul ball that you caught. Is that your best memory as a young Cubs fan?

WP: Yeah, I remember like it happened last week. That day cost me a suspension from school. It was Opening Day of '67 or '68. I think it was April 2nd. My buddy Scott McKay, who now owns a bunch of Nissan dealerships in North suburban Chicago, ditched school to go. We took the El down from Evanston and tried to get tickets. In those days, Opening Day was the only day of the year that was sold out, so all we could find were bleacher seats. I don't know how we did it, but we managed to sneak into the main part of the ballpark. We were looking for open seats, walking from the left field side down behind third base. Kessinger was one of my favorite players. He was hitting from the left side (Kessinger was a switch hitter) and ripped a shot down behind third base. I saw it coming at us and never took my eye off of it. I saved the guy who was right behind us some dental work. I put my left arm up and it hit my wrist. It bounced down a few feet and must have hit something because it bounced right back to me and I grabbed it. I haven't gotten once since, but I did catch a puck at a Blackhawks game many years later.

DM: How was it you got suspended from school?

WP: We got caught ditching. Scott and I both called into school as our dads. (deep voice) "Uh, Hello, this is Mr. Petersen. Bill is not feeling well today and he will not be coming to school." We called from some pay-phone outside some drugstore after we parked our bikes. I was in 8th grade and Scott was only in 7th so I had it all figured out. It was some Catholic school and they checked up on stuff like that so you had to make it sound good.

DM: So how did you get caught?

WP: The game was on WGN. Everybody watched Opening Day. They saw us on TV. If it would have been the next day or the day after, nobody would have known because nobody cared much after that.

DM: Did you keep the ball?

WP: Yeah, I still have it. About a month went by and I thought to myself, "This thing needs to be signed," but there was no way I was going to get Don Kessinger to sign it so I signed it as Don Kessinger and told people he had signed it. How was I going to get a hold of Kessinger? I wound up telling him the whole story on some radio show. . . .

DM: (interrupting) That would be my radio show, not some radio show.

WP: Sorry. Yeah, your show. That was the only time I ever got to Kessinger. He was somewhere down South. Alabama, I think.

DM: Mississippi. Selling real estate. We talk to him almost every year before the Cubs and White Sox play because he played for both and also managed the White Sox.

WP: That sounds right.

DM: So was it worth getting suspended?

WP: Yeah. I've got a story now.

Sorry for the verbosity, but we must establish criteria. A movie produced in Chicago, but not set in Chicago, is disqualified. I loved *Hoffa* as much as anybody. Not a Chicago movie. A movie that includes a scene or two in Chicago, but is primarily set elsewhere, is disqualified. Sorry *When Harry Met Sally* fans. You're out. If a movie is set in Chicago, but was produced somewhere else, it is eligible for consideration, provided it captures the feel of this awesome town.

The film industry long has embraced Chicago as a perfect backdrop. And why wouldn't it? We possess awesome architechture, a breathtaking skyline, and a rich history, although not all of it good. It was incredibly difficult to limit this one to 10, but here are my 10 favorite "Chicago" movies.

10. *Nothing in Common*. '86. Comedy/Drama. Directed by Garry Marshall. Jackie Gleason and Tom Hanks are the father and son who fail to connect. When dad and mom (played by Eva Marie Saint) split, Hanks' character drops his commitment to his career to become a real son. This is a hysterically funny film that also includes many sad realities that define the human condition. It is amazing to me this one slipped so far under the radar. Great dialogue with many vivid views of the city.

9. *Ferris Bueller's Day Off*. '86. Comedy. One of the many John Hughes adolescent gutbusters. Matthew Broderick is Ferris, who finds a dozen ways to get into trouble while playing hookey. Alan Ruck plays Cameron Frye, Ferris's best friend. Maybe I was a smidge too old to "get" this film completely when it was released, but I must include it for fear of being kidnapped one of the millions of fans who adore it.

8. *The Blues Brothers*. '80. Comedy/Musical. This is classic Chicago. Dan Aykroyd not only delivered a brilliant performance as Elwood Blues, he helped write the film with director John Landis. Aykroyd and John Belushi (Jake Blues) turn in a magnificent tag team effort in this worthy comedy. Any time I see an old Plymouth driving down the road, I think of Jake and Elwood. And sorry Elvis, "Jailhouse Rock" never sounded as good as it did when it was peformed by The Blues Brothers.

7. *The Breakfast Club*. '85. Comedy. John Hughes strikes again. "Brat-Packers" Emilio Estevez, Anthony Michael Hall, Ally Sheedy, Molly Ringwald and Judd Nelson spend a Saturday in detention at Shermer High. It proves to be one of the most meaningful days of their young lives. The principal is played by the late Paul Gleason, who is the perfect dickhead to supervise the delinquent teens. I still get an enormous kick out of this movie and have passed it on to my teenage sons.

6. *The Break-Up*. '06. Comedy/Drama. Finally something worthy has been produced in Chicago in this century. This is kind of an updated version of *About Last Night*, but I believe it is funnier and, at times, much sadder. Vince Vaughn and Jennifer Aniston are equally devilish in their dysfunctional relationship that ultimately goes belly up. Jon Favreau is a stitch as Vaughn's best friend while Judy Davis delivers a hysterical role as Aniston's boss. Directed by Peyton Reed, *The Break-Up* captures the spirit of young singles in the big city. And it also gives us a cameo from the still-easy-on-the-eyes Ann-Margret, a native Chicagoan. This movie is full of Chicagoans and is Chicago.

5. *The Untouchables*. '87. Drama. Any list of Chicago movies that doesn't include an Al Capone film is not credible. Capone is played by the great Robert DeNiro. If you haven't seen the spine-tingling scene where he ball bats a disloyal member of the gang, you're missing out on all the best that gangster movies have to offer. Kevin Costner turns in one of his best performances (tall midget award?) as Elliot Ness, the cop determined to bag Capone at whatever price. Brian De Palma directs this thrill ride, which also includes fantastic efforts by Sean Connery and Andy Garcia.

4. *Ordinary People*. '80. Drama. My tear ducts are active just thinking about this sad story of a typical family anywhere in America, in this case, north suburban Chicago. Donald Sutherland is Calvin Jarrett, a successful, loving father who lets his selfish wife, Beth (Mary Tyler Moore), push him around. Timothy Hutton is Conrad, the confused son who is struggling to get past his brother's drowning and find his own way. Robert Redford directed this tearjerker, that includes a solid effort from Judd Hirsch as Conrad's psychologist.

3. *The Fugitive*. '93. Suspense/Drama. If you don't know the hook to this one, you must have been living on Mars for the past 15 years. In addition to the tremendous chemistry that is established among Tommy Lee Jones (Marshal Samuel Gerard) and his team, this film captures some remarkably vivid shots of Chicago, both downtown (the lower Wacker scene is my favorite) and in the neighborhoods. Harrison Ford's performance as Dr. Richard Kimble is, for my money, the best of his career. This film is so Chicago, director Andrew Davis even had local newsies (at the time) Lester Holt and John "Bulldog" Drummond play themselves.

2. *Thief*. '81. Suspense. The most underrated movie produced *anywhere*. This is a dark, chilling story of an ex-con, played by James Caan, who can't let go of his craft, which is high-line burglary. Caan is assisted by James Belushi and the duo, previously self-employed, ultimately join a crew, which is run by Robert Prosky's character, Leo. Chicagoan Michael Mann is the director of this brilliant movie, which includes a peek at the Green Mill Lounge on Lawrence Ave. and several other off-the-beaten path Chicago landmarks. Tuesday Weld is Caan's love interest. Willie Nelson is Caan's mentor. Both were spectacular. And *Thief* includes some of the earliest performances of Chicago natives Dennis Farina and William Petersen. Watch this movie!

1. *The Sting*. '73. Drama/Suspense. Normally I wouldn't point to a film's acclaim to back a recommendation, but when seven Oscars grace a résumé, it's difficult not to take notice. Robert Redford and Paul Newman are at their best, even better than in *Butch Cassidy and the Sundance Kid*. Robert Shaw turns in his second best role ever (sorry, I'm a "Quint" man). The wardrobe and sets dramatically capture a bygone era. George Roy Hill proves in *The Sting* why he is among the greatest directors in film history. There is nothing about this bait-and-switch classic *not* to like. Now that I've wrapped up this list, I'm going immediately to the 60-inch Sony for a date with this legendary classic.

The Best of Ozzie Guillen :: ES

The White Sox manager is incredibly outspoken on any topic and isn't afraid to throw a player—or the entire team—under the bus. Here is the best of Ozzie with many bleeps just in case the kids are reading.

14. When sworn in as a U.S. citizen, Ozzie was asked who was the Mayor of Chicago: "I said Ozzie Guillen."

13. Ozzie at spring training in 2006 as the manager of the World Series champions, as opposed to being a rookie manager in 2004: "Now there are 30 or 40 reporters around to see how big my mouth really is."

12. Ozzie on whether his kids were involved in a Cubs-Sox brawl: "If my kids were on the field, they're going to get their [rear-end] kicked. What's Ozzie Jr. going to do? Eat somebody? My other one is 20 pounds, and the other one is only 14."

11. Ozzie not hiding his feelings about Jay Mariotti: "He's a garbage. He's always been a garbage. And he will die a garbage."

10. On Rob Mackowiak playing centerfield: "I don't think you're going to see Mackowiak in centerfield that much—I want to keep my job. And I think Mackowiak wants to keep his job, too."

9. On Buck Showalter criticizing Guillen: "There are so many different things he might be jealous [of] . . . I was a better player than him, I've got more money than him and I'm better looking than him."

8. On a bad streak: "We have to apologize to the fans watching this thing because I'm tired of watching this day in and day out. Wow. You thought I was a good manager. Well, look at me now. I'm not that good. You're as good as your players are."

7. On steriods revelations: "When I see Wally Joyner, Ken Caminiti and Jose Canseco talk about it, they make me puke. They're full of (bleep). You know why? Whatever happens in the clubhouse stays in the clubhouse. I see these former players talking (bleep) about the game, and it's not right."

6. Feuding with Magglio Ordonez: "Why do I have to apologize to him? Who the (bleep) is Magglio Ordonez? Why ever talk about me? He doesn't do (bleep) for me. But if he thinks I'm his enemy, he has a big enemy. He knows me."

5. On managing: "It's a horse(bleep) job. If you win, you get paid two million dollars. If you lose, you get fired."

4. On sports-talk radio: "They think they know baseball, but they don't know (bleep). If people on the radio were so smart, they'd be in the (bleep) dugout with me. Every time the media second-guesses you, it's after something happens, not before.

3. Venting on treatment of Sox compared to Cubs: "We won it a couple years ago, and we're horse(bleep). The Cubs haven't won in [100] years, and they're the (bleeping) best. (Bleep) it, we're good. (Bleep) everybody. We're horse(bleep), and we're going to be horse(bleep) the rest of our lives, no matter how many World Series we win.

"We are the (bleep) of Chicago. We're the Chicago (bleep). We have the worst owner [Jerry Reinsdorf]. The guy's got seven (bleeping) rings, and he's the (bleeping) horse(bleep) owner."

2. Player-manager relationship: "I don't care about [players' feelings]. . . . They don't care about mine. I never heard any player come to me and say, 'How are you feeling today?' Only my wife told me this morning, 'How do you feel?' I feel fine."

1. The essence of Ozzie: "Sometimes I create my own problems too. I'm not going to make any excuses. That's the way I am. That's me. I'm going to say what I have to say. Some people say the same stuff I say, but they don't get attacked like I do."

Da Coach :: ES

Mike Ditka is many things, but nobody will ever call him dull. He has his unique philosophy on how the game should be played, and how people should live. He often begins his mini sermons with "In life," or "Don't get me wrong." Here is a sampling of the best of Ditka.

15. "It's football, it's not brain surgery. Have some fun."

14. "What's the difference between a 3-week-old puppy and a sportswriter? In 6 weeks, the puppy will stop whining."

13. "He's a young guy [Dave Wannstedt] with a lot of enthusiasm and he's really proud to be a Pittsburgh guy. And you have to have a Pittsburgh guy here. You don't need any more California guys here, gang. We don't need any of that crap. They come and go like the flies."

12. "If God had wanted man to play soccer, He wouldn't have given us arms."

11. "[Jim McMahon and I] have a strange and wonderful relationship—he's strange and I'm wonderful."

10. "I'm not a mean player. You'll notice I never pick on a player who has a number above 30."

9. "I said a long time ago if you want to change the game take the mask off the helmet."

8. "Success isn't measured by money or power or social rank. Success is measured by your discipline and inner peace."

7. "Before you can win, you have to believe you are worthy."

6. "Yesterday's history. Tomorrow's a mystery. Today's a gift, that's why they call it the present."

5. "The ones who want to achieve and win championships motivate themselves."

4. "You're never a loser until you quit trying."

3. "Success isn't permanent and failure isn't fatal."

2. "If you're not in the parade, you watch the parade. That's life."

1. "Those who live in the past are cowards and losers."

The Zen Master :: ES

Phil Jackson is hardly your typical coach. Deep and introspective, Jackson brings a spiritual approach to the game. While much of his Zen-like mantra confused his players at times, he made it work to the tune of six NBA titles in Chicago. Here is the best of Jackson.

17. "Wisdom is always an overmatch for strength."

16. "An acrobatic dunk will make it onto SportsCenter. A simple, unspectacular bounce pass in the rhythm of the offense will not. System basketball has been replaced by players who want to be the system."

15. "Basketball is a sport that involves the subtle interweaving of players at full speed to the point where they are thinking and moving as one."

14. "If you meet the Buddha in the lane, feed him the ball."

13. "Basketball, unlike football with its prescribed routes, is an improvisational game, similar to jazz. If someone drops a note, someone else must step into the vacuum and drive the beat that sustains the team."

12. "Good teams become great ones when the members trust each other enough to surrender the 'Me' for the 'We.'"

11. "The best part of basketball, for those people on the inside, is the bus going to the airport after you've won a game on an opponent's floor. It's been a very tough battle. And preferably, in the playoffs. And that feeling that you have, together as a group, having gone to an opponent's floor and won a very good victory, is as about as high as you can get."

10. "Once you've done the mental work, there comes a point you have to throw yourself into the action and put your heart on the line. That means not only being brave, but being compassionate towards yourself, your teammates and your opponents."

9. "Like life, basketball is messy and unpredictable. It has its way with you, no matter how hard you try to control it. The trick is to experience each moment with a clear mind and open heart. When you do that, the game—and life—will take care of itself."

8. "Despite their tremendous talent, [NBA players] are still, by and large, young adults, seeking validation from an authority figure, and there is no greater authority figure on a team than the coach. Needless to say, in today's warped, self-indulgent climate, too many players couldn't care less about appeasing the coach."

7. "Yes, victory is sweet, but it doesn't necessarily make life any easier the next season or even the next day."

6. "In basketball—as in life—true joy comes from being fully present in each and every moment, not just when things are going your way."

5. "Winning is important to me, but what brings me real joy is the experience of being fully engaged in whatever I'm doing."

4. "Always keep an open mind and a compassionate heart."

3. "I think the most important thing about coaching is that you have to have a sense of confidence about what you're doing. You have to be a salesman and you have to get your players, particularly your leaders, to believe in what you're trying to accomplish on the basketball floor."

2. "Love is the force that ignites the spirit and binds teams together."

1. "I gave it my body and mind, but I have kept my soul."

The One and Only :: ES

Harry Caray. There will never be another one like him. Chicago fans got the full Harry experience for 27 years—11 years with the White Sox and 16 years with the Cubs. Caray was wild and unpredictable. You never knew what was going to come out of his mouth. Here's Harry on announcing, baseball and life:

11. "I'll tell you what's helped me my entire life. I look at baseball as a game. It's something where people can go out, enjoy and have fun. Nothing more."

10. "Now, you tell me, if I have a day off during the baseball season, where do you think I'll spend it? The ballpark. I still love it. Always have, always will."

9. "This has been the remarkable thing about the fans in Chicago, they keep drawing an average of a million-three a year, and, when the season's over and they've won their usual 71 games, you feel that those fans deserve a medal."

8. "Chicago people are kind of fatalistic but they continue to hope that somehow, some way, the Cubs will shock even them and win it just one time. Their fatalism allows them to enjoy the team's success, knowing that one horrible thing will happen down the line to rip the rug out from underneath them."

7. "I would always sing it ["Take Me Out to the Ball Game"] because I think it's the only song I knew the words to!"

6. "I knew the profanity used up and down my street would not go over the air. So I trained myself to say 'Holy Cow' instead."

5. "My whole philosophy is to broadcast the way a fan would broadcast."

4. "I've only been doing this 54 years. With a little experience, I might get better."

3. "When I die, I hope they don't cremate me 'cuz I'll burn forever."

2. "Oh, what difference does it make (talking about his age)? I figure I had no business being here this long anyway, so what do you care how old I am? I've been on borrowed time for years. You know my old saying: live it up, the meter's running. I've always said that if you don't have fun while you're here, then it's your fault. You only get to do this once."

1. "Booze, broads, and bullshit. If you got all that, what else do you need?"

Great Voices :: by Pat Hughes

Note: Cubs radio play-by-play man Pat Hughes has held his position since 1996. He has put together CD tributes to Harry Caray and Jack Buck among others. Hughes loves nothing more than hearing a great voice behind the microphone. While Hughes has a great set of pipes himself, modesty prevented him from including himself in his list.

Here are Hughes' favorite voices.

7. Pat Summerall. He has such a pleasing manner of speaking. He never was guilty of overhyping a Super Bowl or a Masters. He was just kind of there, keeping things moving. Very, very easy to listen to. A great soothing wonderful voice.

6. Paul Carey. The great voice of the Detroit Tigers. He was overshadowed by Ernie Harwell, understandably. But in terms of just the quality of the voice, it would be hard to imagine a man having a deeper, more authoritative, stronger voice than Paul Carey. Also, a very nice man.

5. Jon Miller. Great voice of the Giants and ESPN. I've been on the air with him doing interviews. When you are actually on the air with him, and his voice is coming through the headphones, you could fully appreciate what a wonderful gift he has.

4. Lon Simmons. He was Russ Hodges' partner in San Francisco on the Giants' broadcasts. He also was a great voice for the 49ers. He was one of those guys I grew up listening to. I still can remember coming home, and my parents had this small stereo in the living room, and I'd sit down in front of the speakers and be mesmerized by his voice. Lon had such a deep, soothing baritone. He always was a funny man. He reminded you that sports should be fun. I learned a lot from him.

3. Mel Allen. The first real great baseball voice. The fact that he was the Yankees' announcer was big. In those days, the networks had a deal where the local announcers would call the World Series. A lot of people thought Mel was a network announcer, because he happened to be on the World Series year after year. An incredible voice.

2. Harry Kalas. Not only an unbelievably great voice, but he combined a superior work ethic with his God-given talents. That's why he was as special as he was.

1. John Facenda. He did as much to popularize the NFL as any player, coach, or broadcaster. With those tremendous voiceovers on NFL Films, he told the story of the game. What a voice.

Note: Hughes is a true artisan of his craft. While he still is waiting to call a World Series winner for the Cubs, he has enjoyed many memorable moments behind the microphone. Here are his favorites.

11. Cubs at New York Mets, April 2, 2003. Ron Santo burned his hairpiece at Shea Stadium. He stood too close to the electric heater. I looked over and his head was smoking. He goes, "How does it look?" I lied and said, "It doesn't look bad." But it looked like Tiger Woods took a pitching wedge and whacked one off Ronny's noggin.

10. San Diego Padres at Cubs, April 1, 1996. My first game as a Cubs announcer. It was 32 degrees, but the windchill was like 10. Because of the conditions, it looked like the pitchers were throwing about 130 miles per hour. Nobody could make contact. The Cubs won on a single in the 10th by Mark Grace.

9. Milwaukee Brewers at Cubs, June 29, 2007. Aramis Ramirez hit a game-winning homer off Francisco Cordero in the ninth. He hadn't blown a save all season. It was a turning point in the season. We had been down all day. We had no business winning the game.

8. New York Yankees at Cubs, June 7, 2003. The winning pitcher was Kerry Wood. The losing pitcher was Roger Clemens. Eric Karros hit a three-run homer to key the Cubs. It was a Saturday afternoon interleague game. It was one of those magical games that are frozen in time.

7. Cubs at Houston Astros (in Milwaukee), September 2008. Carlos Zambrano throws a no-hitter. It was the third no-hitter I had called in the big leagues. You don't see many neutral-site games in baseball, but it was necessitated by Hurricane Ike. Zambrano was utterly dominant. It was fun.

6. Pittsburgh Pirates at Cubs, September 27, 2003. Cubs win a doubleheader over the Pirates to clinch the division title. A long but very exciting day.

5. Cubs at Milwaukee Brewers, September 23, 1998. The Brant Brown game. The Cubs led 7-0 and lost. Brown drops the ball in left field, we lose. Ron Santo makes that memorable call, "OH NO!" After the game, Ronny is just despondent. In the clubhouse, he's going, "How could he do that in this situation?" I see something that probably never has been seen in the history of American sports. Jim Riggleman, the manager, goes over to Ron and tries to cheer him up. He said, "That's OK, Ron."

A manager trying to console a broadcaster? I don't think Mike Ditka ever tried to cheer up Wayne Larrivee.

4. Florida Marlins at Cubs, October 14, 2003. Game 6 of the NLCS. I can recall many details. I wish I could forget most of them. I remember the Cubs leading 3-0 in the eighth inning, and Mike Mordecai flied out to left to lead off. Little did we know that Mordecai would come up a second time in the inning and crack a three-run double off the vines. What are the odds? Just ridiculous.

3. San Francisco Giants at Cubs, September 28, 1998. The Cubs win the wildcard tie-breaker against the Giants. Michael Jordan threw out the first pitch. The late Rod Beck got the save. Gary Gaetti hit a two-run homer. The Cubs were in last place the year before, so to get in the playoffs the following year was really exciting.

2. Cubs at Atlanta Braves, October 5, 2003. The Cubs beat Atlanta in Game 5 to win the series. Kerry Wood the winner. It was the first Cubs post-season series win in 95 years. It was a thrilling time. I remember seeing Jim Hendry after the game and giving him a big hug. I had hugged him a week earlier when we clinched the division. I told him, "This is two hugs in a week, and I'm starting to like it."

1. Milwaukee Brewers at Cubs, September 12, 1998. Sammy Sosa hits his 60th homer. The Cubs were down 10-2, but they rallied for five in the ninth inning to win 15-12 on an Orlando Merced three-run homer. An incredible game. The real reason why it is the most memorable for me is that I had my daughter Janell (nine at the time) with me at the game. I took her down on the field before the game.

Sosa saw Janell and me standing there. He made a point to leave the batting cage to come over and say, "Who's the pretty girl?" He made her feel very special. Then he goes out and hits his 60th homer. That's No. 1 for me for all those reasons.

The Toughest Bulls :: by Norm Van Lier

Note: Shortly before he passed away in February 2009, we asked the toughest Bull of them all, Norm Van Lier, to compile his list of Bulls who dished it out and wouldn't back down on the floor. First, though, Norm gave us his assessment of himself as a tough guy.

"Because I grew up in Pennsylvania, I was more excited about playing football than basketball. I played basketball as if I was playing football. I had that small-man's mentality. However, the one thing I'm proud of is that I was never called 'Little Norm.' I was always called 'Stormin' Norman.' There was a reason for that."

Here are the rest of the Bulls tough guys, according to Stormin' Norman Van Lier:

10. Andres Nocioni. I like Nocioni, but I'm going to put this in a delicate way. I think he's tough, but he lets his temperament get in the way of his toughness. He gets fouled on one end and tries to show everyone "I'm tough" by knocking someone out. It hurts the team most of the time. I'll never question his toughness, but *when* he becomes tough disturbs me.

9. John Paxson. He was very underrated in the tough department. He was feisty. He wouldn't back down.

8. Cliff Levington. He came off the bench in the Jordan era. His attitude and play showed the team, "Let's go for it."

7. Michael Jordan. He was tough. He used toughness when he had to use it. He was tough because of the play against him. People tried to knock him out, not let him dunk. His actions showed, "I am tough, you can't hurt me. I'm not going to stop dunking on your face." He had to show more toughness by receiving it than dishing it out.

6. John Mengelt. His nickname was "Crash." John had the football mentality. For basketball, he wasn't quick and fast. John had those instinctive moves. I think he really learned that from football.

5. Ricky Sobers. I always thought Ricky was tough. He had the demeanor about him: "I want to kick your butt."

4. Dennis Rodman. He just went after it. Learning from the "Bad Boys" of Detroit, he came in with a reputation of getting after it. He wouldn't be denied in getting the ball or stopping somebody. He had more talent than his one-dimensional game showed. But when you're playing with Jordan, you're not going to get the ball that much.

3. Horace Grant. He was a guy you wouldn't think was tough, but was. When he put forth the effort to start kicking butt and not let people knock Jordan around is when the Bulls starting winning championships. That's my honest opinion. I always say Horace Grant was the guy.

2. Dennis Awtrey. When it comes to big men, Dennis Awtrey comes to mind. He would kick your ass. In those days, we had people who came in who were more or less like the sheriff: "Okay, law and order is here." When Awtrey came in, you knew somebody was going to get knocked down. I never forget he knocked out Kareem Abdul-Jabbar once. Probably was a mistake because Kareem averaged 50 points per game against us after that.

1. Jerry Sloan. When you talk about a tough player, you're not talking about a guy who wants to fight everybody. We're talking about Jerry's determination to shut down someone and not be afraid of contact. Dick Motta used to say, "You've got six fouls, use five of them." That's the way Jerry and I played.

Jerry came out playing and it certainly rubbed off for me to be around him. He was a good old-fashioned tough farm boy. He was just a tough SOB, man.

The Bulls definitely got it right when they selected Michael Jordan with the third pick in the 1984 draft. However, there were plenty of other times when they got it wrong, and the mistakes bit them in the butt for many years. Here is a list of the Bulls' worst busts on draft day.

10. David Greenwood. With a high pick comes high expectations. David Greenwood came to the Bulls as the No. 2 selection in the 1979 draft. The forward out of UCLA had a decent rookie season, averaging 16.3 points per game. But he never developed into a star player and was shipped out of Chicago after Jordan's rookie season in 1985. Too bad the Bulls didn't have the No. 1 pick that year. The Lakers used that choice to take Magic Johnson.

9. Jimmy Collins. Jimmy, we love you for your long-term work as coach at Illinois and UIC. But you didn't cut it with the Bulls. Selected with the 11th pick in the 1970 draft, the guard out of New Mexico State played only two seasons in Chicago, seeing little playing time. Thankfully, Collins had more success as a coach.

8. Ronnie Lester. Technically, the Bulls acquired Lester in a draft-day trade in 1980. The Bulls swapped their fourth pick, guard Kelvin Ransey, with Portland for Lester who was a dynamic guard at Iowa. But he hurt his knee during his first year with the Bulls and was never the same. He lasted only four years with the team.

7. Scott May. The Bulls used the No. 2 pick in the 1976 draft to select Scott May. It appeared to be a sound selection considering the forward was the leader of Bobby Knight's undefeated Indiana team. But May, dogged by injuries, was decidedly underwhelming as a pro, never averaging more than 14.6 points per game in a season. To take May, the Bulls passed on players such as Adrian Dantley, Quinn Buckner and Robert Parish. Ouch.

6. Tyrus Thomas. The jury still is out with Thomas, but the early returns aren't favorable. The Bulls took LaMarcus Aldridge with the second pick in the 2006 draft and then traded the big forward to Portland for the rights to Thomas. Thomas has tremendous athletic ability, but hasn't shown the basketball skills to go with it. To make things even worse, Aldridge has emerged as a solid inside player.

5. Marcus Fizer. Fizer seemed to be a good fit for the Bulls, who took him with the fourth pick in the 2000 draft. He played for Tim Floyd at Iowa State and at 6-8, 260 pounds, he looked to be a big, rugged inside player. However, it turned out he had limited basketball skills and didn't do much of note in four years with the Bulls.

4. Jay Williams. We'll never know how good Williams could have been. Taken with the second pick in the 2002 draft, the former Duke guard showed some flashes, averaging 9.5 points per game as a rookie. Then during the off-season he crashed his motorcycle, severely injuring his leg, and never played again. A big loss for the Bulls.

3. Brad Sellers. Has there ever been a softer man? The Bulls took the 7-footer out of Ohio State with the ninth pick in the 1986 draft. Sellers could shoot, but he was pushed around and not nearly tough enough to hang in a division that included the rugged Detroit Pistons. He was gone after three years. Remember, Jordan wanted GM Jerry Krause to select guard Johnny Dawkins from Duke, who went on the next pick. It would have been a better choice since Dawkins had some good years for San Antonio and Philadelphia.

2. Eddy Curry. Curry's selection proved to be the downfall for Krause. The GM picked the Thornwood product No. 4 in 2001. Then he turned around and traded Elton Brand to the Los Angeles Clippers for Tyson Chandler. Krause thought he had a dominant inside game set for years, but Curry never motivated himself to get any better, and Chandler struggled under a succession of coaches. The master plan was a flop.

1. Quintin Dailey. It still remains baffling why the Bulls picked this controversial guard. He was facing rape allegations when the Bulls used the seventh pick in the 1982 draft on Dailey. Women's organizations picketed the Bulls ticket offices to protest Dailey's selection. This was not a good character guy. Dailey then confirmed it with drug problems and all sorts of other issues as a pro. He actually averaged 16.4 points a game for the Bulls, but they couldn't get rid of him fast enough after four seasons. Just a bad dude.

When I was a kid, my dad used to tease me because I preferred the sports section to the Sunday comics. I knew I was going to be in sports media before I was in Little League. We've been fortunate to have some of the best sports writers in Chicago. These are my faves.

10. Barry Rozner, *The (Arlington Heights) Daily Herald.* I'll give Roz a mulligan for his over-the-top love for the Cubs. He can craft a graceful sentence as well as any suburban columnist. Rozner also speaks hockey, which earns him points in my world. I am a huge fan of columnists who are willing to shift gears and "spray to all fields" and Rozner does that regularly.

9. Ray Sons, *The Chicago Sun-Times.* Too much of a homer but an entertaining read while still in his prime. Sons was among the most well-received sports scribes in an era when the competition for readers was much stiffer than it is today.

8. Gene Seymour, *Copley News Service.* The periphery papers with limited travel budgets picked up Gene's columns on the wire. A South Sider through and through, Seymour could bring the hammer down, but still looked for the good in the athletes he covered. Geno had a condition called Marfans Syndrome and passed away in October of '96. At 43, he left a loving family, colleagues who respected him and readers who enjoyed him. A gentle, sweet man. I haven't set foot on a golf course without reflecting on my friendship with him since he left us way too early.

7. Ron Rapoport, *The Chicago Sun-Times.* Joined the S-T in '77. Also wrote for the *Los Angeles Times* and was a regular contributor to "The Sportswriters" on WGN Radio and National Public Radio. Witty. Brilliantly sarcastic. Rap was an old-school print guy who also had the capability of reaching younger readers with his oft-times cynical perspective.

6. John Schulian, *The Chicago Sun-Times.* When I would come home from college in the early 80s, one of the first things I would do was sift through the papers to see who Schu was bagging. John got me through the White Sox collapse against Baltimore in the '83 ALCS by capturing the disappointment better than anybody else did. A talented, bright man, Schulian chose to paint on a broader canvas when he split town for Los Angeles to create television programs.

5. Bob Verdi, *The Chicago Tribune.* Verd gained the trust of the guys he covered better than any writer I've seen. Joined the *Trib* in '67 and quickly established himself as an outstanding Blackhawks beat guy. Bob still contributes to the paper with a Sunday column. He reduced his role earlier in this decade to take on projects with *Golf World* and *Golf Digest*. A skilled wordsmith and outstanding tavernmate, Verdi could have been even bigger than he was if he were a bit more willing to take the blade to his subjects.

4. Skip Bayless, *The Chicago Tribune*. After a stellar 17-year run in Dallas, Skipper joined the *Trib* in '97. Great football mind, despite attending Vanderbilt. A dispute with management over the length of his pieces led to his resignation in '03. Bayless dug into the stories and the men behind them deeper than any local scribe. He is honest, passionate and prepared. More than any local newspaper man, Skip possesses a comfortable presence on television and contributes regularly to many national shows.

3. Jay Mariotti, *The Chicago Sun-Times*. Between 1991 and 2008, Mariotti was the self-appointed conscience of Chicago sports. And his readers hated him almost as much as his colleagues did. Lost in the madness was Jay's ability to turn phrases and create clever "Jay-isms." His personal war with Jerry Reinsdorf grew old, but the first thing I did in the mornings was read Mariotti. More than anybody, Jay was willing to take on our town's favorite sons, including Michael Jordan. A tireless workaholic, Mariotti would probably benefit from a non-sports hobby and some therapy. My opinion of his work, however, is not swayed by his cantankerous personality. Nobody created more interest and stirred it up more in this decade than Jay.

2. David Israel, *The Chicago Daily News*, *The Chicago Tribune*. In the mid-to-late-70s, when I was writing for my high school paper, Israel was the standard and served as a role model. His columns were vivid and provocative. The '73 Northwestern grad had an uncanny knack for getting under the skin of those he covered. He was fearless in a time when boosterism among writers was the norm. The bright lights of Hollywood unfortunately swayed him away. Israel was involved administratively in the '84 Los Angeles Olympics.

1. Bernie Lincicome, *The Chicago Tribune*. My favorite smart-ass. When the Bears were on their run to immortality in 85, Lincicome's star was at its brightest. Jim McMahon told Bears radio voice Wayne Larrivee that the media were nothing more than puppets and idiots. Lincicome took on the punky QB, writing a scathing piece that began with his dilemma for his tax return: "Am I puppet or an idiot?" Bernie gracefully turned phrases and barbequed the a-holes who had it coming for 17 years. Once a columnist for *The Rocky Mountain News*, Lincicome was always willing to take on icons. And he did it with style, not merely the sledgehammer-over-the-head approach Mariotti employed. Bernie's departure (another management battle) marked a sad day in Chicago sports journalism.

I need to make three things clear: First, this is not Ed Sherman's list; it is mine. Secondly, if any sportswriter or sportscaster who has worked for more than a month doesn't admit that he has a story about an enormous man-root, he is a liar. Lastly, I am 100 percent heterosexual and I don't go into locker rooms to "pecker check." Some visual images, however, simply cannot go unnoticed.

10. Domingo Ramos. His career as a Cubs utility man in the late '90s is less than memorable. Watching him parade through the Cubs clubhouse, on the other hand, is.

9. Kenny Lofton. He played centerfield for both the Cubs and the White Sox. I suspect he has played with many things. Fenway Park is noted for its ridiculously small clubhouse and I can testify to the truth of it: I once walked in and walked right back out because there just wasn't enough room for Lofton and everyone else.

8. Greg Clark. You're asking yourself, "Who?" He was a Bears linebacker in the early '90s and later played for Green Bay. A Packer player who was a teammate of Clark's once asked me "Did you ever see him in the lockerroom?" My answer was "yes." And I knew exactly why he was asking.

7. Steve Smith. Strike one up for the white guys. The Blackhawks defenseman wielded an impressive Sherwood.

6. Dennis Rodman. Madonna really was a "Material Girl."

5. Robert Parrish. When he was with Boston, I covered a Celtics-Pacers game in Indianapolis in '83. I think it was the first time I was issued a credential for a professional sporting event. As I waited for Larry Bird to return to his locker, Parrish emerged from the shower and began a slow walk toward where I was standing. All I could think was "Hail to the Chief."

4. Dennis Gentry. The Bears running back and special teams ace of the '80s was affectionately called "Pinky" by his teammates. Take one guess why.

3. Minnie Minoso. All four of the decades he played in major league baseball were long before I made appearances in clubhouses. I never saw Minoso naked. My friend and former White Sox third baseman Bill Melton did. I'm taking his word for it that Minnie was a nickname, not a condition.

2. Keith Van Horne. Another white guy? Yup. And the former Bears No.1 pick who played right tackle was happy to acknowledge his gift. For reasons none of us quite understood, a local camera toter was rolling when Bears players were exiting the shower after a game against the Vikings in '89. Van Horne arrived at his locker stall and said to the guy "I bet I gave some good footage."

1. Otis Wilson. Legendary. Never saw it, but this many people can't be wrong. His nicknames included "Mama's Boy" and "The Big O." Both made sense but I often wondered, based on the manner in which his man-package has been described, how he didn't wind up "The King of Swing" on his business card.

Chicago fans have a rich tradition of supporting their local teams. However, for some, it wasn't enough. These teams tried but ultimately failed to make it in Chicago.

8. Chicago Fire/Winds. This was our entry in the short-lived World Football League. The team was first dubbed the Chicago Fire for the debut WFL run in 1974. Former Bears and Bengals quarterback Virgil Carter was the big-name player. He wasn't enough to carry the show. After becoming the Chicago Winds in 1975, the team didn't even make it through the season and folded.

7. Chicago Hustle. This team represented Chicago in the Women's Basketball League from 1978-81. Doug Bruno was the coach, and the Hustle was led by Rita Easterling. Most male fans, though, remembered Janie Fincher, and not because of her basketball prowess. The WBL eventually disbanded in 1981, and Easterling and Fincher were gone.

6. Chicago Blitz. This United States Football League team was guided by two of the greatest coaches of all time. George Allen, who had been out of football since 1977, was patrolling the sidelines when the Blitz began in 1983. The team struggled at the gate and Allen only lasted one year. New ownership came in and hired Marv Levy as coach. Unfortunately, the Blitz folded after averaging only 7,500 people per game in 1984.

5. Chicago Stags. Chicago's pro basketball roots are not with the Bulls, but with the Stags. They were the Chicago team for the new pro-league that was formed in 1946. The Stags lost in the Finals in 1947 but were a consistent winner during their four-year run. The team folded, however, after the 1949-50 season. At time, the Stags held the rights to Bob Cousy, but he never played a game in Chicago. Our loss was Boston's gain.

4. Chicago Packers/Zephyrs. Pro basketball gave it another attempt in Chicago during the early 1960s. The expansion Chicago Packers made their debut in 1961-62. Despite having the Rookie of the Year in Walt Bellamy, who averaged 31.6 points per game, they went a mere 18-62. The team changed its name to the Zephyrs the following year, but again they struggled with a 25-55 mark. That was it for Chicago, as the team moved to Baltimore and became the Bullets.

3. Chicago Cougars. The Cougars were a favorite when I was growing up in the 1970s. The Chicago entry in the World Hockey Association had players such as Pat

Stapleton, Ralph Backstrom and Dave Dryden. For some reason, we loved Darryl Maggs. Debuting in 1972, the team played in the old International Amphitheatre. However, during the 1974 playoffs, the Cougars got booted out of the Amphitheatre because of a *Peter Pan* show and had to host the Finals at the Randhurst Twin Ice Arena. The team never recovered and folded in 1975.

2. Chicago Sting. Owner Lee Stern can't be blamed for not doing everything he could to make the Sting and soccer a fixture in Chicago. For one brief moment, the team did have Chicago's attention, winning the title in 1984. Players like Karl-Heinz Granitza and Pato Margetic were popular with fans, as was coach Willy Roy. But alas, they couldn't make it, as the team eventually folded.

1. Chicago Cardinals. Chicago was once a two-football team town. However, the Cardinals were never a match for the Bears. Playing in Comiskey Park, the Cardinals had some great players like Ollie Matson and Ernie Nevers. They even won the NFL title in 1947. But they were dismal in the 50s and after a 2-10 season in 1959, the Cardinals were moved to St. Louis.

Top 5 Moments of the 2008 Presidential Campaign :: by Ben Finfer, ESPN Radio

Note: Ben Finfer, "The Surgeon of Sound," is the most informed Chicago sports-radio personality when it comes to U.S. history and politics. That's kind of a "tall midget" award, but an award nonetheless. We asked Finfer to illustrate the highlights of a Chicagoan's path to the White House.

5. Barack Obama wins the Iowa caucuses. Prior to January 3 it was cute to support the junior senator from Illinois. After, it was cool. Obama opened his victory speech by pronouncing, "They said this day would never come." It might have been more accurate to say, "Holy crap." Would he have defeated Hillary Clinton without winning in Iowa? Unlikely. It took only 162 years in the union for Iowa to contribute something besides corn.

4. John McCain goes out to lunch. No image exemplified the difference between the Republican and Democratic nominees more than John McCain's visit to "Schmidt's Sausage Haus and Restaurant" on July 24. The same day Barack Obama addressed a crowd of more than 200,000 people in Berlin, McCain stood alone in front of the Columbus, Ohio restaurant. Ultimately, it was a sign of things to come. And while McCain may have lost his bid for the presidency, he only needs nine more visits to Schmidt's for a free wiener schnitzel.

3. Barack Obama's acceptance speech in Denver. In 1960, John F. Kennedy accepted the Democratic nomination for president at the L.A. Coliseum. It would be 48 years before another candidate would dare match Kennedy's boldness. Obama delivered his acceptance speech at Denver's Invesco Field (Mile High Stadium) in front of nearly 80,000 people. It was not a surprise to see the Illinois senator sell out a football stadium, but it was indeed a sight to see. Not since John Elway led the Broncos was another human being so raucously received by Denver fans.

2. Katie Couric's interview with Sarah Palin. It was August 29 when McCain selected his running mate and Americans learned that Alaska actually had a governor. It was September 3 when she delivered her acceptance speech and Americans learned she was kind of hot. Next came September 24 when *CBS Evening News* aired Katie Couric's interview with Sarah Palin and Americans learned she was a moron. In that interview, Palin revealed that her foreign policy experience came from living near Russia, misstated the role of the Vice President and struggled to name any Supreme Court decisions besides Roe vs. Wade. Later in the week she could not name any newspapers or magazines that she liked to read. Her stock never recovered. Normally a running mate has very little effect on a campaign. This time it may have sunk the ship. You betcha!

1. President-elect Obama's election night victory speech.

On November 4, the first African-American was elected President of the United States. His first words as the next commander-in-chief would surely have to reflect the enormity of this historic event. Would he quote Abraham Lincoln or Martin Luther King Jr.? The world waited. That night Obama walked to the podium, stared out into the sea of people gathered at Grant Park and shouted, "Hello Chicago!" A World's Fair, the creation of jazz and six NBA championships was no match for the pride brought on by those two words.

These are the players who didn't get as much fanfare as their superstar teammates, but were still vital to their teams' success. They were players you could count on to do their jobs with consistency and class. These men deserve to be recognized too.

10. Lance Johnson. "One Dog," as he was dubbed by Ken Harrelson, served proudly on both sides of town. He played eight years with the Sox as an offensive catalyst at the top of the order. He hit .311 during the Sox AL West champion season in 1993. After a side-trip to the New York Mets, Johnson returned to Chicago in 1997 with the Cubs. He was a spark for them during their NL wildcard run in 1998. "One Dog" got the job done.

9. Ron Harper. A show of hands if you remember that Harper was a starter on the Bulls' last three championship teams. On a team filled with stars, he was an essential role player in the backcourt with Michael Jordan. Harper had been a scorer prior to arriving in Chicago, but he changed his game to fit in with the Bulls. That's the sign of a true pro.

8. Tom Waddle. Local fans know him now for his television and radio work, but Waddle forever endeared himself as a fearless receiver for the Bears from 1989-94. He would sacrifice his body by running routes through the middle of the field. Other receivers had more speed and size, but Waddle made up for it in guts—big-time guts.

7. Greg Walker. As a beat writer for the Sox in the 80s, I have to confess that "Walk" was one of my favorites. He was genuinely a nice guy off the field, and a hard-working solid player on the field. Walker had his best year in 1987 when he hit 27 homers with 94 RBIs. Too bad injuries and a seizure cut short his career at the age of 30. However, "Walk" will always have a special place in my book.

6. John Paxson. When you share the backcourt with Michael Jordan, you tend to get overlooked. But Bulls fans will never forget the way "Pax" stepped up to help the Bulls win their title clinchers in 1991 and 1993. In Game 5 against the Lakers in '91, Paxson scored 10 fourth quarter points to trigger the first victory celebration. Then in Game 6 in '93, Paxson hit the famous game-winner to beat Phoenix. Clutch.

5. Doug Buffone. It is easy to get overlooked as a linebacker when you've got Dick Butkus playing next to you in the middle. Buffone, however, distinguished himself during a 15-year career with the Bears that saw him register more than 1,200 tackles. He was also a true leader, serving as the captain of the defense for seven years.

4. Steve Larmer. "Larms" wasn't as flashy as teammate Denis Savard, but the right-winger was a force during his days with the Blackhawks. Larmer had five 40-plus goal seasons with the Hawks. He was also an excellent two-way player. Too bad he wound up winning a Stanley Cup with the New York Rangers and not the Hawks.

3. Pat Stapleton. Stapleton often found himself in the background on teams that featured Bobby Hull, Stan Mikita and Tony Esposito. However, it would be a mistake to minimize the contributions of "Whitey." The blond-hair defenseman had a knack for finding the puck. The Rangers' Vic Hatfield once said of Stapleton, "We completed more passes to Stapleton than to any of our guys." The Hawks knew they could count on Pat.

2. Glenn Beckert. On teams that featured Ernie Banks, Billy Williams and Ron Santo, it was "Beck" who was the personification of a steady player. He was the perfect No. 2 hitter, never striking out more than 36 times in a season after his rookie year. He was a four-time All-Star and hit .342 in 1971. Day-in and day-out, Beckert showed up to play.

1. Jay Hilgenberg. "Hilgy" came to the Bears as an undrafted free agent in 1981. The scouting report said he was too small and too slow. Turns out they were wrong. Hilgenberg went on to become a seven-time Pro Bowl center as the foundation of that great Bears offensive line. Centers aren't normally recognized in Canton. That's too bad as Hilgenberg had a Hall of Fame career with the Bears.

The Sports-Television Boom in Chicago ::
by Jim Corno

Note: Jim Corno joined SportsVision in 1984 when it was a pay channel with 13,000 subscribers. Since then, he has overseen the evolution and development of Chicago's regional sports cable outlet from SportsChannel to Fox Sports Chicago to Fox Sports Net Chicago to Fox Sports Net to Comcast SportsNet. Here Corno shares his memories on being at the center of an important part of TV sports history in Chicago.

10. Going to HD. That was a big deal for us. We did everything in HD beginning in 2008. That gave us a leg up on a lot of regional networks.

9. The NHL All-Star Game in 1991 at the Chicago Stadium. It occurred right around the start of the first Gulf War. I've never heard it louder at the Old Barn during the National Anthem; U.S. flags and sparklers were everywhere. I still get chills thinking about it to this day.

8. The Hawks Stanley Cup Finals against Pittsburgh in 1992. We did *HawkVision* for their home games in the playoffs. We had a lot of people sign up. There was a lot of excitement around it.

7. The "Sports Writers on TV" phenomenon. It was just the simplest show you could ever put together, but producer John Roach and that amazing cast of characters including Bill Gleason, Bill Jauss, Rick Telander, Ben Bentley and a number of solid fill-in guests over the years made it compelling television, and made it fun for the viewer. Those guys were rock stars if you ask me. That show should also be credited as the catalyst for the sports roundtable discussion shows that can now be found just about everywhere.

6. The firsts. When I came here, I looked at what we were doing and said we should be programming ourselves like we're a television station. We did a lot of firsts for a regional sports network: we were the first to go live to the locker room, we were the first to go 24/7 and we were the first to have a nightly local sports report. I'm proud of that.

5. Adding the Cubs as one of our main pro teams in 1999. There was a lot of speculation about this for quite a while. But when it became official, I gathered our entire staff into our studio and broke the great news to them. The excitement was overwhelming to say the least. The fact that we would now be airing both Cubs and White Sox games during the baseball season was definitely a major factor in our channel's growth and evolution.

DAYGLO.

Shock-Resistant And Bold.

1. GLX5600-4 $99
2. G7900A-7 $99
3. DW6900CC-2 $99
4. GW6900A-7 $130
5. DW6900CC-6 $99
6. G7900A-4 $99
7. GLX5600A-2 $99
8. DW6900CS-7 $89
9. DW6900CC-3 $99

Make a splash with color.

Water & Shock Resistant

1. BG3001-2 $79
2. BG3000-8 $79
3. BG169R-2 $79
4. BG5601-4 $79
5. BG169R-4A $79

6. MSG300C-7B $160
7. BGA101-4 $99
8. BG5601-7 $79
9. BGA101-7B $99

Ba·by-G

4. The conversion from being a pay-service to a basic cable TV service. Our subscriber count jumped immediately and we were finally able to reach a bigger audience, which gave Chicago sports fans an easier and more affordable opportunity to watch our channel.

3. The launch of Comcast SportsNet. We started the channel from scratch in 2004. The channel was going to be owned by the teams (Cubs, White Sox, Bulls and Blackhawks) and Comcast. You couldn't ask for a better group of owners. They're behind us all the way.

2. The White Sox World Series. The success we had doing post-game shows and programming around the games was incredible. We had a big rating after Game 3 (which ended after 1 a.m.). People are conditioned to turn to us after a big game.

1. The Bulls championship years. The excitement. Michael Jordan. It was like following a rock star band. We set a record that might still exist for a regional sports network. We did a 25 rating for a Bulls game in the playoffs. That's just unheard of for sports on cable. Everyone wanted to watch the Bulls and we had them.

Coach Ray :: by Chuck Swirsky

Note: Chuck Swirsky worked 11 years with Ray Meyer as the play-by-play voice of DePaul basketball for WGN. He spent countless hours with the legendary Blue Demons coach, gaining insights into what made him tick. Swirsky talks about the traits that made Meyer a true sports icon in Chicago.

7. Sense of humor. DePaul had a player named Bernard Randolph. During a game, Coach Ray grabs him and says, "Bernard, you're a 40-point scorer. Twenty for us and twenty for them!"

Ray also once met the Pope. He gave me a picture of himself and Marge (Ray's wife) with the his Holiness. He inscribed it, "The Pope says hello."

6. The husband. When I got engaged, I asked him, "How did your marriage with Marge last?" He said, "I would come home and I would always make her feel this was her time even though my head was full of a lot of basketball." Marge was so big in his life.

5. Sense of family. He was great family man. He loved all his kids. He didn't favor any of them. Obviously, we were around Joey a lot. He was respectful that Joey was the coach. The first year was tough on him. After that, he took a step back. Whatever Coach Ray felt in his heart, he never second-guessed his son. Never.

4. Competitiveness. On the air, he was just as competitive as an analyst as he was as a coach. When we started doing games after he retired I said, "Coach, the press notes are up at the table." He replied, "No, the press notes are up here in my head." There was one consistent thing for Coach Ray after a loss. He was so down, but not for himself. He felt so badly for the players.

3. One-on-one. He had the ability to treat people like they were the only person on the planet. I saw him with politicians, entertainers, big-time coaches. But he would make that person who was picking up the programs, cleaning up the trash, feel just as important as the Athletic Director or Al McGuire.

2. Compassion for other people. If you needed something, he would go through a brick wall. He would do it immediately. He wouldn't procrastinate. He would show me letters of people asking, "Coach could you come to our school?" He would pick up the phone and call up a high school kid and say, "This is Coach Ray." On the other end, I could hear this kid screaming on the phone, "Mom, Mom, it's Coach Ray Meyer. He's coming to our school!"

1. Kindness. I never saw him turn down one autograph, one picture request or one telephone request for him to appear on a show. We almost missed so many commercial flights because he was signing autographs. He would get in a cab and he would never pay because the cab drivers would insist: "No, coach, it's on us."

Favorite Athletes to Drink With :: by Mike North

Note: Long-time Chicago radio and television personality Mike North has knocked more than a few back with many prominent athletes. According to Mike, a good drinking partner is "a guy who likes to talk sports, who sees a chick walk by and says she's hot, doesn't get crazy, and likes to hang out and have fun."

Here are Mike's guys:

9. Moe Drabowsky. I worked at a Cubs fantasy camp one year, and drank with all of them. Pepitone, Santo, Beckert, etc. Moe was the best of all. He was a great guy. He and I hit it off really, really well. He was a practical joker. He brought in the snake to the team dinner. He was just hilarious.

8. Freddy Garcia. He's the guy who was a big-timer. Six martinis. Big-game Freddy. When I was with him, he didn't have a game the next day. But who knows? He probably drank like that before he pitched.

7. Kenny Williams. I had a few drinks with him in Detroit. He wasn't talking to me at the time. He came up to me in the Sox hotel and said, "Let's go across the street." We had a few cocktails and we made up. Good guy.

6. Sebastian Janikowski. I had him on my TV show. He was the guy I wanted the Bears to take over Urlacher. I invited him to my house afterwards. He basically drank the cooler dry. He was a pro's pro. That's all bought and paid for when you see his gut.

5. Isiah Thomas. I drank with him at Gibson's. He was a great guy, very polite. When you read about what went on with him in New York, it doesn't seem like the same guy that was here. When he was in Chicago, he was great, effervescent. He was cool.

4. Dennis Rodman. I drank with him at Gibson's and the Crowbar. It was unbelievable. He had dinner with me and my wife (BeBe). He had a gas station shirt on. It said Al on it. B left, but he and I high-tailed it over to the Crowbar. I only stayed for a couple, but I heard he had many shots. The next night he took down 17 boards. Nothing stopped him.

3. Dick Butkus. When he did my TV show, he had a little red wine in him already. He was just hilarious. "Let's do a two-parter," he said. The people got two-for-the-price-of-one. We've been friends ever since. A great, great guy.

2. Mike Ditka. Numerous times we went out. In the 90s, it was ugly. We just didn't stop. We kept going. He was like a magnet. Everyone wanted to say hi. One night we polished off a few bottles of Dom and the valets took us home. I had fun with him.

1. Jeremy Roenick. Hands down, Jeremy was my favorite. A couple times he went to my neighborhood in the Northwest side. One night, Jim Harbaugh was with him. To walk into places like the Edison Park Inn, regular neighborhood joint, with Roenick and Harbaugh, everyone loved it. Jeremy was a regular guy. He was a good drinker and friendly to everybody. A great guy.

Chicago is known around the world as *the* city for pizza. And it is. I prefer thin crust to the stuffed, but I sprayed to all fields here in my Top 10 Chicagoland pizza joints.

10. Gino's East. Give Gino's a fair amount of credit for helping the Windy City develop its reputation as "Pizza City." Gino's prides itself on the deep-dish, which features a chunky tomato sauce. There are four locations in the city and nine in the suburbs.

9. Pizzeria Uno/Pizzeria Due. Since 1943, Uno has been making customers happy with a variety of pizzas, including the "Spinoccoli," which features spinach, broccoli and garlic. Uno has penetrated the Northeastern seaboard, but my favorite store is Due, at 29 E. Ohio.

8. D'Agostino's. Strike one up for a mom-and-pop operation. "Dags" is a great place to go before or after a Cubs game, at 1351 W. Addision. There also is a store at 752 N. Ogden and in Glenview. They offer a devilish cheeseburger pizza and a healthier pie with sundried tomatoes, goat cheese and basil.

7. Ranalli's on Clark. Ranalli's also offers outdoor dining at its 2301 N. Clark operation. If you're a thin crust enthusiast, take it up a notch and sample their super thin crust.

6. House of Pizza/Zuni's. The famous "House" recipe, originally developed at the 7008 Indianapolis Blvd. store in Hammond, has multiplied at all NW Indiana Zuni's locations. Snappy sauce. Real, chunky pork sausage. Crackery crust. Awesome when served cold with a hangover.

5. Lou Malnati's. Lou Mal's has five stores in the city and 24 suburban locations. Two things distinguish Malnati's: the flakey, buttery crust and their awesome gift delivery service. Send "Chicago" anywhere in the world at Lou Malnati's.

4. Chicago Pizza & Oven Grinder Co. In the heart of Lincoln Park at 2121 N. Clark St., Oven Grinders offers the unique "pot pie pizza" with "door knob sized" mushrooms. A must try. A departure from all the rest. Warm, downstairs atmosphere. The Mediterranean bread appetizer kicks it. One of my favorite Chicago spots, but it oddly remains a secret.

3. Village Inn Pizzeria. Located in Skokie at 8050 N. Lincoln Ave. The Village Inn balances the restaurant/sports bar combination better than any establishment in the northern suburbs. Great atmosphere for both sports viewing and family dining. Awesome thin crust pie with healthy options. Awesome full menu, but this is a list about pizza joints.

2. Giordano's. If you have a friend in from out of town and he's never tried the famous Chicago deep-dish, take him to Giordano's for the stuffed special. Consistently the best deep-dish in town. Always fresh, despite the heavy volume they do. Gio's has 13 locations in the city and 27 in the suburbs.

1. Aurelio's Pizza. A South Side tradition. Best thin crust in the world. Zippy tomato sauce over a precisely baked crust. Fresh, chunky pork sausage and just the right amount of cheeses. Aurelio's, founded in 1959 by the late Joe Aurelio, has 43 locations in six states. Find them downtown at 506 W. Harrison, or at my favorite store in Homewood, where it all started. Eating is believing.

Take a look at the Bulls' press guide: you will be astounded just how bad their line-ups were in the early Jordan years. It wasn't until 1989-90 when both Scottie Pippen and Horace Grant were in the starting lineup to open the season that the team showed any promise. It gives you new appreciation for what Jordan was able to do without a strong supporting cast.

These are opening game lineups:

1984-85: Steve Johnson and Orlando Woolridge at forward, Caldwell Jones at center, Michael Jordan and Ennis Whatley at guard.

Caldwell Jones? Are you kidding? Woolridge could only do one thing and that was shoot. Forget about any defense. Whatley was a bust for the Bulls. Jordan knew what he had to do: lead the Bulls in scoring with 28.2 points per game. They were 38-44, losing in the first round of the playoffs to Milwaukee 3-1.

1985-86: Orlando Woolridge and Sidney Green at forward, Jawan Oldham at center, Jordan and Kyle Macy at guard.

The season marked the end of the Oldham era for the Bulls. He averaged 4.8 points per game in four seasons. Green and Macy were college standouts, but didn't do anything in the pros. Jordan, meanwhile, missed 64 games with a broken foot but came back to lead the Bulls into the playoffs (even with a 30-52 record), setting up his memorable 63-point game against Boston.

1986-87: Earl Cureton and Charles Oakley at forward, Granville Waiters at center, Jordan and Steve Colter at guard.

How can you forget the seriously hair-challenged Waiters? He looked about 20 years older than his actual age, and played like it too. Colter was Jordan's third different backcourt mate in three years, and Cureton was just a journeyman. At least Oakley gave an inkling that some quality help might be on the way. Jordan did it all, leading the league in scoring with 37.1 points per game. The Bulls were 40-42 and got swept in the first round in three games by Boston.

1987-1988: Brad Sellers and Charles Oakley at forward, Artis Gilmore at center, Jordan and John Paxson at guard.

Sellers proved to be a huge first-round bust. He might have been one of the softest big men to ever play the game. Gilmore was way past his prime in his second go-around with the Bulls, averaging only 4.2 points in 24 games. Paxson was still in the early stages of his Bulls run. The team, however, was better, going 50-32 as Jordan averaged 35 points per game. They defeated Cleveland in five games on the "shot" by Jordan. Then they lost in five games to Detroit.

1988-89: Brad Sellers and Horace Grant at forward, Bill Cartwright at center, Jordan and Sam Vincent at guard.

Finally, the Bulls starting lineup was starting to take shape. Grant replaced Oakley, who was traded for Cartwright. Still, Jordan's backcourt mate was Sam Vincent, who lasted only two years with the Bulls, and they still were trying to do something with Sellers. The Bulls finished 47-35 behind Jordan's 32.5 points per game and advanced to the Conference Finals before losing to Detroit. The following year, the big three of Jordan, Pippen and Grant, would be in the opening-night lineup together for the first time, and the Bulls were on their way.

The No-Man Show (the Post-Jordan Years) :: ES

After the Bulls won their sixth title in 1998, the team scattered and the dark ages returned in Chicago basketball. Just look at some of these horrid opening night line-ups in the post-Jordan era, and you'll know why the Bulls were so bad until returning to the playoffs again in 2004-2005.

1998-99: Toni Kukoc and Mark Bryant at forward, Andrew Lang at center, Ron Harper and Brent Barry at guard.

Bryant was rather big and puffy, which doesn't work well in basketball. Unfortunately, Brent Barry wasn't as good as his father, Rick. Even if he was, it wouldn't have matched all the fire-power they lost. The Bulls went 13-37 in a strike-shortened season.

1999-2000: Toni Kukoc and Elton Brand at forward, Dicky Simpkins at center, Randy Brown and Hersey Hawkins at guard.

Bet you forgot that Simpkins once played for the Bulls. Kukoc was eventually traded to Philadelphia and Brown and Hawkins couldn't do much as role players. Brand was impressive, but he couldn't prevent the Bulls from suffering through a franchise worse 67 losses.

2000-2001: Ron Artest and Elton Brand at forward, Michael Ruffin at center, Khalid El-Amin and Ron Mercer at guard.

The Bulls picked up Mercer as a free agent hoping he would help. He didn't. El-Amin was actually a second-round pick who cracked the starting lineup. Not a good thing. Ruffin was a beefy guy who contributed two points per game. Artest was still a few years from going crazy, not that the sanity helped. The Bulls lost 67 games again.

2001-2002: Ron Mercer and Charles Oakley at forward, Brad Miller at center, Greg Anthony and Fred Hoiberg at guard.

Oakley was washed up in his second go-around with the team. Miller would grow into a decent player elsewhere, and returned to the Bulls in 2009. Hoiberg could shoot, but he wasn't a starting NBA player. The Bulls go down hard again with a 21-61 mark.

2002-2003: Jalen Rose and Tyson Chandler at forward, Eddy Curry at center, Jay Williams and Trenton Hassell at guard.

Jerry Krause's kids, Chandler and Curry, crack the opening night lineup. Too bad they played like kids, and did throughout their ill-fated tenure with the Bulls. Williams did show some flashes in his rookie year. However, he decided to jump on his motorcycle in the off-season, getting in an accident and ending his career. The Bulls improve a bit, but still dreadful at 30-52.

2003-2004: Scottie Pippen and Lonny Baxter at forward, Eddy Curry at center, Jamal Crawford and Jalen Rose at guard.

Pippen was brought back for old-time sake, but he couldn't play anymore. Baxter and Rose were shipped out in mid-season. The Bulls lost 59 games, but help was on the way in the form of rookie Kirk Hinrich. The dark ages would end the following season, as the Bulls made the playoffs in 2004-2005.

There have been many occasions when bizarre conditions turned sports events into almost surreal experiences.

6. Snow ball. The Sox were the guests for the first baseball game in Toronto in April, 1977. Since this is Canada, naturally it snowed. What, you were expecting sun and 80 degrees? However, with a full house at the legendary Exhibition Stadium, officials weren't about to call the game. The Sox and Blue Jays played through the snow. The immortal Dane Ault hit two homers in Toronto's 9-5 victory.

5. The last College All-Star Game. I have vivid memories of this game because I was there. In 1976, the champion Pittsburgh Steelers took on the All-Stars. It wasn't much of a match-up, as the Steelers held a comfortable 24-0 lead in the third quarter. Then the skies opened up and we were pelted with torrential rains. It felt like being in India during a monsoon. Since the Steelers were winning so big, officials decided to call the game. And that was that. There was never another College All-Star game.

4. Flooded. Just before the 1987 Western, Butler National in Oak Brook was flooded with what was described a 100-year rain. An estimated 67 million gallons of water had washed over the course. Only nine holes were available for play at Butler. However, rather than cancel the tournament, officials used nine holes from Oak Brook Golf Club, which runs adjacent to Butler. Somehow, the tournament was completed, with D.A. Weibring edging Greg Norman and Larry Nelson by a stroke.

3. 8/8/88. After playing day games for an eternity, Wrigley Field was set to finally enter the 20th Century with the first night game on August 8, 1988. The build-up for the Cubs-Philadelphia game was huge, and tickets were at a premium for the big event. The lights went on and the place went up for grabs. However, the karma train arrived during the fourth inning as monsoon rains washed away everything. The first night game was a rainout. Traditionalists took it as a sign that God favored afternoon baseball.

2. Lightning strikes. The 1975 Western Open almost turned into a major tragedy when Jerry Heard, Lee Trevino and Bobby Nichols were struck by lightning. Heard said every muscle in his body convulsed and his hands involuntarily turned into fists. Each player was lucky to be alive. However, they each suffered physical problems from the incident that dogged them for the rest of their careers. The incident should be a cautionary tale for all golfers: Don't mess around when lightning is in the area.

1. "The Fog Bowl." Nothing tops surreal when it comes to this game. On December 31, 1988, the Bears hosted the Philadelphia Eagles in a playoff game. As the game went on, a thick fog blew in over Soldier Field. By the second half, nobody in the stands could see a thing. The TV pictures were just one big cloud. You could barely make out mere images of players running around, but that was about it. Incredibly, the officials let the game continue. Head referee Jim Tunney announced the down and distance for each play on a wireless microphone. Somehow, the Bears wound up winning 20-12. One fan summed up the day by making an impromptu sign: "What the fog is going on?"

America has had a long-standing love affair with Wrigley Field. The ivy. The charming old scoreboard. Baseball in the sunshine. I say "Keep it." I'll take the ballpark that sits hard off the Dan Ryan expressway, seven miles south and a smidge west of Wrigley. Here are 10 reasons why.

10. The Jumbotron. Call me crazy, but updated stats on players and teams, replays, trivia contests, etc. enhance the experience of attending a professional sporting event. Wrigley's scoreboard doesn't even possess enough room to include a full slate of out-of-town scores.

9. The restrooms. There are more of them. They are cleaner. The lines move faster. No primitive troughs, but a personal urinal. I like that.

8. The food. It's edible at the Cell. From salads to bratwursts to ice cream treats (the "Winning Ugly Is Sweet" stand on the concourse behind third base is a must-stop every time) the fare at U.S. Cellular Field is not only the best in town—it's in baseball's Top 3. If you eat anything in a foil wrapper at Wrigley, you're consuming only warm germs.

7. The sightlines. Constructed in 1990 and opened in 91, the Cell offers its patrons a better look at the game. No I-beams that obstruct your view. Wrigley has too many seats before you get to the aisle and the concrete steps aren't as steep as they are the Cell, which impairs the view for those of us who are vertically challenged.

6. Getting there. Unless you live in the neighborhood or take the El, Wrigley's location is a colossal pain-in-the-ass. The only public transportation I take has wings. The Cell has convenient entrances and exits and both the Dan Ryan and Stevenson expressways are practically in spitting distance.

5. Roger Bossard. "The Sodfather" is the Michelango of groundskeepers, hence the Cubs "stealing" him to re-do Wrigley's cow pasture after the 06 season. I've walked the meticulously manicured grass at the Cell and have also had the privilege of standing at the dish and taking a dozen swings following a Sox game in 03. Those were nothing shy of spiritual experiences.

4. The concourses. Ever try to find shelter during a rain delay at Wrigley? It's tantamount to a cattle drive. The concourses at the Cell are decidedly wider and offer the aforementioned great choices for food and beverage.

3. The P.A. system. Gene Honda's booming voice. The high voltage rock and roll riffs offered by soundman Chris Hubble between innings and as batters approach the dish. That beats the hell out of Wrigley's tin-can speakers, which I think were upgraded last on the day Gabby Hartnett hit "the Homer in the Gloamin."

2. Asphalt. What a novel idea it is to provide 40,000 baseball fans a place to park their cars. Spacious lots envelop the Cell and the ballclub encourages tailgating. Nothing beats standing over hot Kingsfords on a gorgeous day before the Sox host the Cubs three times every summer.

1. The Banner. On a rainy night in April of 2006, the White Sox unveiled their 2005 World Series championship banner behind the left-center field concourse. Top that.

Note: My first Cubs game was 1975, when I was an impressionable 4-year-old. I left thinking that Wrigley was the greatest place on earth. Well, at least the second best place on earth—next to Kiddieland on North Ave. Willie McCovey and the Giants were in town. How good were the Cubs in my mind then? I thought his name was McCubbie. Didn't everyone want to be a part of my team? I was hooked. I later learned that my team wasn't exactly "all that and a bag of chips." My ballpark? I've had my ups and downs with it over the last 34 years. All in all, my time at Clark and Addison has been a historical roller coaster ride. From the neighborhood clean up in the early 80s, to the transition, to "building a new tradition" in 1984, to lights in 1988, to Sosa's HR chase of '98, to five outs away, to bleacher expansion of 2006.

Through good and bad—a lot more bad—I'm happy to call Wrigley Field my ballpark and a place I've grown up. Like me, it's not perfect. Quirks and all, I wouldn't trade it for anything. Here's why:

10. Blow me. I'm talking about the wind here. There is no park in baseball where wind consistently plays a bigger role. Wind blowing out, get ready for lots of home runs. Wind blowing in, it's one of the toughest places to hit a homer. It changes day-to-day and sometimes inning-by-inning. You never know what you're going to get. Check the flags on the scoreboard the moment you walk in.

9. The scoreboard. Where else do those same flags give you the standings of each National League division? Each team's pennant is positioned in order of record atop the scoreboard. Where else can you look at a scoreboard in a ballpark or stadium and know where you are by just looking at it? And where else can a simple "W" flag fly atop the scoreboard and tell you all you need to know? It's old school, yes. But my grandfather looked out at that same scoreboard. It's a landmark, looking at it inside or outside the park. No replays? When your team hasn't won a World Series in 100 years, keep the replays. They're mostly bad.

8. The Box Seats. No ballpark has the fans sitting closer. Whether you're up against the brick wall or directly above the field in the upper deck. Oh yeah, we've never debated the color of our seats. Didn't those blue seats look great at the Cell?

7. Traditions. "Left field sucks." "Throw it back." "Take me out to the ball game." Wooing. The Ivy. The "W" Flag. They're not all good, but it's better than the tradition of the "Running of the Ligues."

6. The Press Box. It's not the actual structure, but look who has sat there: Jack Quinlan, Jack Brickhouse, Vince Lloyd, Harry Caray, Lou Boudreau. The Cubs have had legends broadcast their games.

5. The Organ. Is Gary Pressey better than Nancy Faust? Maybe not. But we let our organist play EVERYDAY like a real ballpark should.

4. History. It's a place for all seasons. When the NHL and the Blackhawks wanted to showcase the greatest Winter Classic yet, the obvious choice was Wrigley. Not the Cell, Not Soldier Field. Babe Ruth called his shot here. Sayers and Butkus played here. George Halas won Championships here. Bill Veeck—your Sox owner—planted the ivy before he owned the Sox and watched games here after he sold the Sox. This was HIS park. Not Comiskey. Wrigley is now 95 years old and will be open for business for many more.

3. Sunshine. Sure, there have been lights since '88 but there's still something magical about day baseball. 52 times each year. A FULL ball park, despite most people being at work and or at school. Walking UP the ramp at Wrigley and seeing the colors pop out from the grass and the ivy. Greenest green you've ever seen.

2. The Bleachers. Plain and simple, they're the most famous seats in sports.

1. It's always an event. Because of everything stated above and an entertainment district that's rivaled only by Vegas and New Orleans, going to Wrigley Field, day or night, isn't just about going to a game. It's an event.

The 10 Best Things About Wrigley Field :: by Gene Wojciechowski

Note: ESPN.com sports columnist Gene Wojciechowski spent a year hanging around Wrigley Field in 2004 for his book *Cubs Nation*. Like everyone else, he fell in love with the place. He shares some of favorite things about Wrigley Field.

10. Wayne Messmer. Nobody sings the National Anthem better than Wayne. Plus, as PA announcer, he actually introduces himself when it comes time to sing the Anthem.

9. Grilled hot dogs and onions inside the concourse. Never buy from the concession stand. Always go to the small grills. It's a longer line, but worth the wait.

8. The grounds crew actually uses scissors to trim the ivy on the walls.

7. Aerobic exercise. If you don't wuss out and take the lone elevator near the left-field corner of the stadium, then you have to walk the steps and/or ramps to the upper deck. K2 has less elevation.

6. Being a Ballhawk during batting practice. Follow the vets on Waveland or Sheffield to figure out the best place to stand for homers hit during BP. There's even a spray-painted spot down from Waveland where Sammy Sosa hit one about 600 feet.

5. The metal urinal troughs in the men's room. Old School, baby.

4. How can you not love a place that flies a W or L flag after every game. You always know where you stand with the Cubs.

3. Beer vendors who remember your name.

2. The Bleachers. Sort of like a baseball Mardi Gras, but without the beads.

1. A scoreboard from heaven. Even better than the oldest ballpark, Fenway.

Top Closers :: ES

Game on the line. You need a few precious outs to secure the victory. Summon the closer. These star relievers finished the deal for the Cubs and White Sox. Two of them even went to the Hall of Fame. Here are the best closers ever to play in Chicago.

10. Ed Farmer. "Farmio" had a short, but distinguished run as a closer for the White Sox. Acquired from Texas in mid-season 1979, Farmer finished strong with 14 saves in 42 games. Then, in 1980, he earned a trip to the All-Star game with 30 saves. Alas, Farmer was gone after the 1981 season, but he returned to close games in the Sox broadcast booth.

9. Phil Regan. "The Vulture" had a few shining moments in the Cubs bullpen. Acquired from the Dodgers in 1968, he sparkled with a 10-5 record, 25 saves and 2.20 earned run average. Regan opened the 1969 season strong but he, like every other Cub, wilted down the stretch in the infamous collapse.

8. Gerry Staley. Staley anchored the Sox bullpen on their great teams during the late 50s. In 1959, he went 8-5 with a 2.24 earned run average and 14 saves. More importantly, he was on the mound working the last inning in the Sox pennant clincher against Cleveland.

7. Eddie Fisher. One of the Sox's great knuckleball pitchers, Fisher had a stellar year in 1965. Working 82 games, he went 15-7 with a 2.40 earned run average. The save rules were different back then, but keep in mind he finished 60 games, recording 24 saves. Fisher had such an impact on the Sox second-place finish, he wound up fourth in MVP voting.

6. Randy Myers. Myers went to three All-Star games during his three years with the Cubs. The hard-throwing lefthander shined in 1993, recording 53 saves. But Cubs fans will remember him most for what happened after a particular blown save: A fan was so upset, he rushed the field and tried to attack Myers. Cubs fans take these things pretty hard.

5. Bobby Thigpen. "Thiggy" played outfield in college, but it was his arm that made him a star for the Sox. Owner of a dominating fastball, he had a career year in 1990, recording 57 saves. It stood as the Major League record for 18 years. All told, Thigpen had four 30-plus save seasons with the Sox.

4. Bobby Jenks. Jenks is easily General Manager Kenny Williams' best pick-up. Claimed off waivers from the Angels in 2005, Jenks went from Double-A that season to closing games for the Sox in the post-season, including the World Series clincher. He continued to dominate from there, tying a Major League record when he retired 41 straight batters in 2007.

3. Hoyt Wilhelm. The Sox acquired the veteran knuckleballer in 1963 at the age of 40. Washed up? Hardly. Wilhelm gave the Sox six seasons of superb work. In five of those seasons, his earned run average was under 2.00, bottoming out at 1.31 in 1967. The run helped Wilhelm get inducted into the Hall of Fame in 1985.

2. Lee Smith. At 6-foot, 6-inches, Lee Arthur Smith was an imposing presence on the mound for the Cubs. His overpowering fastball helped him pile up a Cubs record 180 saves in eight seasons. He had a 1.65 earned run average in 1983 and collected 36 saves in 1987.

1. Bruce Sutter. Sutter was unhittable during his five seasons with the Cubs. His split-finger fastball overwhelmed batters, making him as close to a sure thing as the Cubs ever had. He won the Cy Young Award in 1979 with 37 saves and a 2.22 earned run average. He should have gone into the Hall of Fame with a Cubs hat, but they wouldn't pay him and he was traded to St. Louis in 1980. So now his bust features a Cardinals cap. Too bad.

For various reasons, two individuals are paired together for all time. One couldn't have done it without the other. Some did it on the field, and some did it off. Note: This list doesn't include announcing teams. We had our own special section for that on p. 41.

10. Glenn Beckert and Don Kessinger. In 1965, Glenn Beckert took over at second base and Don Kessinger became the regular shortstop for the Cubs. For the next nine years, they would become a fixture as the Cubs' reliable double play combination. During that period, Kessinger was selected for five All-Star games and Beckert went to four. They also manned the top of the order, with Kessinger at lead-off followed by Beckert.

9. Ray Meyer and George Mikan. Few coach-player relationships did more for both parties than the Meyer-Mikan pairing at DePaul. Meyer was a 28-year old coach when Mikan arrived at DePaul in 1942. Mikan was tall but extremely awkward and didn't look to possess any basketball skills. But Meyer saw something in Mikan and turned him into a player. Mikan went on to become a two-time NCAA player of the year and lead DePaul to the 1945 NIT title, back when that tournament meant something. Thanks to Mikan, Meyer established himself as a top coach.

8. Red Grange and C.C. Pyle. Grange was a huge college star at Illinois, but it was a Champaign promoter who turned him into a rich man. C.C. Pyle, otherwise known as "Cash and Carry," arranged a post-college tour after the 1925 season that saw Grange play 19 games in 66 days. A crowd of 73,000 people saw Grange and the Bears play at the Polo Grounds and 75,000 fans packed the LA Coliseum to get a first-hand look at "The Galloping Ghost." That proved to be a solid partnership.

7. Jerry Reinsdorf and Eddie Einhorn. When Bill Veeck sold the White Sox after the 1981 season, the team went to a couple of brash, daring businessmen. It didn't take long for Reinsdorf and Einhorn to make their impact felt. For better (the team won the AL West in 1983) or worse (a new pay-TV concept and many controversial statements), the pair always seemed to be in the news. Often they were called "Reinshorn" or "Eindorf." On the other hand, they were never called dull.

6. Jerry Sloan and Norm Van Lier. Has there ever been a tougher backcourt than Sloan and Van Lier? Sloan, "The Original Bull" and "Stormin' Norman" Van Lier formed a wall for the Bulls during the 1970s. Sloan was named All NBA Defensive first team four times while Van Lier made three appearances. Players knew they would get a beating if they tested Sloan and Van Lier.

5. Nellie Fox and Luis Aparicio. One of the greatest double play combinations of all time, Fox and Aparicio were the backbone of the great White Sox teams during the 50s and early 60s. They were Gold Glovers in the field and also manufactured runs at the top of the lineup. How good were they? Both players have their busts in Cooperstown.

4. Walter Payton and Roland Harper/Matt Suhey. Payton was blessed to have two solid backs clearing the way for him during his great career. First, it was Harper, a 17th round draft pick who ran in the backfield with Payton. In addition to his blocking ability, Harper could also run a bit, rushing for a career-high 992 yards in 1978. After Harper departed, Suhey picked up the slack as an effective blocker and pass receiver out of the backfield.

3. Joe Tinker and Johnny Evers. They were so outstanding, the Cubs' doubleplay combination had a poem written about them. Technically, you have to throw in Frank Chance, but really all the first-baseman did was catch the relay. Tinker, the shortstop, and Evers at second did all the hard work in anchoring a Cubs team that won two World Series titles. But here's my favorite tidbit about the duo: They didn't talk for 33 years. Who says you need to get along to be great?

2. Bobby Hull and Stan Mikita. OK, technically they didn't play much together since they skated on different lines. But when you talk about the greatness the Hawks had in the 60s and 70s, it always comes out as "the Hull-Mikita teams." They are forever linked in history as the Hawks' greatest players.

1. Michael Jordan and Scottie Pippen. For all his greatness, Jordan doesn't fill his fingers with championship rings without Pippen. In Jordan and Pippen, the Bulls had two of the league's top 5 players when both were in their prime. Like Jordan, Pippen could play a myriad of roles on the floor and created match-up problems that teams couldn't overcome. One-plus-one wound up equaling six for Jordan and Pippen—as in six NBA titles.

For the most part, Chicago teams haven't been very active in the free agent market through the years—and that's probably a good thing. The track record isn't great as plenty of these expensive pick-ups proved to be money down the drain. Here's the worst of the worst.

9. Bob Probert. Despite all of Probert's personal problems, which eventually got him suspended for a year, the Blackhawks brought him into the fold for the 1995-96 season. "Probbie" continued his brawling ways as an enforcer, but he did little else after scoring 19 goals in his first season with the Hawks.

8. Ron Blomberg. The White Sox picked up Blomberg in 1978 during Bill Veeck's "Rent-A-Player" regime. It was hoped that the DH would make up for the power loss of Richie Zisk and Oscar Gamble, who departed after the 1977 season. It started well, as Blomberg hit a game-winning, opening day homer. But that was it, as Blomberg hit .231 with only five homers in 61 games before calling it a career.

7. Mel Rojas. The Cubs signed him after he saved 36 games for Montreal in 1996. It seemed like a good move at the time. But Rojas was a complete disaster in 1997, going 0-4 with a 4.64 ERA and only 13 saves in 54 games. Cubs fans hated him, and Rojas was mercifully traded to the Mets in August later that year.

6. Todd Hundley. Since Randy Hundley did well with the Cubs, they decided to take a chance on his son, Todd. The Cubs signed the catcher to a four-year, $24 million contract going into the 2001 season. Big mistake. Hundley hit only .187 in 2001 and .211 in 2002. He complained about playing time and not getting his No. 9 jersey. He even flipped off the fans at one point. The Cubs dumped him after the 2002 season. Turns out Todd was no Randy.

5. Jamie Navarro. White Sox fans are still trying to forget this free agent bust. After winning 15 games for the Cubs in 1996, he signed a four-year, $20 million deal with the Sox. He should have given the money back after going 9-14 with a 5.79 ERA in 1997 and 8-16 with a 6.36 ERA in 1998. The Sox finally dealt him to Milwaukee in 1999, but it was two years too late.

4. Eddie Robinson. This guy was a true bum. No other way to put it. Bulls GM Jerry Krause gave Robinson a 5-year, $32 million contract in 2001 even though he averaged 7.2 points per game in two years with Charlotte. Krause liked his athletic ability. Too bad the GM didn't do a more thorough check on his heart. Robinson never averaged more than 9 points per game for the Bulls and missed more than 102 games in three seasons. Krause's replacement, John Paxson, bought out Robinson from the last two years of his contract. Good riddance.

3. Bryan Cox. Cox was a loud-mouth linebacker when he arrived with the Bears in 1996. At least with Miami, his play backed up his mouth. It wasn't that way with the Bears, as his on-field temper tantrums got old real quick. The Bears released him prior to the opening of camp in 1998.

2. Albert Belle. It seems crazy to call a player who set the Sox single-season record with 49 homers and 152 RBIs in 1998 a bust, but that's exactly the case. The Sox signed Belle to a 5-year, $55-million contract going into the 1997. They anticipated teaming him with Frank Thomas to produce a lethal 1-2 punch. It never happened. Belle got off to slow starts in both seasons with the Sox. Then once the Sox were out of it, he heated up to pad his stats. Luckily for them, he invoked an out-clause and left after 1998.

1. Ben Wallace. The Bulls thought they finally had their big man when they signed Wallace to a four-year, $60 million deal in July, 2006. Instead, he was nothing more than a big disappointment. Either his legs were gone or he missed being in the Detroit system. For whatever reason, Wallace often disappeared in games for the Bulls. Finally, the Bulls dumped him on Cleveland in February, 2008. The search for a big man continued.

1985 also was a big year for me. I went from writing about the Illinois state high school badminton tournament in the spring to covering the Bears in the Super Bowl in January. At only 25, I received my first big assignment: serving on the *Tribune's* reporting team for the Bears. Talk about good timing. All the major stories from that season are well-known while others remained quiet—until now. Here are some of my most obscure memories and observations from covering the Bears in 1985.

8. Raw meat. Midway through that season, I was assigned to chronicle a week in the life of offensive lineman Tom Thayer. Thayer was, and still is, extremely gracious. One night I went back to his apartment. His mother was making dinner for him and teammate Keith Van Horne. The photographer thought it would be great to get a picture of the guys eating the steaks. However, he didn't have time to wait for them to get cooked.

The photographer told the guys not to worry, because the steaks would look cooked in the paper. So we staged the photo. Sure enough when the paper came out, the steaks appeared about as raw as can be.

"Thanks," Thayer told me, "Now everyone thinks we eat raw meat."

7. Bear trap. It was the night before the famous Bears-Miami Monday night game. Bears PR director Ken Valdisseri wanted to take 12 of us to the famous Joe's Stone Crab. When we pulled up, it looked like there were about a thousand people trying to get into the place. We wanted to go somewhere else but Ken said, "Just give me a minute." A few moments later, he was waving us inside.

"How'd you do that?" I asked.

"I gave the Maitre D' two tickets to the game," he said.

Through subsequent trips, I have learned that the highest paid person in Miami is the Maitre D' at Joes.

6. Stumbling. I can't say I saw any wild, out-of-control incidents involving Bears players. Guess I wasn't in the right place. However, I'll never forget a sight I saw during a trip to San Francisco. Several ex-Bears stayed at the team hotel. As we were returning to our rooms one night, we witnessed a prominent ex-Bear literally slamming into the walls. He was so drunk we had to help him back to his room for fear he either would damage himself or one of the walls. To think we grew up idolizing the guy. It definitely changed our perception.

5. Ghostbuster. The highlight I have following the NFC title game came from my interview with Matt Suhey outside the Bears lockerroom. I talked to him for about five minutes, not taking notice of the man standing next to me. Finally, Suhey turned to him and said, "Hey, thanks for coming." I looked up and noticed that the man was Bill Murray, one of my comic heroes. I quickly thanked Suhey and started talking to Murray.

4. Name calling. One thing always stuck out for me in talking to Mike Ditka. He always addressed you by your name while answering a question. It would be, "Well, Ed, I think. . . ." Considering most coaches don't even care if you have a name, I always was impressed Ditka had that trait.

3. A quiet moment with Fridge. I think I may have had the last one-on-one interview with William Perry before he became a national mega-star. A few days prior to the Packer game that made him famous, I sat with the "Fridge" in the lockerroom. Still a raw rookie, he was extremely quiet and some of his answers were barely audible. I remember that Steve McMichael overheard a question I asked Perry. He bellowed, "Don't be askin' him stuff like that." I'm not sure what I asked, but obviously nothing came out of it. A few days later Perry scored a touchdown against the Packers, and you then would have to go through the Bears PR department to get an interview with the "Fridge."

2. Super Sunday. I can't say I remember much from the actual Super Bowl game. It seemed like everything was going in fast motion. Once the Bears took the big lead, I began typing frantically. My main assignment was to write about Buddy Ryan, who would be leaving the Bears after the game to become coach at Philadelphia. As I went downstairs to the lockerroom, I was also told to do a piece on Richard Dent. Everyone had assumed that Jim McMahon would be the game's MVP, and Bob Verdi had him covered. Dent, though, got the award to everyone's surprise. That meant I had to scramble to get both Dent and Ryan in the chaos of the lockerroom. Not sure how I did it, but I did.

1. Payton's place. Any reporter who dealt with Walter Payton knew getting him to sit still for an interview was as difficult tackling him in the open field. My first contact with him came when I was doing a story on Suhey. Since Suhey blocked so well for Payton, I thought it would be a no-brainer to get him to cooperate. Not so.

But with the help of Valdisseri, he arranged for me to have a moment with Payton. I remember he was sitting on his motorcycle outside of Halas Hall. He fidgeted while giving me brief, sometimes silly one- and two-word answers. Then he did something I'll never forget: He started to read the serial number off the motorcycle. I gave up after about five minutes. When I told my story to the veteran Bears reporters, they laughed. They had been through it with Payton before.

While assembling this collection of talent, it became obvious to me that an entire book should be dedicated to homegrown talent that lit it up in comedy, television and/or film. I will not be remiss and ignore the work of dearly departed comedic actors such as Redd Foxx, John Belushi or Bernie Mac. Foxx, who attended Du Sable High School, was the main attraction on one of television's funniest programs, *Sanford and Son*. Belushi, once a middle linebacker at Wheaton Central, was one of driving forces behind the early success of NBC's *Saturday Night Live*. Bernie Mac, who passed away in August of '08, was one of the funniest actors in this decade and, before Barack Obama was elected President, was the White Sox's most recognizable super fan.

Then there's Richard Pryor (Peoria is close enough to claim him) and Karl Malden (the oldest living actor to receive an Oscar for best male lead or supporting role). John C. Reilly (Brother Rice High School) is one of the industry's most promising of a new-breed of comedic stars. And I must acknowledge the great Bob Newhart, whose television program still is regarded by many sitcom enthusiasts as among the most gut-busting of all time.

This difficult assignment requires a special two-fer appetizer section for two legends who left us in this decade.

Charlton Heston. With his wife of 64 years, Lydia, by his side, Heston succumbed to pneumonia in April of '08. He was 84. The Northwestern alumnus is perhaps best known for his role as Moses in *The Ten Commandments*, but he copped the Oscar for best actor with his portrayal as Judah Ben-Hur in *Ben-Hur*. Heston was also magnificent in the galvanizing role of Col. George Taylor in *Planet of the Apes*. Initially a democrat, the legendary actor later swung to the right and became president of the National Rifle Association. A WWII veteran, his career was also marked by well-received performances in the theatre, playing the title role in *Macbeth* and Mark Antony in *Julius Caesar*.

Marlon Brando. Ask 10 guys to list their 10 favorite movies and chances are *The Godfather* will appear on every list. Brando's portrayal of Vito Corleone was nothing shy of remarkable. He bagged an Academy Award for it. In his younger days, Brando was a Hollywood hunk (that would be part of the reason Marilyn Monroe spent quality time with him) and starred as in popular films such as *A Streetcar Named Desire*, *On the Waterfront*, *The Young Lions* and *Mutiny on the Bounty*. Brando was born in Nebraska in '24, but moved North to suburban Chicago and attended Libertyville High School. He was expelled, however, for driving his motorcycle down the school's hallways, then was shipped off to military school in Faribault, Minnesota. Brando was a woman's man (married three times) and a man's man, who admitted to having homosexual relationships. Diabetes and obesity plagued the star later in his life, but not before getting in one last terrific role, opposite Robert DeNiro, in *The Score*.

5. Vince Vaughn. A staple at Wrigley Field with his leading "Take Me Out to the Ballgame" during the 7th Inning Stretch. Comedic actor Vince Vaughn is among the most influential actors in this young century. Born in Minneapolis in 1970, Vaughn's family moved to Buffalo Grove, then to Lake Forest where he attended Lake Forest High School. Success came quickly for Vaughn and he burst onto the national scene for his role in *Swingers* in '96. He then brought the house down opposite Will Ferrell in *Old School* in '03 and continued to star in comedy smashes such as *Dodgeball* in '04, *Wedding Crashers* in '05, and *The Break-Up* in '06. A big Cubs and Notre Dame fan, Vaughn is charming enough to get female attention, while also making every man who watches his work want to go grab a beer with him. He has been active in the U.S.O. Tour, entertaining soldiers in Afghanistan, Kuwait and Iraq. The sky is the limit for V-Squared.

4. William Petersen. Full disclosure first: We're friends and I must confess it is difficult to be completely objective here. Nonetheless, nobody can argue that Evanston native "Bill" Petersen has enjoyed more television success than any actor in the last 10 years. His brainchild, *CSI: Crime Scene Investigation*, has been a smashing success at CBS. Petersen, who played "Grissom," appeared in and helped produce 192 episodes. Born February 21, 1953, Petersen had disciplinary problems and was sent off to live with an older brother in Boise, Idaho, where he was an outstanding high school athlete. He would later become active with Chicago's Steppenwolf Theatre Co. before finding film success as the lead character in *To Live And Die In L.A.* ('85) and *Manhunter* ('86), which was the prequel to the '91 thriller *The Silence of the Lambs*. An avid sports fan, Bill and his wife, Gina, return to Chicago several times every year to check on his beloved Cubs and terrorize fine golf courses in the Northern suburbs. Petersen also turned in outstanding performances in *Fear* and *The Rat Pack*, in which he played JFK.

3. John Malkovich. This Benton native attended both Illinois State and Eastern Illinois. We're claiming him as ours. Malkovich, like Petersen, Joan Allen and Gary Sinise, were big players at Steppenwolf. Also an outstanding host when invited by NBC to serve as frontman for *Saturday Night Live*. Malkovich has been nominated twice for Academy Awards—*Places in the Heart* ('88) and *In the Line of Fire* ('94), in which he plays a chilling role as a former intelligence operative whose objective is to assassinate the president. For my money, John's finest moment was his role as "Teddy KGB" in the '98 film *Rounders*. I regard *Rounders* as the best "guy movie" of the 90s and I know I'm not alone. Malkovich, Matt Damon and Edward Norton sizzle in this suspense-thriller based on a man's commitment to his high school pal, whose addiction drags them both into the gutter. Malkovich, who lived in France for 10 years, also gained critical acclaim for his work in *Being John Malkovich* and *The Killing Fields*.

2. Bill Murray. There is no "guy movie" quoted more than *Caddyshack*. And Murray's role as assistant head greenskeeper Carl Spackler is one of the biggest reasons why. "It's a Cinderella Story." "Cannonball . . . cannonball comin'." "I was unavoidably detained." "Bark like a dog. . . ." "It's a little harsh." I could keep going, but you catch my drift. *Caddyshack* made Murray, but it was just the beginning of his brilliant career as a comedic actor. *Ghostbusters*, *Stripes* and *Groundhog Day* followed. The kid from Wilmette was a global star. Murray, who prepped at Loyola Academy and was the frontman for a band called "The Dutch Masters" in his teens, was David Letterman's first guest when Letterman's late-night talk show debuted on NBC in '82. Murray would have that same distinction when Letterman moved to CBS in '93. Wild Bill has made several attempts at more dramatic roles and found success in the '04 production *Lost in Translation*, for which he was nominated for an Oscar. Sadly, Murray's character in *Lost* hits a bit too close to home as Murray's personal life has crashed, largely because of substance abuse.

1. Harrison Ford. Some would say Ford is more of a movie star than an actor. I understand that point of view, but if you dismiss Ford, you're an idiot. Harrison Ford put his signature on two of the largest grossing film series in history: *Star Wars* and *Indiana Jones*. Neither is my cup of tea, but their success is undeniable. Steven Spielberg saw something in Ford, a 1960 Maine East High grad, when he pleaded with director George Lucas to get him a piece of *Star Wars*. Ford happened to be working on the set as a carpenter and was also helping actors with their lines. Han Solo was born. And so was Ford's career. Indiana Jones would follow. My Ford faves are Chicago-produced *The Fugitive* and *Witness*, for which he received an Oscar nomination (his only) in '85. In the summer of '08, it was estimated that Ford's lead-role films have made more than $3.4 billion in the U.S., topped only by Eddie Murphy. Other must-see Harrison Ford movies include *Patriot Games*, *Clear and Present Danger*, *The Mosquito Coast*, *Air Force One* and *Blade Runner*. And by the way, if anybody ever asks you who broadcast the first sportscast ever on student-run WMTH radio at Maine East, tell 'em it was some guy named Harrison Ford.

Top 10 Blackhawks "Policemen" in the 1980s ::
by Judd Sirott

Note: Judd Sirott has been a fixture in local hockey circles as the long-time voice of the Chicago Wolves. He knows as well as anyone that the 1980s were a wild time for the Blackhawks. Most of the focus was on the offensive wizardry of Denis Savard, but somebody had to do the dirty work. The period also produced some memorable enforcers for Chicago. Now working with the Blackhawks radio coverage, Sirott ranks the Hawks' top tough guys from the 80s.

10. Mike Peluso. He broke in with the Blackhawks in 1989-90 and by 1991-92, held the franchise record with 408 penalty minutes.

9. Gary Nylund. A punishing checker at 6-foot-4 and 220-pounds; limited by knee injuries.

8. Terry Ruskowski. "Roscoe" had three 200 penalty-minute seasons including 1979-80 when he led the team in scoring and PIM.

7. Dave Hutchison. He rode shotgun for Doug Wilson during his 1981-1982 Norris Trophy season as the NHL's best defenseman (he went on stage with Wilson when the award was given out).

6. Wayne Van Dorp. He piled up 303 PIM in 1989-90. Also launched Darren Pang's broadcasting career by falling on his knee.

5. Bob McGill. "Big Daddy" kept everybody honest and could deliver one-liners with the best in the game.

4. Curt Fraser. He had huge mitts; some Blackhawks from that era felt he might have been the toughest guy on the team.

3. Behn Wilson. His own teammates were careful around him.

2. Dave Manson. "Charlie" Manson put the fear of God in any opponent crossing the Blackhawks blueline.

1. Al Secord. He had a devastating left hand and one of only three Blackhawks to ever record a 50-goal season.

Most Defining Moments In Northwestern Men's Basketball :: DM

5.

4.

3.

2.

1.

Michael Jordan made "23" a special number in Chicago. However, there have been other notable 23s who have enjoyed considerable success with that number on their backs as well.

9. Lenny Walterscheid. Yes, the former Bears defensive back wore No. 23 from 1977-82 He wasn't a star, but he did have seven career picks. Plus, he had a great name so we included him in this list.

8. Pete LaCock. Speaking of guys with great names, it would be hard to top LaCock, who wore No. 23 for the Cubs in 1975 and '76. He was the son of Peter Marshall of *Hollywood Squares* fame, making him the answer to a popular trivia question.

7. Carmen Fanzone. OK, he wasn't a big star, but if you're a Cubs fan, how can you forget Carmen Fanzone, an infielder for the Cubs in the 70s? He was also an accomplished horn player who once played the National Anthem before a game. Now that's something Jordan couldn't do.

6. Stu Grimson. He didn't have many skills as far as skating and handling the puck. But he was big and tough as a Blackhawks winger from 1990-93. During the 1991-92 season, he scored all of four points but piled up 234 penalty minutes. Those qualities endeared him to Hawks fans during his run with the team. We like them tough and mean in Chicago.

5. Shaun Gayle. He wasn't a big name like some of his teammates, but he proved himself to be a steady player as a safety for the Bears defense during the late 80s. Gayle was involved in a big play during the 1985 playoff game against the Giants: When Sean Landetta fanned on the punt on the cold, windy day, Gayle snapped up the ball and ran it in for one of the Bears' best gift touchdowns of all time.

4. Robin Ventura. The Sox's first-round pick 1988, Ventura went on to become one of the most consistent and popular players in team history. You could always count on Robin to hit between 20-30 homers, drive in around 90 runs and play Gold Glove defense at third base. You also wanted Ventura at the plate with the bases loaded. He hit 18 Grand Slams in his career, tying him for third on the all-time list with Willie McCovey when he retired in 2004.

3. Jermaine Dye. He came over from Oakland in 2005 with plenty of uncertainty, as he had been plagued by injury problems. Dye went on to become one of Kenny Williams' best acquisitions. He was named the World Series MVP in 2005, banging out the game-winning hit in Game 4. In 2006, he had one of the best seasons ever in Sox history, hitting .315 with 44 homers and 120 RBIs. Then after a down year in 2007, he bounced back in 2008 with 34 homers.

2. Devin Hester. And you thought Gale Sayers was special as a kickoff and punt returner? It's hard to imagine that anybody could blow away Sayers, but Hester did it in his rookie year, when he ran back five for touchdowns. Hester's presence altered game plans, as the other teams quickly learned to kick away from him. He's been the most exciting player in a Bears uniform since, well, Sayers.

1. Ryne Sandberg. If not for Jordan, he would be this town's most successful 23. Picked up from Philadelphia in Dallas Green's best trade, Sandberg went on to have a Hall of Fame career with the Cubs. All he did was win nine Gold Gloves and hit 282 homers, including a league-leading 40 in 1990. He was the National League Most Valuable Player in 1984. Although "Ryno" was probably one of the worst quotes in the game as a player, he certainly made a bunch of noise on the field.

Chicago has a great collection of campy, yet memorable songs that have become synonymous with the respective teams. Here are our favorites. Try to hear the music in your head as you read a sample of the lyrics.

7. Go U Northwestern! It doesn't rank up there with Michigan's "Victors" on the all-time list, but Northwestern's fight song does have a catchy melody.

Go U Northwestern!

Break right through that line.

With our colors flying,

We will cheer you all the time,

U Rah! Rah!

Go U Northwestern!

Fight for victory,

Spread far the fame of our fair name,

Go! Northwestern win that game.

6. Go Cubs Go! The Cubs actually have two theme songs. This is the modern version written by ultimate Cubs fan Steve Goodman in 1984. Cubs fans now sing this song after a victory. As a result, it seems a bit strange to say, "The Cubs are gonna win today" when they've already won. No accounting for the logic of Cubs fans.

Baseball season's underway

Well you better get ready for a brand new day.

Hey, Chicago, what do you say

The Cubs are gonna win today.

They're singing.

Go, Cubs, go

Go, Cubs, go

Hey, Chicago, what do you say

The Cubs are gonna win today.

Go, Cubs, go

Go, Cubs, go

5. Hey-Hey! Holy Mackerel! This version by jazz magician John Frigo was written in 1969. It combines Jack Brickhouse's signature "Hey-Hey" and Vince Lloyd's "Holy Mackerel." Listening to the song brings back images of Santo, Beckert, Banks and Williams. An oldie but a goodie.

Hey, hey, holy mackerel,

No doubt about it,

The Cubs are on their way!

The Cubs are gonna hit today,

They're gonna pitch today,

They're gonna field today,

Come what may,

The Cubs are gonna win today!

Hey, hey holy mackerel,

No doubt about it,

The Cubs are on their way!

They've got the hustle,

They've got the muscle,

The Chicago Cubs are on their way!!!

4. Let's Go-Go-Go White Sox! How can you not love a song written by Captain Stubby and the Buccaneers? Penned in 1959, this classic was mostly forgotten until the Sox revived it during their World Series run in 2005. Now the park shakes when it comes on. Love the tuba carrying the beat.

White Sox!

White Sox! White Sox!

Go-Go White Sox!

Let's Go-Go-Go White Sox

We're with you all the way!

You're always in there fighting,

And you do your best.

We're glad to have you out there in the Middle West.

We're gonna root-root-root-root White Sox.

And cheer you on to victory.

When we're in the stands,

We'll make those rafters ring;

All through the season,

You will hear us sing.

Let's Go-Go-Go White Sox,

Chicago's proud of you!

3. Bear Down, Chicago Bears! This classic was written by Jerry Downs in 1941 to celebrate the Bears' epic 73-0 victory over Washington in the 1940 title game. Generations of Bears fans have sung this tune after a Bears touchdown. Considering the ineptness of the Bears offense, there have been plenty of times when we've wished for that T-formation.

Bear down, Chicago Bears! Make every play clear the way to victory!

Bear down, Chicago Bears! Put up a fight with a might so fearlessly!

We'll never forget the way you thrilled the nation with your T-formation.

Bear down, Chicago Bears, and let them know why you're wearing the crown.

You're the pride and joy of Illinois. Chicago Bears, bear down!

2. Here Come the Hawks! Dick Marx wrote this song in 1969 and the words and melody still stands up after all these years. If you're a true Hawks fan, you still get chills every time it is played before a game.

Here come the Hawks, the mighty Blackhawks!

Take the attack and we'll back you Blackhawks!

We're flyin' and now let's wrap it up!

Let's go you Hawks, move out!

Here come the Hawks!

1. The Super Bowl Shuffle. The legendary song from the legendary season. Don't forget that the Bears made the music video the day after their loss to Miami. Call it audacity or call it confidence. Whatever, the Bears backed it up. Thankfully, the "Shufflin' Crew" played better than they sang and danced.

We are the Bears Shufflin' Crew

Shufflin' on down, doin' it for you.

We're so bad we know we're good.

Blowin' your mind like we knew we would.

You know we're just struttin' for fun

Struttin' our stuff for everyone.

We're not here to start no trouble.

We're just here to do the Super Bowl Shuffle.

The Most Significant Chicago Bands :: DM

Plausible arguments could be made that our city's global influence on rock and roll, when compared to Chicago's rich history in jazz and blues, has been underwhelming. That said, I don't think Chicagoans who rock need to apologize to any other American cities for the tunage produced by the four bands chronicled below.

Honorable Mention, REO Speedwagon. While students at Illinois in '67, these boys began by covering cool stuff in local gin mills. REO was a band riddled by dysfunction. They had three different lead vocalists on their first three albums. When Oak Lawn's Kevin Cronin finally settled in, REO reached new heights. Their *Live: You Get What You Play For* album in '77 went certified platinum. Peoria's Gary Richrath was a gifted guitarist, but was ultimately asked to leave. The band played on and in 1980 their release *Hi Infidelity* was the No.1 album in America for three months, but left early fans of the band a bit saddened. Poppy, cheesy ramblings like "Take It on the Run" and "Keep On Loving You" paled to early numbers such as "157 Riverside Avenue," "Keep Pushin'" and "Golden Country." The Wagon would have chugged more efficiently and longer had it been managed more heavenly and didn't write such pussy songs after some success arrived.

3. Styx. Originally "The Tradewinds." Spawned by twin brothers Chuck and John Panozzo and their neighbor Dennis DeYoung in '70 in the Roseland section of the city's Southeast side, Styx were a phenomenally successful band. In the early years, Styx recorded on the Wooden Nickel label before landing a deal at A&M. *Styx II* included the classic "Lady," but it took two years before the band got air play for the tune. Guitarist James Young swooped in and gave the band a "hook" sound. When Tommy Shaw joined Young in '75 for *Equinox*, Styx was off to the races. They reeled off four consecutive multi-platinum albums between '76 and '81. *Paradise Theater* in '81 reached No.1 on Billboard and it birthed five hit singles, including "The Best of Times" and "Too Much Time on My Hands." The old familiar struggle for creative control spun Styx out of control, however, and the band embarrassed itself with the techno disaster that was "Mr. Roboto." They should have kept their secret a secret. Give me "Light Up" or "Mademoiselle."

2. Cheap Trick. You bet a Rockford band counts—as it would for 80s adult film star Ginger Lynn if we were doing that list. Best described as "power pop," Epic Records signed Cheap Trick on Aerosmith's producer Jack Douglas' recommendation. A bit gimmicky with an army of guitars (and bass) on stage and Rick Nielsen's incessant pick flipping, but a really, really fun band. Especially for those of us who were on board when it began for CT. I loved them at the Hammond Civic Center in '77 (I was 16) following the release of their second album, *In Color*. All of Cheap Trick's first three albums went gold in Japan. *Live at Budokan* went triple platinum in the States—it made them. It was a vessel for some good songs that just sounded better live. What better place than Japan: they were beloved there. Suddenly, "I Want You To Want Me" and "Surrender" penetrated America because every rock station in the country insisted. Front man Robin Zander had a velvety, versatile voice, but sadly sounded far too comfortable crooning the band's cheesiest songs. And they had some dog food that sold, too. If I hear "Dream Police" again I may have to call the police. My faves are "ELO Kiddies" from the debut album, and "Downed" and "So Good To See You" from the second helping offered by Cheap Trick.

1. Chicago. Many wonder how high Chicago could have gone if guitarist Terry Kath had not fatally shot himself in '78, reportedly while cleaning his gun. Originally a DePaul cover band who called themselves "The Chicago Transit Authority," Chicago emerged in '67 and exploded quickly. According to *Billboard*, Chicago was the leading U.S. singles chart act of the decade of the 70s. The band, which featured a spirited horn section, sold more than 120 million albums. Five of Chicago's albums reached No.1 and it produced 21 Top 10 hits. Bassist/lead vocalist Peter Cetera was a master craftsman. His voice was an extension of the band's already soulful nature. Columbia Records was fortunate to have Chicago in its stable. Tracks like "Does Anybody Really Know What Time It Is?," "Make Me Smile," "Saturday In The Park," and "Beginnings" are timeless classics. If you went to a high school dance in the 70s or 80s, chances are excellent you looked for a snuggling partner for "Colour My World." At every dance. For many years. I must confess I never had a strong desire to see Chicago and I don't own a bunch of Chicago's library, either. But this isn't about me. Anybody who would deny Chicago its rightful place in rock history would be ignorant.

The guys who swap thoughts (and insults) on the message boards at chicagosports-fan.com are not shallow dudes. Nope. Their waters run pretty deep and their passions include more than sports. When it comes to music produced after the mid-80s, I'm out. So, with thanks to Doug from Evergreen Park, Wheaton Zach and Frank Coztansa for the following text, here is a list of Chicago's best musical acts, with a rock and roll bend, since 1990.

Honorable Mention: Liz Phair. Phair is easily the most successful female rock artist from Chicago. She has two Grammy nominations, a gold record and is one of the most sexually confident women in rock. Her music has been featured in commercials for Gatorade and promotions for the NCAA women's basketball tournament. Men buy her albums for her music, not because she's pretty.

5. Local H. A "local" favorite, they are the brainchild of Scott Lucas, who uniquely blended the concept of bass and guitar into one instrument. Local H landed two gold records and added two Top 20 singles to highlight their catalogue. They are not the most successful rock stars from the Chicago area, but their albums and shows never disappoint.

4. Ministry. Founded by Al Jorgensen, Ministry created 14 albums over a 27-year span. Their music covers the gamut between synth-pop and industrial metal, though focusing heavily on the latter. A show-stealing Lollapalooza veteran, Ministry helped bring industrial music to the mainstream in the 90s. Plus, there were upwards of 37 different band members or "collaborators" during their career.

3. Kanye West. Kanye is controversial and brash, yet willing to poke fun at himself. His music and arrangements are fantastic. West is a multiple Grammy winner and has sold millions of albums worldwide. The guy headlines Lollapalooza in his hometown. Enough said.

2. Wilco. Founded from the ashes of Uncle Tupelo, Wilco exploded into the independent music scene in the mid 90s. They are a critically acclaimed band with two Grammys during their 15-year career. Internationally successful and part of many top-album lists, Wilco is the major-label-indie-band that reinvented the genre of alternative-country music. And they headlined Lollapalooza.

1. The Smashing Pumpkins. Led by Billy Corgan and recently celebrating 20 years, The Smashing Pumpkins are the most commercially successful alternative-era rock band from Chicago. Hands down. The Pumpkins have won a Grammy Award, have upwards of 20 million albums sold (including nine million units from a double album) and were featured on an episode of *The Simpsons*. These Lollapalooza veterans, for better or worse, have always practiced artistic integrity while pushing the boundaries of what is acceptable in rock music. And they have the most recognizable t-shirt ("Zero") in the history of music.

White Sox general managers have fleeced opposing teams more than a few times over the years. Here is a look at their best trades.

10. Carlos Quentin acquired from Arizona. It seemed to be a minor trade on December 3, 2007 when the Sox picked up Quentin from the Diamondbacks for a prospect. Quentin hadn't done much in Arizona and almost didn't make the Sox out of spring training. But given the opportunity to play, Quentin made the most of it, hitting 36 homers and 100 RBIs in 2008 before being sidelined with a wrist injury in early September. If Quentin stayed healthy, he probably would have been AL MVP.

9. Hoyt Wilhelm, Pete Ward and Ron Hansen acquired from Baltimore. On January 14, 1963, the Sox did the unthinkable in trading the future Hall of Famer Luis Aparicio to the Orioles. However, in return the Sox received knuckleballer Hoyt Wilhelm, who would cement his Hall of Fame bid in Chicago, third-baseman Pete Ward, a solid power hitter, and the steady fielding Hansen at shortstop. Those players led the Sox to three straight 95-plus win seasons.

8. Dick Allen acquired from the Los Angeles Dodgers. General Manager Roland Hemond turned around a listless franchise on December 2, 1971 when he traded pitcher Tommy John to the Dodgers for Dick Allen. Sure, John would go on to have a long career and flirt with getting into the Hall of Fame. But Allen revived the franchise with an electrifying MVP year in 1972. It was worth the price.

7. Sammy Sosa and Wilson Alvarez acquired from Texas. On July 29, 1989, General Manager Larry Himes stunned Sox fans by sending fan favorite Harold Baines in a package to the Rangers, getting minor leaguers Wilson Alvarez and Sammy Sosa in return. Alvarez became a reliable starter, throwing a no-hitter in 1991. We all know what became of Sosa. If the Sox had kept him, this trade would have been ranked much higher.

6. Ozzie Guillen acquired from San Diego. This one also was a stunner when it was announced on December 6, 1984. General Manager Roland Hemond sent 1983 Cy Young winner LaMarr Hoyt in a multi-player swap to San Diego with the Sox getting a skinny shortstop who had yet to play in a big-league game. It seemed like a terrible trade at the time, but it proved to be one of the best as Guillen starred with the Sox as a player and then won a World Series for them as a manager.

5. Paul Konerko acquired from Cincinnati. On November 11, 1998, the Sox dealt centerfielder Mike Cameron to the Reds for Konerko; a young, but struggling power hitter. Cameron would go on to have a decent career, but Konerko would develop into a force in the middle of the Sox lineup, ultimately becoming a 2005 World Series hero. He also is one of the classiest players to wear a Sox uniform.

4. "Shoeless" Joe Jackson acquired from Cleveland. On August 20, 1915, the Sox shipped two players and $31,500 for Jackson. That was a considerable sum of money back then, but Jackson was worth it as he continued to hit everything in sight for the Sox. That includes the 1919 World Series, which he supposedly threw despite hitting .375.

3. Minnie Minoso acquired from Cleveland. In a three-way deal between the Philadelphia A's and Cleveland in April, 1951, the Sox wound up acquiring a rookie outfielder-third baseman in Minoso. Minoso would go on to become one of the Sox's most popular players.

2. Billy Pierce acquired from Detroit. On November 10, 1948, the Sox traded catcher Aaron Robinson for a 21-year-old Pierce. The lefthander became the anchor of the Sox rotation during the 1950s, winning 186 games over 13 years. If the Sox had won more than one pennant during his run, Pierce might be in the Hall of Fame.

1. Nellie Fox acquired from Philadelphia. It will be hard to top this trade. On October 19, 1949, the Sox dealt journeyman catcher Joe Tipton to the Philadelphia A's for a young second-baseman named Nellie Fox. All Fox did was go to 10 All-Star games, win the AL MVP in 1959 and earn a spot in Cooperstown. Now that's a good trade.

Sammy Sosa is the White Sox equivalent of the "Brock-for-Broglio" disaster that beset the Cubs. Unfortunately, it wasn't the only bad trade in Sox history. Here are the worst of the worst.

9. Todd Ritchie acquired from Pittsburgh. On December 13, 2001, Sox GM Kenny Williams picked up Ritchie from the Pirates in a package that included Kip Wells and Josh Fogg. Wells and Fogg would go on to become fair-at-best starters, so it wasn't as if they were major losses. Rather this trade is on the list because Ritchie turned in one of the worst performances ever by a Sox starter in 2002. He went 5-15 with a 6.06 earned run average. It was painful to watch.

8. Doug Drabek dealt to the Yankees. Drabek was a minor league pitcher for the Sox when he and Kevin Hickey were traded to the Yankees for Roy Smalley Jr. on July 18, 1984. Smalley hit .170 during the last half of that season and was gone. Drabek, meanwhile, went on to become an ace for Pittsburgh.

7. Eddie Lopat dealt to the Yankees. Lopat was an effective starter for the Sox, but they traded him to the Yankees on February 24, 1948 for catcher Aaron Robinson. The trade would come back to haunt the Sox, as Lopat would beat them several times as a Yankee into the 1950s.

6. Tommie Agee and Al Weis traded to the Mets. After finishing just short in the 1967 American League pennant race, the Sox decided they need some hitting. So on December 15, 1967, they sent Agee, the 1966 AL Rookie of the Year, and Weis to the Mets in a deal that saw them land Tommy Davis. It turns out Davis was a bust, as he lasted only a year with the team. Agee and Weis went on to become heroes of the 1969 "Miracle Mets" World Series team.

5. Bobby Bonilla dealt to Pittsburgh. As the White Sox beat writer, I was actually there when Hawk Harrelson traded Bonilla for Jose DeLeon on July 23, 1986. I remember Bonilla being extremely emotional about leaving the team. It turned out it was the Sox who wound up crying as Bonilla went on to become one of the top hitters in the National League.

4. Earl Battey dealt to Washington. The next three entries are linked. After winning the pennant in 1959, owner Bill Veeck wanted to repeat. So they traded a bunch of promising young players for established, but aging veterans. Battey was dealt in this deal in April, 1960 in return for Roy Sievers. Sievers had a couple good years

with the Sox, but they never won with him. Battey, meanwhile, became a five-time All-Star catcher with Minnesota. If the Sox had kept him and the other young players on this list, there's little doubt they would have won another pennant or two in the 1960s.

3. Johnny Callison traded to Philadelphia.

Again, the Sox went for veterans when they traded Callison to the Phillies for third-baseman Gene Freese on December 8, 1959. Freese didn't do much for the Sox. Callison, meanwhile, became a fixture for the Phillies as a four-time National League All-Star.

2. Norm Cash traded to Cleveland.

The Sox continued to purge themselves of young players on December 6, 1959 when they traded Cash in a package to Cleveland for Minnie Minoso. Sox fans loved having Minoso back in the fold, but he was 39 in 1960. Cash, meanwhile, eventually moved to Detroit, where he hit the bulk of his 379 career homers.

1. Sammy Sosa dealt to the Cubs.

This trade didn't look so bad when it was made on March 30, 1992. Sosa hardly did anything to distinguish himself with the Sox. So dealing him for an established power hitter like George Bell seemed like a good idea at the time. Bell, though, only lasted two years with the Sox, hitting .217 in 1993 before calling it a career. As for Sosa, who was only 23 at the time, I seem to recall hearing about him hitting about a zillion homers for the Cubs. Also makes the list for "Cubs' best trades" on the next page.

The Cubs' history says they probably get it wrong more than right when it comes to making deals. But they have had a few winners, enabling them to pick up future Hall of Famers in the process. Here are their best trades.

10. Gary Matthews and Bob Dernier acquired from Philadephia.
On March 26, 1984, Dallas Green went back to his old stomping grounds and traded Bill Campbell and Mike Diaz for Matthews and Dernier. Both players would go on to patrol left and centerfield and solidify the Cubs lineup. They were key factors in the Cubs' run to the 1984 National League East title.

9. Derrek Lee acquired from Florida.
On November 25, 2003, the Cubs took advantage of the fire sale that the Marlins were having by picking up Lee for Heep Seop Choi. Choi was a top prospect for the Cubs, but he never amounted to anything. Lee, meanwhile, became a fixture for the Cubs, winning the National League batting title at .335 in 2005.

8. Rogers Hornsby acquired from the Boston Braves.
The Cubs enjoyed another fire sale on November 7, 1928. This time, they took advantage of the financially-strapped Boston Braves, sending five no-name players and $200,000 (a huge sum of money back then) for Hornsby. One of the greatest hitters of all time responded in 1929, hitting .380 with 39 homers and 149 RBIs to lead the Cubs to the National League pennant.

7. Rick Sutcliffe acquired from Cleveland.
This falls under the old adage of "sometimes you have to give something to get something." On June 13, 1984, the Cubs traded prize prospect Joe Carter, along with Mel Hall, to the Indians for Sutcliffe. Carter went on to have a huge career, hitting nearly 400 homers. Sutcliffe, though, was unhittable with the Cubs in 1984, winning the Cy Young Award with a 16-1 record. He would have several steady, if not spectacular seasons from there. This goes down as a good trade.

6. Hank Sauer acquired from Cincinnati.
Sauer was 32 when the Cubs acquired him on June 15, 1949 for Harry Walker and Peanuts Lowery. But he still had plenty left, as he went on to become one of the Cubs' most popular players after winning the NL MVP award in 1952.

5. Randy Hundley and Bill Hands acquired from San Francisco.
Hundley and Hands were rookies on December 2, 1965 when the Cubs picked them up in a package that included reliever Lindy McDaniel. Hundley would go on to become an All-Star catcher and Hands was a solid No. 2 starter behind Fergie Jenkins, winning 20 games in 1969.

4. Aramis Ramirez acquired from Pittsburgh. On July 23, 2003, the Cubs fleeced the Pirates. Knowing Pittsburgh couldn't afford to keep him, they essentially gave up nothing to pick up Ramirez. The deal also included Kenny Lofton, who would spark the Cubs' offense during the second half of their 2003 playoff run. But it was Ramirez who would become an anchor in the middle of the Cubs' lineup.

3. Ferguson Jenkins acquired from Philadelphia. On April 21, 1966, the Cubs traded 35-year old pitcher Larry Jackson and 37-year-old Bob Buhl to the Phillies in a package that saw the Cubs receive the 22-year-old Jenkins. Big mistake for the Phillies. In 1967, Jenkins peeled off the first of six straight 20-win seasons. In 1991, Jenkins went into the Hall of Fame wearing a Cubs hat.

2. Ryne Sanberg acquired from Philadelphia. Sanberg was actually a throw-in on January 27, 1982 when Dallas Green traded Ivan DeJesus for Larry Bowa. Green, who came over from the Phillies, knew what he was getting in Sandberg. In 1984, Sandberg was named the NL MVP and was well on his way to building a career that would land him in Cooperstown. It was easily Green's biggest trade for the Cubs.

1. Sammy Sosa acquired from the White Sox. The worst trade in Sox history is the Cubs' best. On March 30, 1992, General Manager Larry Himes shipped George Bell across town for Sosa. It was the second time Himes traded for Sosa; he picked him from Texas while with the Sox. Himes obviously saw something in Sosa. While Bell's career was nearing an end, Sosa found glory with the Cubs, for better and some worse. The rest, as they say, is history.

Everyone always points to the Brock-for-Broglio trade but trust me, there were other clunkers that wound up costing the Cubs, big time. Here are some of the worst trades in Cubs history.

10. Larry Gura traded to Texas. On August 31, 1973, the Cubs traded Gura to the Rangers for pitcher Mike Paul. Gura hadn't done much with the Cubs, winning only three games in four years. But he eventually found himself as key starter with some fine Kansas City Royals teams. He wound up with 123 career victories.

9. Burt Hooton traded to Los Angeles. On May 2, 1975, the Cubs sent Hooton to the Dodgers for pitchers Geoff Zahn and Eddie Solomon. The owner of the "knucklecurve" was only 25 at the time and had thrown a no-hitter in 1972. Sure enough, he blossomed with the Dodgers, winning 18 games in 1975 and 19 games in 1978. Zahn would go on to have a nice career, winning 111 games. However, only two of them were with the Cubs.

8. Bill North traded to Oakland. On November 21, 1972, the Cubs sent North to the A's for Bob Locker. Locker, who had some good years with the Sox, was 35 at the time and only pitched for one season with the Cubs. North, meanwhile, was 25 and went on to become the starting centerfielder for two World Series champion teams in Oakland.

7. Willie Hernandez traded to Philadelphia. On May 22, 1983, the Cubs traded Hernandez to the Phillies for Dick Ruthven. Hernandez had some good years as a reliever for the Cubs, but little did they know he would later hit the jackpot with the Detroit Tigers. Hernandez saved 32 games for the World Series champs, winning both the MVP and Cy Young awards. Ruthven wound up winning only 22 games in four years with the Cubs.

6. Bill Madlock traded San Francisco. This December 11, 1976 trade was motivated by money, pure and simple. After winning back-to-back batting titles in 1975 and 1976, Madlock wanted more cash. The Cubs weren't willing to open their wallets. So the third-baseman was off to the Giants for Bobby Murcer and Steve Ontiveros. Neither did much of note in Chicago, while Madlock would go on to win two more batting titles.

5. Bruce Sutter traded to St. Louis. Again, the December 9, 1980 deal was about the mighty dollar. The Cubs didn't want to pony up for Sutter and wanted to get something for him before he became a free agent. Trouble is, they didn't get enough. Leon Durham was the main guy the Cubs got in return. While he had some OK numbers, he never emerged into a big star—certainly not enough to offset losing Sutter, who would go on to solidify his Hall of Fame credentials with the Cardinals.

4. Rafael Palmeiro and Jamie Moyer traded to Texas. On December 5, 1988, the Cubs dealt Palmeiro and Moyer in a nine-player trade that saw them get Mitch Williams in return. Williams had a big year in 1989, saving 36 games for the NL East champs. But that was about it for him in a Cubs uniform. Palmeiro went on to hit more than 500 homers, and steroids or not, they counted. As of this writing, Moyer is a World Series winner with the Phillies and may pitch until he is 90.

3. Lee Smith traded to Boston. On December 8, 1987, the Cubs sent Smith to the Red Sox for Calvin Schiraldi and Al Nipper. The Cubs made the move in the hopes of shaking things up. Can't blame them for that. However, Schiraldi and Nipper, two mediocre pitchers, hardly were worth the price. Frank Robinson said it best: "The Cubs traded a horse and got two ponies." Schiraldi and Nipper both were gone within two years, while Smith still had more than 300 saves left in him.

2. Dennis Eckersley traded to Oakland. On April 3, 1987, the Cubs sent Eckersley to the A's, getting three prospects who never put on their uniform. At the time, Eck appeared to be washed up as a starter, going 6-11 in 1986 at the age of 31. Little did they know that Eckersley would be converted to a star closer in Oakland by manager Tony LaRussa. His dominating run earned him a spot in Cooperstown. Yes, this one hurt.

1. Lou Brock traded to St. Louis. This June 15, 1964 move actually involved six players, but Brock and Broglio were the key components. On the surface, it didn't look like a bad trade. Broglio was only 27 and coming off an 18-win season in 1963. Brock, at 25, struck out a ton and didn't hit higher than .263 in part-time action over two seasons with the Cubs. Of course, everyone knows the rest of the story. Brock would go on to record more than 3,000 hits, break many stolen base records and earn his way to Cooperstown. Broglio would hurt his arm and go 7-19 during his 2 ½ years with the Cubs. Brock for Broglio: A trade that will forever live in Cubs infamy.

Note: Listeners to Dan Bernstein's radio show on WSCR-AM can expect him to cut through all the crap and get to the heart of the matter. His insights are among the best in the business. Here is Dan dissecting the top myths in Chicago sports.

10. The Butkus-era Bears inflicted pain on opponents. "You knew you had played Butkus and those Bears," the saying goes. Yes, probably because you had won. Several highlight tackles have made people forget the 48-74-4 record, and that they never made the playoffs. Some of those mean hits must have happened in the end zone after opposing TDs.

9. The 2005 Sox won the title by "grinding" and playing "Ozzie-ball." It's nice to celebrate small-ball and the little things, but the Sox won the World Series by hitting 200 homers, and leading the league in both complete games and saves. Timely power, a spectacular bullpen and dominant starting pitching (historically so in the play-offs) forged their true identity.

8. Ron Santo is loveable. The bumbling, incompetent broadcaster has become a Cubs mascot, as the city has forgotten or ignored his past. A great player, and an angry hot-head who fought with managers, teammates, opponents, umpires and media. His postgame antics in 1969 were not cute to most in baseball. There are reasons why an otherwise deserving HOF candidate has been kept out so far.

7. Michael Jordan is a great businessman. Then so is Chef Boy-ar-dee. Jordan is a brand, not a mind. He lends his name and image to products so they sell. When he has been given actual responsibility (Wizards, Bobcats), he has shown no aptitude or desire to do any real work. He is obscenely rich only because he achieved global fame by putting a ball in a basket.

6. Sammy Sosa. Myth incarnate, this puffed-up megalomaniac hijacked a base-ball franchise to indulge his own vainglory. His statistical achievements are the emptiest in the city's sports history. Complicit, too, are the Cubs' bosses who enabled his hopping, chest-tapping circus act and the MLB brass who obfuscated the corked-bat aftermath.

5. "Bear Weather." Detailed historical analyses of the Bears' success relative to gametime temperature show no advantage for them in the cold. This does not stop people from believing otherwise, apparently because they want to. The Bears have won in the cold in the years when they were good at blocking and tackling, and have lost in the cold in the years that they were not.

4. Cub fans are yuppie sissies, and Sox fans are blue-collar tough guys. Nope. Actually, both teams' fans are a complicated mix of income levels, education levels, age, gender, and ethnicities, according to a well-publicized study. While the neighborhoods around the respective parks do differ, the actual fan bases are nearly identical. The stereotypes do not hold.

3. Mike Ditka was a great coach. Good coach for the right team at the right time, fine. But even Ditka himself admits they should have won at least another Super Bowl. His gluttonous pursuit of every last endorsement dollar set the tone for the team to fracture. His 15-33 run leading the Saints was embarrassing. His legacy? A screaming, mustachioed archetype that haunts coaches in this town to this day.

2. Jerry Krause single-handedly dismantled the Bulls. Krause is short, fat, unattractive and paranoid, and that put him at a disadvantage in the public-relations battle over how the Jordan era ended. The massive egos and conflicting desires of Krause, Phil Jackson, Jordan and more came together after the final Finals, and the most easily-demonized participant took the brunt of the blame. It was going to end sometime, and it wouldn't have ended cleanly in any scenario. Krause was at fault, but so were others.

1. Chicago sports fans are tougher than those in other cities. Though this phenomenon also occurs elsewhere, there is some fundamental insecurity among fans in Chicago that creates a need for the validation of their toughness. No evidence exists that wearing a Bears hat or a Hawks t-shirt, or waving an "It's Gonna Happen" placard makes one tougher than the average sports fan from Los Angeles, Miami, Vancouver, London, Moscow or Mumbai.

There wasn't a more challenging part of writing this book than narrowing down a list of Chicago heartbreaks to 10. An entire book could be committed to disappointments. I've chosen to restrict these heartbreaks to on-the-field events and to provide balance with both baseball teams represented equally. Truth be told, the only knee-buckler for me that involves the Cubs would be the '69 collapse. It was shortly after that season when I joined a 12-step recovery group and defected to "the dark side" to root for the White Sox.

10. Super Bowl XL: Colts 29, Bears 17. Nobody was terribly shocked, just terribly disappointed. Peyton Manning is a pretty good player and his skills compared to those of Rex Grossman's were the biggest reason Indianapolis was favored. The Bears, however, made it look easy in the NFC title game against Drew Brees and New Orleans and the Colts were the league's worst defense against the run. Optimism abounded when Devin Hester took the opening kickoff 92 yards for a score, but it was all Indy after that. The Bears turned it over five times and we spent a long night in a Southern Florida monsoon.

9. The '01 White Sox. Have to go with the collective disappointment of a season riddled with frustration. The Sox were supposed to go the proverbial next level after winning the AL Central with a young nucleus in 2000, but a 14-29 start put the them behind the 8-ball and they never recovered. Newcomer David Wells, acquired for popular fellow southpaw Mike Sirotka, was a bust and a clubhouse distraction. Frank Thomas was hurt most of the year. The Sox finished third with an 83-79 record.

8. Seattle sweeps the White Sox in '00 ALDS. The White Sox hit all season. They won 95 games and finally snapped Cleveland's streak of division titles at five. Frank Thomas, Paul Konerko, Magglio Ordonez, Carlos Lee, Ray Durham and the clutch Jose Valentin had Sox fans optimistic this would be the year. It wasn't. The Mariners' staff—which included Game 2 starter, the immortal Paul Abbott—looked like the Braves' staff of the 90s and the Sox scored just seven runs in 28 innings.

7. Padres beat the Cubs in the '84 NLCS. A magical year on the North side as the Cubs won 96 games and the National League East. Acquired by GM Dallas Green in mid-stream, Rick Sutcliffe went 16-1 and won the Cy Young. Ryne Sandberg was the NL MVP. Jim Frey was NL manager of the year. The team had speed (center-fielder Bobby Dernier), power (Gary Matthews, Leon Durham, Keith Moreland and Ron Cey) and depth on the pitching staff. After the Cubs embarrassed San Diego in Games 1 and 2 at Wrigley, they were kicked in three straight at Jack Murphy Stadium in the then best-of-five format. Cubs bats went silent in Southern California, where Mr.

America Steve Garvey played long ball against Chicago pitching. First baseman Durham, who booted a ground ball, was perceived to be the goat, but the collapse was a textbook team loss.

6. Orioles beat the White Sox in '83 ALCS. Most impressive second-half to a season in Sox history. They smoked the pack and won the AL West by a record 19 ½ games. Gary's Ron Kittle was Rookie of the Year with 35 HRs and 100 RBIs and Lamar Hoyt was AL Cy Young winner. With high expectations, the Sox took the opener in Baltimore, but dropped three straight after that. Eddie Murray's three-run homer in the first inning of Game 3 at Old Comiskey may have landed in Lake Michigan had the upper deck not broken the baseball's flight. In Game 4, the great Tito Landrum delivered a clutch homerun off hard-luck loser Britt Burns in the 10th. Sox utility man Jerry Dybzinski authored one of the great baserunning blunders in Chicago history. The Sox scored only one run in the final 30 innings of the series.

5. Penguins sweep the Blackhawks in '92 Finals. This was particularly hard to swallow for those of us who prefer hockey over hoops because the Bulls were en route to their second straight championship. Just as Mike Keenan's Hawks were gaining momentum and attention, following a sweep of the Oilers in the old Campbell Conference Finals, Pittsburgh put the brakes on a great postseason run. Eddie Belfour had been, in hockey parlance, "standing on his head" and the Hawks were getting enough offense from a group led by Jeremy Roenick, Steve Larmer and defenseman Chris Chelios. In fact, the Hawks looked like they were onto another victory in Game 1 at The Igloo, but they blew a 3-0 lead and Mario Lemieux and the Penguins blitzed them in rude fashion. Watching the Pens pass the Stanley Cup around on Chicago Stadium ice left many of us breathless.

4. Redskins 27, Bears 13. January 3, 1987. We have to give the '86 Bears credit for overcoming adversity and injuries on the heels of their Super Bowl XX season. Amidst chaos, including the departure of beloved defensive coordinator Buddy Ryan, the Bears went 14-2 and hosted Washington in a divisional playoff game. Jim McMahon was hurt and the unpopular (among teammates) Doug Flutie didn't have enough for a Redskins team that came to play. DE Charles Mann and DT Dexter Manley both had big days. Flutie was 11-of-31 for 134 yards with a TD and a pick. The assumption of a Bears' dynasty died that day. And it was evident Walter Payton would be best served by calling it a career. Payton carried 14 times for 38 yards. He returned for one more Un-Sweetnesslike season and it only took another playoff loss to the 'Skins to convince him to hang it up.

3. Games 6 and 7 of the '03 NLCS. Five outs from the elusive World Series and the Cubs (and their fans) pissed it away. Yes, you can blame the dorky Steve Bartman—and anybody who sat near him who also didn't notice Cubs leftfielder Moises Alou closing on that foul ball. You can also blame Cubs shortstop Alex Gonzalez for kicking a groundball in the same inning. The finger could also be pointed at Cubs folk hero Kerry Wood, who started Game 7 and didn't get out of the fifth inning. And don't spare Dusty Baker. When the Marlins needed relief help in a win-or-go-home scenario, the venerable Jack McKeon was giving the ball to his best starters. Baker gave the ball to career journeyman David Veres. There is no collapse—once already advanced to the big stage—that dispirited this city more than this in the NLCS of '03. Even as a Sox fan, the memory of this performance makes me want to turn off the phone and take a long nap.

2. The 1969 Cubs. Remember in *The Silence of the Lambs* when Lecter asks Starling "What is your worst memory of childhood?" What a nightmare August and September of '69 were. Big lineup. It included Hall of Famers Billy Williams and Ernie Banks. Third baseman Ron Santo was solid. Jim Hickman could play several positions and could stroke. Don Kessinger and Glen Beckert were solid middle infielders and ter-rific tablesetters. The staff? Awesome. HOFer Fergie Jenkins, Kenny Holtzman, Bill Hands. Bullpen anchored by Ted Abernathy and Phil Regan. We all went to bed that summer with sweet visions of sweeping the Orioles in the World Series. Then came a black cat lurking near Santo at Shea Stadium. A bobble by centerfielder Don Young. A near-perfect game by the Mets' Tom Seaver. Rough series against the Pirates, who were also red hot. As the leaves turned autumnal red, so did our faces. The big August lead evaporated to just 4½ games as September arrived. Banks hit one homer in September. Santo hit just two. The Mets won the East, the National League and the World Series. Some have been damaged for life. I chose the White Sox.

1. The '90-'91 Blackhawks lose in the first round. On the heels of the most impressive regular season in Hawks' history, the fourth-place Minnesota North Stars took the Hawks out in six games. Reflecting on it makes me physically ill. Keenan's Hawks accrued a league-best 106 points and earned home ice advantage all the way through the Cup Finals. They were healthy, but they were tired. And the Stars succeeded in getting under their skin. They coaxed defensemen Chris Chelios and Dave Manson into dumb penalties. Minnesota veterans Dave Gagner, Brian Bellows and Neal Broten played smart hockey and Stars' goalie Jon Casey was terrific. When I left Chicago Stadium after an emotional win over the Blues on St. Patrick's Day, I was convinced the Hawks were going to be Stanley Cup champs. They were physical, relentless, solid on the power play and had enough goaltending to win it all. And then came a team with 68 points and a game plan. God damn those North Stars, who went on and fought the good fight until Pittsburgh got 'em in the Finals.

Note: How ya' doing, everybody. It's Chet Coppock. You know, I've been a Bears fan right from the cradle. In 2008, I went to my 58th consecutive Chicago Bears home opener. I've seen at it all. You know how it is with the Bears; some good, but a lot of heartbreak too. Here's my all-time list of rip-your-heart-out days on and off the field suffered by the Monsters of the Midway.

10. January 6, 1984. The NFC title game: San Francisco 23, Bears 0. Just seven days after beating Joe Theismann and the Washington Redskins at RFK Stadium, the Bears were dropkicked off the Golden Gate Bridge. The Bears, a team that "thrived on distractions," tried to avoid distractions by holing up in California wine country about 60 miles from Frisco. As game day approached, any well-informed 10-year-old from Des Moines could sense that the Bears were in for a miserable afternoon. The victory over the Skins had made the Bears season. They didn't really believe they could knock off the 49ers.

9. January, 1987. The firing of Jerry Vainisi. Another Michael McCaskey gem. The Bears didn't repeat as Super Bowl champs in 1986, but they were an impressive 14-2 before getting licked by the Redskins in the playoffs. McCaskey, convinced that he was a "football man," decided Vainisi had to face the firing squad. (Side note: Jerry told me at a TV taping at Fox-32 that he was finished two days before the firing was announced.) As Ditka's shoulder to lean on, Vainsi was a superb contract negotiator and the man who structured George Halas' will to save the McCaskeys a huge fortune in tax revenue. The move was stupid beyond words.

8. January 8, 1989. NFC title game: San Francisco 28, Bears 3. All week Mike Ditka and the Bears preached a double-dip gospel that should not have been spoketh. One, that the NFC road to the Super Bowl ran through Chicago and two, that the 49ers would certainly wave the white flag in weather conditions that were the coldest I've ever experienced during any game at Soldier Field. The script was given to rewrite. Jerry Rice hauled in two first-half touchdown passes to give the 49ers a 14-3 lead at the break. Honest to gosh, half the crowd left Soldier Field before the third quarter. Mongo McMichael will tell you it was the longest fourth quarter of his life.

7. November 13, 1960. Baltimore 24, Bears 20. The essence of Johnny U. Johnny Unitas connects with Lenny Moore in the final minute of a brutally tough football game to give the Colts the win. But wait. Why wasn't a flag thrown on Moore who clearly pushed off Bears defensive back J.C. Caroline to create space for the reception? The play left Bears fans dazed and Coach Halas mad at the world. As the Colts departed Wrigley Field, hundreds of fans crowded the Colts team bus just begging for a glimpse of Unitas.

6. The renovation of Soldier Field. I don't have to tell you the "Old Soldier Field" was no great shakes. In fact, it's the only NFL stadium I've been to where it actually rained under the stands. You want more? In 1976, while doing PA on a Bears-Vikings game, I lost sound because a rat had chewed through the electrical wiring that controlled my microphone. However, the new joint is a Lake-front monstrosity that has all the warmth and charm of a two-week vacation in Siberia.

5. January 15, 2006. NFC playoffs. Carolina 29, Bears 21. Another playoff swan dive. The Bears now had gone 11 years without a post-season win. You had an idea it was going to be Carolina's day when Jake Delhomme hooked up with Steve Smith on a 58-yard touchdown two minutes into the game. It was dramatically clear after the game that Lovie Smith and D-coordinator Ron Rivera were operating on different pages.

4. December 15, 1968. Green Bay 28, Bears 27. A raucous afternoon under dark, gray skies at Wrigley Field. The Bears, in Jim Dooley's first year as head coach, mounted a sensational comeback that falls just short and cost the Bears a playoff spot in the season's final regular season game. Dooley's team was decimated by injuries. Gale Sayers, who was leading the league in rushing, had gone down earlier in the year with torn knee ligaments against the 49ers.

3. The Mike Ditka firing. A tenure that began in 1982 with back-to-back losses to the Lions and Saints; peaked with a Super Bowl in 1986; ended with a classless firing by the Bears after the 1992 season. When Ditka twisted in the wind—knowing full well he was going to get blown out of the gym—Michael McCaskey went on a skiing trip. A freakin' skiing trip?! The great irony: Ditka remains the essence of Chicago, a larger than life football man, salesman and showman. McCaskey, meanwhile, was exiled to the closet at Halas Hall after he botched the Dave McGinnis hiring in 1999. And just who put the blade to Michael? Virginia, his mom.

2. October 24, 1971. Bears 28, Detroit 23. A sense of disbelief. Bobby Douglass plays the finest game of his career to the lead the Bears to a road win over the Lions at old Briggs Stadium. But that's far from the story. I watched from the press box as Lions wideout Chuck Hughes collapsed and died on the field. The sound of the ambulance carrying Hughes from the field was nothing less than the sound of a funeral. My most vivid memory: Dick Butkus and Ed O'Bradovich reduced to tears on the team plane carrying the Bears back to Chicago.

1. January 10, 1988. NFC playoffs. Washington 21, Bears 17. The end of an era. Walter Payton rushes for 85 yards in the final game of his career. At game's close, Payton, burned by the loss and facing the realization that the party is over, sat with his head in hands for nearly 20 minutes on the Bears bench. Walter was at once bewildered and suddenly vulnerable.

Everyone else is checking in with their favorite moments. I figured I would indulge myself too. I spent 27 years covering sports for the *Chicago Tribune*. It was a dream job, and I loved every minute of it. The job gave me memories for a lifetime. Often they centered on my brushes with the rich and famous. Here are some of them.

10. Badminton snub. I've been blown off by many prominent athletes, but this one always stood out. In 1985, I was assigned to cover the Illinois High School Badminton tournament. I was in a foul mood since it wasn't exactly my dream assignment. Then it got even worse when after the first day, the No. 1 player said she wasn't talking. I was stunned. I remember thinking, I just got blown off by a badminton girl? I'll never forget it. Whenever I need to be humbled, I'll always think of her.

9. An evening with Charles and Magic. In 2006, I went down to TNT in Atlanta to spend an evening in the studio with Charles Barkley. Sir Charles was a hoot. While watching the NBA games on one screen, he had the technicians put up *House* on the other screen. "Can't miss *House*," he said. Magic Johnson also was there. He came up to me and said, "Good to see you again," even though we hadn't met. We talked for an hour about basketball, Michael Jordan, business, etc. Charles and Magic in the same night. As I left the building, I couldn't help but think of the people who would have loved to have traded places with me.

8. The Buckner game. By Game 6 of the 1986 World Series, I was exhausted and just wanted to go home. I thought I had my wish when the Red Sox were one out away from wrapping up the title in the 10th. Then everything went haywire, climaxing in Bill Buckner's blunder. It went down as perhaps the most infamous play in World Series history. However, through all the chaos I'll always remember that Buckner met the avalanche of reporters head on and offered no excuses.

7. Make my day. After Tiger Woods won his sixth straight tournament at the 2001 AT&T at Pebble Beach, I saw Clint Eastwood at the side of the green. I went up to him for a quote. He didn't have much to say, but he quickly found me useful. As the autograph seekers came up to him, he used me as a shield, saying: "Can't right now. Doing an interview." When we got to his Mercedes, perhaps feeling guilty, he asked if I needed a ride. I passed since I only had to walk a few more feet. To this day, my biggest regret is that I didn't get in that car with Clint Eastwood. I should have made him drive me all around Monterrey.

6. Miami-Notre Dame. I covered national college football for six years. I loved the atmosphere on campus for a big game. There's nothing to match it in sports. The best I saw was the Miami-Notre Dame game in South Bend in 1988. With plenty of hate on both sides, both teams—undefeated at the time—played their hearts out. Miami missed a two-point conversion in the final minutes, allowing the Irish to hold for a 31-30 victory. Best game I ever saw.

5. Bulls win first title. When the Bulls met the Lakers in the 1991 NBA Finals, it wasn't certain that they would win the championship—let alone six. With the series tied 1-1, I got to be part of the crew that covered the last three games at the LA Forum. There were stars and cleavage all over the place. That made for good viewing. The games were terrific, especially Game 5. When the Bulls pulled it out, the atmosphere in the lockerroom was an amazing mix of joy and tears. That first title will always be the best in my book.

4. Tiger wins the Masters. The first golf tournament I covered was the 1997 Masters. Trying to be bold, I predicted in a front-page article that there was no way Tiger Woods would win playing for the first time as a pro. He never made the cut as an amateur. Well, to quote Maxwell Smart, he "Missed it by that much." Woods produced a performance for the ages, winning by 12 strokes and setting a course record. As a result, I had to eat a heaping portion of crow. It didn't matter. My journey with Tiger had begun.

3. Summer Olympics in Australia. The 2000 games were my first Olympics. I knew they were big, but I truly didn't expect to be overwhelmed by the experience. Walking to the opening ceremonies, you heard all the different languages and saw people representing virtually every country in the world. It was an incredible feeling. I loved covering events I had previously seen on *Wide World of Sports*: ping-pong, weightlifting, cycling, etc. I also loved Sydney. I would vote for every Olympics to be held there.

2. White Sox in the 2005 World Series. As a die-hard Sox fan, I never thought the day would come when I would see them in a World Series. Our dreams came true in 2005. The entire run was incredible, but the first two games in Chicago had special meaning. My father made the trip up from Florida. He wasn't in the best shape, and traveling was extremely difficult for him. But there was no way he was going to miss his Sox play in a World Series. He watched those games with my brother and both of my sons. Shortly thereafter, his health declined and he passed away in 2007. However, I always will be heartened that the last two Sox games he saw in person were World Series games.

1. The 1985 Bears. My first pro beat was as the No. 2 man to Don Pierson for the 1985 Bears. Talk about great timing for a 25-year-old reporter. I was with the team from the first day of training camp in Platteville to the Super Bowl in New Orleans. The story just kept getting bigger with McMahon, Payton, Ditka, the Fridge, etc. I couldn't wait to get to Halas Hall every day. The 1985 Bears were the biggest story in Chicago sports history. I knew no matter what I did the rest of my career, it never would match that season with the Bears.

How do you "rank" the level of sadness when it comes to death? You don't. These heartbreakers are the ones that hit me the hardest, in no particular order.

Matt Hartl, 23, Northwestern fullback. Hartl was the soul of the Northwestern offense when the Wildcats arose from the ashes and shockingly claimed the Big Ten championship in '95. The ruggedly handsome Denver native was diagnosed with Hodgkins disease when doctors found a tumor in his chest two months before Northwestern went to the Rose Bowl. Hartl missed the '96 season, but his cancer was in remisssion and Matt courageously returned to the NU football program in '97. Ultimately, Hodgkins returned and claimed his life on August 31, 1999.

Rod Beck, 38, Cubs closer. "The Shooter" was one of the more colorful figures in Cubs history. Beck saved 51 games in '98 and helped the Cubs earn a wild card berth. Honest. Playful. Charitable. Unfortunately, Beck sank deep into the throes of addiction. He lived too hard and when police searched his Northeast Phoenix home after his death on June 24, '07, they found evidence of cocaine use and other drug paraphernalia. Beck was a three-time All-Star and a guy whom I considered a very fond acquaintance for the short time he was here.

Ben Wilson, 17, Simeon High basketball star. I was home from college on Thanksgiving break when I learned of the tragic shooting of the Simeon standout. I remember where I was driving on November 21 of '84 when I heard the unspeakable news on the radio. Wilson led Simeon to the state championship his junior year. *Sporting News* listed him as the nation's No. 1 recruit. Former NBAer Nick Anderson wore jersey No. 25 to honor Wilson. Simeon named its basketball arena "Ben Wilson Memorial Gym."

Matt Heldman, 23, Illinois basketball player. Heldman was a four-year letterman ('95-'98) for the Fighting Illini. He was among three killed, including his father, Otis Heldman, on October 10, '99, in a two-car, head-on collision near his Libertyville home. Alcohol was involved. Shortly after his passing, Illinois created the "Matto Award," given to the the Illini player who demonstrates the most hustle.

Michael Williams, 7, Highland (Ind.) Little Leaguer. Neuroblastoma is a rare form of cancer that all too often claims the lives of children. Michael was everything a sports-minded guy like his father, Lou, dreamed of for his son. Mike loved baseball, fishing and golf. His cancer, diagnosed when he was 4, was put in remission, but returned and claimed his brief life in September of 2001. The Little League field in Highland was dedicated to his memory and is called "Michael Williams Field of

Dreams." For information on neuroblastoma research and fundraising, please visit neuroblastomacancer.org.

Keith Magnuson, 56, Blackhawks defenseman, head coach, Alumni Association. As a player ('69-'79) "Maggie" was a fierce competitor and the most willing participant when it came to dropping the gloves. He usually lost, but he'd go with anybody and was an insipiration to his teammates and to Hawks fans. Magnuson continued his association with the club long after his career as a player and coach were finished and he was instrumental in the development of the Blackhawks Alumni Association. Maggie and fellow former NHLer Rob Ramage were overserved, sadly, and Ramage got behind the wheel in suburban Toronto and a nasty accident claimed Keith's life in mid-December of '03. The Blackhawks honored Magnuson's loyalty to the organization by retiring his No.3, along with Pierre Pilote, in November of '08.

Ricky Byrdsong, 43, Northwestern basketball coach. Byrdsong was jogging near his home in north suburban Skokie when a white supremacist fatally shot him on July 2, '99. I didn't know Ricky (other than an occasional phone interview with him), but I cried hard when I learned of the hate crime, which happened in the presence of Byrdsong's young son and daughter, ages 8 and 10 at the time. The shooter, whose name I have chosen to omit, later shot himself.

Randy Walker, 52, Northwestern football coach. As if Northwestern hadn't experienced enough tragedy. Coach Walk was a straight shooter and a damn good football coach. Many coaches speak of their programs becoming "a family." Walker meant it. He spent seven years as the head master in Evanston before a heart defect claimed his life on June 29, '06. Randy spoke at a fundraiser I hosted for my high school football program almost immediately after he was named as Gary Barnett's successor. I liked him right off the start. His message that night, "point the thumb before you point the finger." Like many, I always will miss his spirit, his dedication and his sense of humor.

Most Interesting Assistant Coaches :: DM

In Chicago, we have been fortunate to have a high volume of assistant coaches to share the media responsibilities with the head master. Often it has been the case that the sidekicks were much more engaging than the big boss. It was difficult for me to pare this list to 10. I have decided to punish several worthy candidates who worked the Bulls bench as assistants, primarily because a high percentage of NBA coaching types comport themselves like they're solving terminal diseases or world hunger. So, my apologies to long-time Bulls assistant John Bach, the architect of the Bulls' "Doberman defense" during the title runs. Strength coach Al Vermeil, who made out on Horace Grant, also gets snubbed because of the unmitigated arrogance of coaches such as Phil Jackson. And John Paxson, now the general manager, was a Bulls assistant and he always has been one of the truly good guys in Chicago sports.

10. Ferguson Jenkins, Cubs Pitching Coach and Minor League Instructor. Cooperstown class of '90, Jenkins was a beast as a major league chucker. He reeled off six consecutive 20-win seasons with the Cubs and was the '71 NL Cy Young winner. Fergie served a couple of short stints as Cubs pitching coach and also toiled in the lower levels. Jenkins always was thoughtful, mostly honest and a magnificent source for hard core baseball conversation. He has spoken candidly about his '80 arrest for possession of cocaine, hashish and marijuana at the Canadian border as well as the tragedy of losing his ex-wife and daughter to tragic deaths.

9. Buddy Ryan, Bears Defensive Coordinator, '78-'85. Understated, but colorful. Ryan called rookies by their number, refusing to acknowledge names. Ditka resented the accolades given to the architect of the Bears famed "46" defense. Asked why the two didn't shake hands in '86 when Ryan was the Eagles head coach, Ditka snapped " 'Cuz I would have ripped off his arm and shoved it up it his ass." Ryan was loved by his players. That's why Ditka was so envious. In his spare time, Buddy raised horses on his farm in Kentucky.

8. Dick Pole, Cubs Pitching Coach, '88-'91. The old man is still at it, handling the Cincinnati staff. Pole was instrumental in the early development of future Hall of Famer Greg Maddux. Dick was a bit monotone, but gave good information. Above all else, however, I have to admit to just loving introducing the audience to a man named Dick Pole.

7. Rich Preston, Blackhawks Assistant Coach, '90-'95. Preston was a scrappy player for the Hawks in the early 80s. Terrific penalty killer who later served as an assistant under both Mike Keenan and Darryl Sutter in the early to mid-90s. Still on Keenan's staff in Calgary. Ritchie was a great guy to have a beer with and he wouldn't hedge on what was really going on with the teams on which he served.

6. Greg Walker, White Sox Hitting Instructor '03-present. Despite being questioned publicly by manager Ozzie Guillen after a bad mid-summer series against Tampa in '08, Walk remains the Sox hitting instructor. And he wasn't bashful about firing back at the skipper after Guillen called him out. The '09 season is his ninth with the South Siders. A career .260 hitter with Chicago and Baltimore, Walker's Georgia drawl, with his warmth and insight, make every interview worth a listen. In the clubhouse, my best conversations with the former first-sacker center around fishing and football. A man's man.

5. Billy Williams, Cubs Hitting Instructor, Bench Coach. The '87 Hall of Fame inductee was a hero of mine as a kid and I'm not too jaded to still get a kick out of sitting in the Cubs' dugout or around the batting cage just bullshitting with the "Sweet Swinger." Williams has always been kind and honest. His recollections of the Cubs teams he played on in the 60s and early 70s are vivid and interesting. Whistler, Alabama's favorite son has had a couple of stints on the Cubs staff and remains in uniform when the team trains in Mesa, Arizona in March. He is a great ambassador for the Cubs and is one of the most approachable megastars in Chicago sports history.

4. Greg Blache, Bears Defensive Coordinator '99-'03. One of the most quotable wingmen of all time. In an interview on my show, Blache pissed off Bears fans when he declared local media and fans know nothing about football and that he should host a seminar for the remedial in the offseason. An avid hunter, Blache drew the ire of the NFL when he placed bullets at the locker stalls of players who made impressive "kills" on Sundays. Love him or hate him, nobody could ever contend the ND alum was dull. And his Bears defense in the 13-3, '01 season was the NFL's best scoring defense, allowing just 203 points.

3. Don Cooper, Sox Pitching Coach, '03-present. A journeyman big-league pitcher with a thick, East coast accent, Cooper's draw is his unpredictability. He can be engaging and he can be a surly prick. That's his appeal. He earned high marks from sports-radio consumers in June of '07 when he called *The Score's* Mike North "a jerkoff" in a bumpy interview on North's morning show. Cooper's magnum opus as a pitching tutor unquestionably is the four consecutive complete games authored by his starters in the '05 ALCS against Los Angeles.

2. Tony Wise, Bears Offensive Line Coach, '93-'98. Dave Wannstedt's top lieutenant. Fiery and intense at every turn. Scratchy voiced. The semi-portly Wise cares about nothing more than his beefcakes protecting the A gap. He lives for it. My favorite Wise quotes are topped by "Every sack is a specific occurrence." I asked him why Bears draftee Octus Polk pronounces his name Otis. "The 'c' in Texas is silent," he quipped. Wise followed Wannstedt to Miami ('01-'04), where the Dolphins produced two of the most prolific rushing offenses in franchise history. He now assists Wannstedt at Pitt, where it all started for Wise as a grad assistant making peanuts. Tony slept in the bowels of the stadium. Any football fan who spends three minutes with Tony Wise likes him. A must-interview in every city in which he has worked.

1. Dave McGinnis, Bears Linebackers Coach, '86-'95. There isn't a nicer guy who's ever worked an NFL sideline. McGinnis now coaches linebackers and is the assistant head coach for Jeff Fisher in Tennessee. In '99, the Bears botched his hiring as head man when they announced it prematurely. McGinnis had not agreed to the contract and hadn't notified his family or his boss in Arizona, former Bears defensive coordinator Vince Tobin. It was a dark day for all Chicago media and fans who had come to love his candor and warmth. When the Bears trained in Platteville, Wisconsin, Coach Mac gave me "full access" to his linebacker drills. Sometimes he would comment to me directly during practice or even solicit my opinion. His players loved him and would put their nuts on the line for him. Though his tenure as head coach with the Cardinals was underwhelming (17-40), McGinnis still is considered one of the finest defensive assistants in the last 20+ years.

Summer in Chicago invariably means golf for many of us. And if you wanted, you could play hooky at work and fill in almost every day on the June, July and August calendars with a charity golf event. Typically, the format calls for a paying foursome with one celebrity "captain" to entertain the "commoners." What makes for a desirable celebrity captain is a combination of golf skills, a sense of humor and, in some cases, the ability to party. In some of these cases, the penchant for silly male bonding is so high, golf aptitude doesn't matter.

10. Dan Plesac. The quirky left-hander spent two of his almost-20 big league seasons in a Cubs uniform and likely is better known for his pre- and post-game work on Comcast Sports Net. "Sack," who grew up in Crown Point, is delightfully silly and tells vivid stories of his professional baseball experiences. Danny's passion is harness racing and for any horse enthusiast, he is the right man to captain the foursome. A bright guy with the ability to relate to people of all socioeconomic backgrounds.

9. Dale Tallon. The ex-Blackhawks General Manager is one of the best golfers on the local celebrity scene. And like a high percentage of hockey players, he is cordial and down to earth. Tallon can be brutally honest and is a great storyteller. When he came to the Hawks in a trade with Vancouver in the early '70s, he made the mistake of wearing No. 9. That number previously was worn by the great Bobby Hull. Tallon was booed unmercifully and still tells funny stories about that experience and others.

8. John Paxson. Since he's taken the reins of the Bulls, Paxson has been less visible on local tracks. Pax reached hero status by canning big jumpers against the Lakers in the title-clinching fifth game in '91 and the game-winner in the final against Phoenix in '93. On top of that, he has maintained tremendous perspective over the years. Pax is a real guy. Very grounded. He is a decent golfer, but more importantly, Chicago fans who play in his group will tell all their friends for months because Johnny Jump Shot is a class act.

7. Steve McMichael. Hanging with Steve is not for the faint of heart. "Mongo" is as physically intimidating as they come, but he's really a teddy bear. He isn't a good golfer, but nobody cares. He tells dirty jokes, regales fellow players with '85 Bears stories and parties like there is no tomorrow.

6. Jim McMahon. You quickly learn Mac's reputation wasn't a fabrication when you spend time with him on a golf course. A refreshing flake. He usually plays barefoot. He also has played naked. In front of a large crowd. There is no lying in Jim McMahon. What you see is what you get. He's a lot of fun, if you're capable of taking the plane to the highest altitude possible while on the golf course.

5. Any other member of the '85 Bears. May as well get 'em all in here. No team in Chicago sports history ever has been more universally appealing than the 18-1, World Champion Bears. Almost 25 years later, people are still awed by their presence. I don't think any of them—except 7-time Pro Bowl Center Jay Hilgenberg—can play golf worth a shit. Nobody minds. Jimbo Covert, Tom Thayer and Jim Morrissey are among my favorite ex-jocks of all time and I consider them friends. And Dave Duerson is a great storyteller and a very bright guy. Say it with me: "Da Bearsss."

4. Hawk Harrelson. Of all the preferred celebs, the Hawk is the most capable of assisting a highly competitive group in its desire to win the event. Harrelson still drives the ball a mile and is uncanny when approaching the green. Harrelson is best suited for old school baseball fans. His stories about Denny McLain, Yaz and life in the American League in the 60s are compelling. He's a warm guy, a terrific baseball mind and very good with people.

3. Kenny Williams. The White Sox General Manager prefers to keep a low profile. He's very guarded. When Kenny decides to relax and let his hair down, however, all bets are off. I've closed establishments with Williams and was left wanting more of his company. He's a cigar aficionado and enjoys fine vodkas. He is also a very intelligent man with football acumen. KW grew up in a rough part of Oakland and has solid perspective on family and life.

2. Norm Van Lier. Stormin' Norman will be in the charter class of the Chicago Party Boys Hall of Fame when it gets erected. Norm always looked the part on a golf course. His pants pleated nicely. His Footjoys always spotless. Van Lier's best attribute, however, is he would make everybody else in the group feel better about their game. He'd hit five balls consecutively and fail to get the club face on all five. But he didn't care. He was there for the party and anybody who was lucky enough to have Stormin's company on the golf course would relish a chance to have it again.

1. Denis Savard. The Blackhawk Hall of Famer and former head coach is the perfect mix of golf skill, ability to mingle and partyability. A group captained by Savy claimed the championship at one of our Mac, Jurko and Harry golf outings to benefit autism research and treatment at Bolingbook Golf Club in the summer of '04. Savy sat on the terrace for hours drinking with the boys and re-living every birdie. When he was a player, Savard was much more reserved. Almost bashful. Not the case anymore. Anybody who spends a few minutes over a beverage with Denis Savard tells all of his friends about it in glowing terms for the next several weeks. When we write the book on "Men's Men" in Chicago sports, we will begin with Savard.

The first White Sox manager was none other than Charles Comiskey. He guided the Sox to an 82-53 record and a first-place finish in 1900. "The Old Roman" then stepped aside to run the club. Some of the managers he picked worked out, and the same holds true with his successors. Here is our ranking of the best Sox managers.

7. Paul Richards. Richard had two spins with the Sox, managing them from 1951-54 and then again in 1976. He was a brilliant baseball man, helping to launch the "Go-Go Sox" era in the 50s. He once had his pitcher move to third base for one batter so he could bring in lefty Billy Pierce to pitch to Ted Williams. The strategy worked as Williams popped out. Richards departed at the end of the 1954 season in a dispute with general manager Frank Lane. Bill Veeck brought him back for an encore in 1976, but he had a terrible team which lost 97 games.

6. Chuck Tanner. Tanner was an unknown manager who inherited a team that lost 106 games in 1970. Tanner's positive approach had immediate results, as the Sox battled the powerful Oakland A's into September in 1972 before falling short. Tanner's biggest achievement was getting the most out of the moody Dick Allen. He let Allen have an extra long leash, and for the most part, the strategy worked.

5. Jimmy Dykes. Dykes was the White Sox winningest manager, compiling 894 victories from 1934-1946. Despite not being blessed with great talent, he still led the Sox to six first-place division finishes. The Sox were frugal back then and often over-hauled their roster year after year. Who knows what Dykes would have done if he had better players?

4. Tony LaRussa. LaRussa was only 34 when Bill Veeck tabbed him to take over in August of 1979. He quickly established himself as a winning manager, leading the Sox to the American League West title in 1983. I covered the Sox and LaRussa in 1986. His relationship with new General Manager Ken Harrelson seemed doomed from the start, as he was fired in June of that year. I remember telling LaRussa he wouldn't be out long. Sure enough, Oakland snapped him up quickly. Since then, he went on to win two World Series and make numerous post-season appearances. I'm sure of all the decisions owner Jerry Reinsdorf regrets the most, firing LaRussa has to be at the top of his list.

3. Fielder Jones. How can you not like a manager named Fielder? Jones led the White Sox from 1904-1908, compiling a .593 winning percentage. Jones was at the helm for one of the Sox's finest moments, guiding "The Hitless Wonders" in 1906. Despite a team batting average of .228, the Sox won the pennant then upset the powerful Cubs in the World Series, giving their fans bragging rights for more than a century. Jones called it quits after the 1908 season.

2. Ozzie Guillen. Guillen is easily the most outspoken and controversial manager in Sox history. If he stays around long enough, he might just be the best. Guillen's style is blunt and brutally frank. He isn't afraid to throw a player under the bus. But he also gets them to play for him too. When you win the team's first World Series in 88 years, you obviously know what you're doing. When he steps away from the Sox, I fully expect that his No. 13 will be retired.

1. Al Lopez. "The Señor" is the only manager to win an American League pennant during the Yankees period of dominance from 1949-64. He did it with Cleveland in 1954 and then with the Sox in 1959. Unfortunately, he didn't do it enough, as the Sox finished second to the Yankees five times during his run from 1957-65. However, the Sox, built on pitching and defense, were a long-running perennial contender under Lopez. That makes him the best in our book.

When you go 88 years between World Series titles, you can be sure the leadership was lacking at times. The Sox have had their share of bad managers. Here are the worst of the worse.

7. James Callahan. At age 29, Callahan was the Sox youngest manager. Clearly, though, he wasn't ready for the job when Charles Comiskey tabbed him in 1903. The older players resented him and Callahan's weight and drinking problems were hardly out of Manager 101. After a 60-77 mark in 1903, Callahan resigned early in 1904 season. Comiskey brought back a more mature Callahan in 1912 for three mediocre seasons.

6. Don Kessinger. Kessinger had his best days with the Cubs, but it was the White Sox who gave him a chance to manage in 1979. Turns out he wasn't up for the task. Kessinger, who played under Leo "Nice Guys Finish Last" Durocher, said he thought a nice guy could win in the dugout. That might be true for some guys, but Kessinger couldn't make it work. With the Sox wallowing at 46-60, Kessinger stepped down in August of that year. His replacement? Tony LaRussa.

5. Ray Schalk. Schalk had an illustrious career as a catcher for the White Sox, earning a trip to the Hall of Fame. However, it was different story as a manager. Schalk took over the Sox in 1927 and went 102-125 in just under two seasons. He was never able to command the respect of the players as a manager.

4. Lew Fonseca. The Sox have had three 100-loss seasons in their history. Fonseca was at the helm for one of them, as the Sox went 49-102 in 1932. Fonseca, though, did have a memorable moment when he punched out an umpire who had been goading the Sox players after a loss. At least he stuck up for his team.

3. Ted Lyons. The great Sox pitcher was another Hall of Famer who didn't measure up as a manager. He took over in May of 1946 and went 64-60 the rest of the way. However, things only got worse from there. In 1948, Lyons' team plunged to 51-101. His days as a manager were done.

2. Terry Bevington. Other Sox managers had much worse records, as Bevington compiled a .509 winning percentage in nearly three years as manager of the Sox. However, his teams had considerable talent making them woeful underachievers. Bevington was clearly overmatched on the field and often feuded with the media. Sox fans wanted his ouster from the beginning. His Sox career will forever be defined by the day he signaled down to the bullpen to make a pitching change. Trouble was, he had no one warming up.

1. Don Gutteridge. It is unfortunate that Gutteridge occupies this spot because he had a long and distinguished career as a Sox coach from 1955 to 1966. When Al Lopez resigned because of health problems in May, 1969, the Sox turned to a reluctant Gutteridge. He was content to be a career coach. Instead, he inherited a terrible team and he couldn't stop the free-fall. He was the manager for the bulk of their 56-106 season in 1970 (he was fired in September), the worst in team history. Unfortunately, that wound up being his legacy with the Sox.

Considering the Bears had one coach for 40 years, it is hard to form a long list here. But they did have a few other successful coaches besides George Halas. Here they are.

5. Jack Pardee. The Bears were a disaster when Pardee took over the team in 1975. Pardee, however, had the good fortune of coming in just as the Bears drafted Walter Payton. After a 4-10 season in 1975, Pardee, thanks to Payton, led the Bears to a 9-5 mark in 1977 and their first playoff appearance in 14 years. But when Pardee's former team, the Washington Redskins, called after that season, he left Chicago. It probably wasn't his best move, as he lasted only three years with the Redskins. Who knows what would have happened if he stayed with the Bears.

4. Hunk Anderson and Luke Johnsos. When George Halas went into the service in 1942, he appointed Anderson and Johnsos to be co-coaches. They had their moment of glory in 1943 when they led the Bears to an 8-1-1 record. Then the Bears beat Washington 41-21 to win the NFL title. However, after the pair went 3-7 in 1945, they were pushed aside as Halas once again took the helm.

3. Lovie Smith. The Bears tabbed the defensive specialist to replace Dick Jauron after the 2003 season. Smith found the winning combination quickly, leading the Bears to the playoffs in 2005 and then the Super Bowl in 2006. Lovie can be stifling and dull and many of his moves can be questioned, such as dumping defensive coordinator Ron Rivera after the Super Bowl season. On the other hand, the Bears have had only two coaches who have taken them to the big game—and Smith was one of them.

2. Mike Ditka. What can you say about Michael Keller Ditka? In his last act shortly before he died, Halas went with his gut and brought in a man with a questionable résumé to lead the Bears in 1982. But it was Ditka's guts that Halas was banking on to revive the Bears. Sure enough, he did. Ditka's record speaks for itself. He went 112-68 in 11 years, and, of course, won the Super Bowl in 1986. Ditka's impact went beyond his record. His style and personality defined not only the Bears, but the city as well.

1. George Halas. It is interesting to note that George Halas tried to hand over the reins on three different occasions, only to go back to the sidelines again. He couldn't sit back and watch somebody else do it when he knew he was the best man for the job. Halas won eight NFL titles and 324 games. He still was going strong in 1963, when he led the Bears to championship at the age of 68. Papa Bear was simply the best.

Besides George Halas and Mike Ditka, the Bears haven't been blessed with a wealth of good coaches. Some of them have been downright terrible. Here are the worst of the worst.

5. Dick Jauron. Jauron took over the Dave Wannstedt disaster in 1999 and didn't make it much better, going 6-10 and 5-11 in his first two seasons. His 2001 team did catch lightning and went 13-3 in a year when they seemingly caught every break. However, Philadelphia thrashed the Bears in the playoffs, and they slid back downhill from there. After two more losing years, making it four out of five, Jauron was fired following the 2003 season.

4. Neill Armstrong. Jim Finks brought in Armstrong to replace Jack Pardee following the 1977 season. Armstrong's four-year tenure was among the dullest in Bears history, with the exception of their playoff team in 1979. Armstrong had the great Walter Payton, but couldn't figure out anyone to go along with him. He was never able to settle on a quarterback and after a 30-35 record in four years, he was dumped in 1981.

3. Dave Wannstedt. Ah, Wanny. A Jimmy Johnson protégé, he arrived in Chicago in 1993 expecting to do the same thing for the Bears that Johnson did in Dallas. The Bears gave him control of the entire package, which also put him in charge of player personnel. Wannstedt wasn't up to the task. He made the incredibly stupid move of trading a first-round pick to Seattle for Rick Mirer, who was terrible. He was never able to live down his infamous "The pieces are in place" proclamation, when clearly they weren't. Often, Wannstedt looked confused and befuddled on the sidelines. It was reflected in his 41-57 record, which had him waving bye-bye after the 1998 season.

2. Jim Dooley. When Halas finally retired for good after the 1967 season, he turned to the 38-year-old Dooley. The Bears nearly made the playoffs in 1968 despite losing Gale Sayers in mid-season. Then disaster struck in 1969 when the Bears plummeted to 1-13, the worst season in their history. Dooley put his team in the hands of the erratic Bobby Douglass. He even moved in with him for a week to try to help the quarterback learn the playbook. It didn't work. Dooley compiled a 20-36 record during his four years and was fired after the 1971 season.

1. Abe Gibron. The overweight Gibron was a colorful and engaging figure. Everyone loved him. Too bad he couldn't coach. Tabbed by Halas to replace Dooley in 1972, Gibron was mostly remembered for the losing battle he fought in trying to keep his pants up on the sidelines. If only somebody had given him a pair of suspenders. Gibron's teams went 4-9-1, 3-11, and 4-10. Halas finally put him out of his misery after the 1974 season. Still, we love Abe.

Yes, despite their miserable history, the Cubs have had a few successful managers. Not a lot, but enough to justify doing a list. Here are the best.

8. Jim Frey. Frey rode into town in 1984 and nearly took the Cubs to the World Series, falling, of course, one game short. He was a good manager, but injuries decimated his entire starting rotation in 1985. GM Dallas Green got impatient and fired him in 1986. Frey did, however, return as General Manager and put together the 1989 playoff team.

7. Don Zimmer. How can you not love Zim? He looked like a cartoon character, not a manager. Zimmer did have one moment of glory as he made all the right moves in 1989 in leading the Cubs to the NL East title. However, success was fleeting, as he was fired in May, 1991. Regardless, Chicago will forever have a soft spot for Zimmer.

6. Lou Piniella. At the time of this writing, Piniella is coming off leading the Cubs to back-to-back NL Central titles. Of course, he also is coming off back-to-back playoff clunkers in which the Cubs got swept both times. So the jury is very much out on Sweet Lou.

5. Fred Mitchell. I always used to kid to *Chicago Tribune* columnist Fred Mitchell that he aged well considering he managed the Cubs from 1917-1920. The other Mitchell led the Cubs to the 1918 World Series, where they lost to the Boston Red Sox and their hot pitcher, Babe Ruth. Since Mitchell is one of only four Cubs managers to win a National League pennant, he makes the list.

4. Leo Durocher. I debated whether to place Leo on the worst list because of the way he alienated players like Ernie Banks and Ron Santo. And he definitely was a large factor in the 1969 meltdown by over-using his regulars. However, "The Lip" did help lift the Cubs from the depths. After losing 103 games in his first year in 1966, Durocher's Cubs posted five straight winning seasons before he was fired in 1972. Cubs broadcaster Jack Brickhouse had the best quote about Durocher: "In those early days, he was an SOB, but a sharp SOB. But by the time he was finished in Chicago, he was just an old SOB."

3. Joe McCarthy. McCarthy, one of the great baseball managers of all time, got his start in the dugout with the Cubs in 1926. McCarthy was a big success thanks in part to his ability to handle the hard-living Hack Wilson. McCarthy's Cubs won the pennant in 1929, losing to the Philadelphia A's in the World Series. However, after coming up short with a second-place finish in 1930, the Cubs fired McCarthy. It was the best thing that ever happened to the skipper, as he went on to win seven World Series with the Yankees. Nice move, Cubs.

2. Charlie Grimm. "Jolly Cholly" had three different stints as manager of the Cubs, leading them to pennants in 1932, 1935, 1938, and 1945. Too bad, Grimm went 0 for 4 in the World Series. But hey, at least he got them there four times. He was a Cub through and through. When he died, his wife scattered his ashes in Wrigley Field.

1. Frank Chance. Known as the "Peerless Leader," Chance became manager of the Cubs in 1905 at the age of 27. At the time, he already was a steady .300 hitter. A stern, no-nonsense manager, his Cubs teams dominated baseball in the first decade of the 20th century. They won three pennants and back-to-back World Series titles in 1907 and 1908. The Cubs are still waiting for the second-coming of the "Peerless Leader."

Where to begin? When you have a history of losing like the Cubs, there are no short-ages of candidates for this category. Here are the worst of the worst.

9. Rabbit Maranville. Maranville was a Hall of Famer as a player and a goof ball as a person. He was a hard drinker and played silly practical jokes. Yet the Cubs still hired him to be their manager in 1925. They quickly realized their mistake and fired him after only 53 games during a season in which they would finish last in the National League for the first time.

8. Rogers Hornsby. Hornsby was another Hall of Famer who was miserable as a manager. The Cubs hired the great hitter at the end of the 1930 season. He was beyond strict, banning everything in the clubhouse from reading to smoking and eating. His players despised him. Hornsby was eventually fired in August, 1932. His successor, Charlie Grimm, went on to lead the Cubs to the pennant that year. In one final act of revenge, Hornsby's players did not give him a World Series share.

7. Dusty Baker. Why is Baker on this list? Didn't he lead the Cubs to within five outs of the World Series in 2003? Yes he did, but it all went downhill from there for ol' Dusty. His managerial moves in that fateful eighth inning of Game 6 will be forever questioned. Then in 2004, he failed to control the clubhouse whining over announcers Chip Caray and Steve Stone. The distraction contributed to a meltdown in the stretch, costing the Cubs a playoff spot. It completely unraveled with a 96-loss season in 2006, leading to his firing. It could have been so much better for Baker in Chicago.

6. Tom Trebelhorn. Trebelhorn took over in 1994. He got off to a brutal start and never recovered. The Cubs lost their first 12 games at Wrigley Field that year and didn't win a home game until May 4. However, Trebelhorn was a stand-up guy. After yet another home defeat, he met with angry fans in the fire station across the street. He was put out of his misery by being fired after the season.

5. Don Baylor. Everyone seemed enthused when the Cubs hired Baylor in 2000. He led the Colorado Rockies expansion team to the playoffs and was one of the most respected men in baseball. But his tenure with the Cubs was mostly a failure. His team finished last in 2000. Then after an 88-victory season in 2001, they lost 95 games in 2002. Baylor didn't make it to the finish line that year, as he was fired before the season ended.

4. Lee Elia. Elia posted a 127-158 mark in just under two seasons as manager of the Cubs. His tenure would have been forgotten if not for his memorable profanity-filled tirade after a Cubs defeat in 1983. It still gets replayed every year, earning Elia a permanent spot in Cubs history.

3. Joey Amalfitano. Amalfitano was a faithful soldier as a long-time coach who deserved better as a manager. He took over the job on an interim basis twice, once when Herman Franks was fired in 1979 and again when Preston Gomez was fired in 1980. The Cubs finally let him have his own season in 1981, but it didn't go well. They went 38-65 in the strike-shortened season. Amalfitano's winning percentage of .363 was the lowest for any Cubs manager who worked more than 200 games.

2. Frankie Frisch. Yet another Hall of Famer who failed big-time as manager of the Cubs. He took over as skipper during the 1949 season. He was often disinterested and it clearly showed: the Cubs finished last, next-to-last, and last during his three-year tenure.

1. The College of Coaches. If this isn't the dumbest idea ever conceived in baseball, it has to be in the top five. In 1961, Cubs owner Phillip Wrigley decided instead of having one manager, he would install a rotating series of coaches who would assume control of the team over a certain period. The Cubs press guide lists seven different "coaches" who led the team in 1961 and 1962. It was chaos, as rules changed during the season, and pitchers were used differently depending on the coach in charge. The result of this great experiment: the 1962 Cubs lost 103 games. The College of Coaches, along with the Lou Brock trade, will forever be a testament to Cubs futility.

Gee, I wonder who is going to be No. 1? Could it be the coach who won six NBA titles? You'll have to read on to find out. Here are the best Bulls coaches.

6. Ed Badger.
Badger makes this list for one memorable run. During his first season, the Bulls closed by winning 20 of their last 24 games in 1977. It was an exciting time as the Chicago Stadium rocked like it never did in the Dick Motta years. The streaking Bulls took the eventual champion Portland Trailblazers to the limit before losing in the playoffs. However, it didn't last for Badger. The following year, the Bulls went 40-42 and Badger was fired.

5. Johnny Kerr.
"Red" Kerr will always be one of the faces of the franchise. He was the team's first coach in 1966 and set the tone in leading the expansion Bulls to the playoffs. Kerr was named NBA Coach of the Year for that accomplishment. He lasted only one more season as coach, but eventually returned as a popular analyst for Bulls games on T.V. and radio. The Bulls never had a soldier more faithful and passionate than "Red."

4. Scott Skiles.
The Bulls were mired in the post-Jordan mess when the fiery Skiles took over at the beginning of the 2003 season. One year later, they won 47 games and were back in the playoffs. In 2006-2007, Skiles' team advanced to the semifinals before losing to Detroit in six games. Skiles looked to be in for a long run, but when the team got off to a slow start in 2007, he was fired in mid-season.

3. Doug Collins.
Under Collins, who took control in 1986, the Bulls started to take their first steps on the road to greatness. In his second year, they won 50 games, and in his third year, they won their first playoff series, defeating Cleveland on "The Shot" by Jordan. Collins was starting to weave young players such as Scottie Pippen and Horace Grant into the mix, and it looked like they were on the verge of taking a bigger step. However, it would be without Collins, who was mysteriously fired following the 1989 season. Would the Bulls have won six titles with Collins as coach? We'll never know.

2. Dick Motta.
Motta was the unknown coach from Idaho who took over the Bulls in 1968. Quickly, he transformed the relatively new franchise into a perennial contender with a stifling defense. Beginning in 1970, the Bulls rattled off four straight 50-win seasons. Then in 1975, they appeared to be on the verge of the NBA Finals with a 3-2 lead in the semifinals against Golden State. Alas, Motta's Bulls never got over the hump, and he was fired in 1976. He did, however, win his NBA title with Washington in 1978.

1. Phil Jackson. Everyone assumes that any old coach could have stepped in and won all those championships with a team that featured Michael Jordan. They would be wrong. Jackson was the piece that pulled it all together. He got those stars to play as a unit. He got them to buy into all that Zen stuff. He was able to handle Dennis Rodman. He rescued Scottie Pippen after his famous "I'm not going in" blunder in the playoffs against the Knicks. Jackson somehow thrived despite working with a General Manager in Jerry Krause who didn't want him around after the first few titles.

Sure, another coach might have won a title or two with this bunch. But not six. And surely not with the class and insights that came with having Jackson on the bench.

Worst Bulls Coaches :: ES

If you're a Bulls fan, you know who is No. 1 on this list. The fellow who followed Phil Jackson had a bit of a rough time in Chicago. Here are the worst Bulls coaches.

6. Jerry Sloan. Sloan ranks as one of the most successful coaches in NBA history for his work at Utah. However, he would like to forget his brief coaching stint in Chicago. The Original Bull took over as coach at the age of 37 in the 1979-80 season. His first team went 30-52. Then after improving to 45-37 the following year, the Bulls went backwards again in 1981-82. The Coach took the fall, as he was fired in midseason with a 19-32 mark. Fortunately for Sloan, he got another chance and made the most of it.

5. Stan Albeck. He never really had much of a chance during his one-year run in 1985-86. Michael Jordan broke his foot during the third game of the season. Management wanted him to remain out for the entire year, but Jordan insisted on coming back in March, just in time to lead the Bulls into the playoffs. Albeck got to witness Jordan's famous 63-point game against Boston, but that was it. He was dismissed after the season.

4. Kevin Loughery. Thank God Loughery wasn't a very good coach. Otherwise, the Bulls never get Michael Jordan. Loughery took over in 1983 and the Bulls sputtered to a 27-55 record. That enabled the Bulls to get the No. 3 pick in the 1984 where they selected MJ. Loughery let Jordan run wild during his rookie season, as the Bulls improved to 38-44. Still, the front office didn't think he was the guy to guide Jordan, and they fired him after the season.

3. Larry Costello. Costello was a highly successful coach with the Milwaukee Bucks, winning an NBA title. He wasn't as successful with the Bulls, however, during a short stint in the 1978-79 season. He resigned halfway through with a 20-36 record. It seems Costello was a better coach when he had a player like Kareem Abdul-Jabbar playing for him.

2. Paul Westhead. Westhead had won an NBA championship with the Lakers in 1980. So there was reason for optimism when he signed on to coach the Bulls in 1982. Westhead's team had gunners like Reggie Theus and Orlando Woolridge, but they played little defense. The end result was a 28-54 record and Westhead was gone after one season.

1. Tim Floyd. He was at the helm for the darkest period in Bulls history. Was it all his fault? No. When he took over after the Bulls won their sixth title in 1998, the team had been gutted. Gone were Michael Jordan, Scottie Pippen, Dennis Rodman, etc. GM Jerry Krause wanted to show everyone his true genius by rebuilding the team from scratch. Floyd definitely was in the wrong place at the wrong time. His teams lost more than 65 games twice, as the Bulls resembled a junior varsity squad playing in the NBA.

Floyd, though, did nothing to stop the bleeding. Finally, he had enough, resigning on Christmas Eve, 2001 with the Bulls sitting at 4-21.

The Blackhawks have had some interesting coaches behind the bench. Here are the best Hawks coaches in history.

6. Tom Gorman/Bill Stewart. They would have been mere footnotes in the Hawks record books except for one thing: they both won Stanley Cups. Gorman was the coach when the Hawks won in 1934. Stewart, meanwhile, salvaged a 14-25-9 season in 1937-38 by winning the Cup in 1938. He was fired after 21 games the following year. Still, if you win one of the three Hawks' Stanley Cups, you merit a spot on the list.

5. Darryl Sutter. Sutter was one of the most respected Hawks as a player and coach. He took over from Mike Keenan and led the Hawks to 47 victories in 1992-93. He guided the Hawks to the Conference Finals in 1995 but lost to Detroit in five games. Sutter lasted another season in Chicago before quitting because of family reasons. He went on to have success as coach with San Jose and Calgary.

4. Bob Pulford. I have mixed emotions about Pully. He stayed around too long, gummed up the works, and was one of the reasons why the Hawks went into a long exile during the last part of Bill Wirtz's ownership. Everyone was thrilled when Wirtz's son, Rocky, finally cut him loose in 2007. Still, Pulford is second on the coaching list with 182 victories. In 1985, he took over for Oval Tessier and led to the Hawks to the Conference Finals, where they eventually lost to the Wayne Gretzky-led Edmonton Oilers in six exciting games. So, as a coach, you would have to give Pulford a passing grade.

3. Mike Keenan. Keenan has been the NHL's version of Larry Brown, coaching many teams but never staying too long in one place. There is little question Keenan can coach, even if his style puts some people off. In four seasons with the Hawks, he led them to the NHL's best record in 1991, although a shocking first-round playoff exit to Minnesota tarnished that season. However, the Hawks bounced back in 1992 to advance to their first Stanley Cup Finals in 19 years. They lost three 1-goal games getting swept by Mario Lemieux's Penguins. Keenan was then forced out, losing a power struggle with Pulford.

2. Rudy Pilous. Pilous had the good fortune of taking over the Hawks midway through the 1957-58 season, the same year a rookie named Bobby Hull made his debut. Besides Hull, Pilous also nurtured other young stars such as Stan Mikita, Pierre Pilote and Chico Maki. It all came together in the 1961 playoffs when the Hawks beat Detroit to win the Stanley Cup. That gave Pilous his spot in Hawks history.

1. Billy Reay. For more than 14 seasons, Reay and his dapper chapeau was a fixture on the Hawks bench. Reay owns the record with 516 games as coach, and in 1967 he led the Hawks to first place for the first time in franchise history. He was the steadying force for all those great teams when Chicago Stadium rocked in the 60s and into the 70s. However, he never got the Hawks to the finish line, losing three times in the Stanley Cup Finals.

Still, he remains the most successful Hawks coach ever. Said Mikita of Reay: "He treated us like men. He was great to play for, and beyond that, he was a good friend."

When you have a coach named Alpo, you have an automatic candidate for the No. 1 spot on this list. But the Hawks had other coaches who failed to measure up as well. Here are the worst Hawks coaches in their history.

6. Herb Gardiner. During one season as Hawks coach, they went 7-28-8 in 1928-29. But here's the astounding stat: They scored only 33 goals for the entire season. Cracked noted Hawks writer Tim Cronin, "Perhaps it was the NHL's dead-puck era."

5. Ebbie Goodfellow. Can't say I know much about Ebbie Goodfellow other than he had a name that makes for an easy punchline. He wasn't a good fellow (Ha! Ha!) as a coach, finishing last in 1950-51 and 1951-52. The Hawks then said good-bye to Goodfellow.

4. Sid Abel. Known as "Old Bootnose" (isn't that a lovely nickname?), Abel enjoyed a Hall of Fame career skating with Gordie Howe on the great Red Wings teams. However, he hardly enjoyed a Hall of Fame spin as coach of the Hawks. Near the end of his career, he was traded to the Hawks in 1952. He served two seasons as player-coach. In 1953-54, the Hawks had one of their worst seasons ever at 12-51-7. That was it for Abel in Chicago.

3. Keith Magnuson. Maggie remains one of the most beloved players ever to wear the Indian on his jersey. He was the tough guy who took on all comers as a player. Unfortunately, the success didn't continue with him behind the bench. Magnuson went 52-61-26 in just under two seasons and was fired midway through the 1981-82 season. However, everyone still remembers him as a player, as his No. 3 hangs from the rafters at the United Center.

2. Dirk Graham. Graham was a tireless worker who eventually served as captain of the Hawks 1992 Stanley Cup Finals team. The Hawks expected those leadership traits would serve him well when he was named coach in 1998. However, Graham's brief tenure was a disaster, as he was fired after posting a 16-35-8 record. You could also throw Trent Yawney in the same category. Groomed to be a coach, he failed miserably, getting fired early in his second season in 2007.

1. Alpo Suhonen. The Hawks should have known they had problems when they hired a coach named Alpo. He truly was a dog (did you see that line coming?). Hired in 2000 by his old pal Mike Smith, Suhonen was ill-prepared and never earned the respect of his players. The Hawks won 10 of their first 32 games, and it got worse from there. They went 29-40-8 and missed the playoffs. Mercifully, Alpo was sent to the doghouse after that season.

I've heard people lament how much they miss Chicago Stadium. It was a more inti-mate setting than the United Center. It was a loud, electric, classic building. The Stadium, however, needed to meet the wrecking ball and I'm glad it did. Does any-body really feel cheated because they don't get to tip-toe through others' urine when they hit the restroom during intermission at a Blackhawks game? The feature com-forts offered by the U.C. offset any of the Old Barn's charms.

New Comiskey Park, now U.S. Cellular Field, also was the target of many criti-cisms when it opened in April of '91. South Siders complained it was too antiseptic and failed to capture any "old-time ballpark" feel. They were right, but over the past 15 years, the White Sox have made many improvements to the Cell. Those adjust-ments included whacking the top several rows that extended to the heavens, painting the seats green, the addition of a fan deck in centerfield, capturing the feel of an era gone by with old-style font on section signs, etc. These days, the park is the recipient of very few negative comments.

The mistake that will not subside is what the Bears and the Chicago Park District did with Soldier Field when it was "rebuilt" in '02. The Bears played their home games in Memorial Stadium in Champaign that season, much to the chagrin of Monday Night Football play-by-play man Al Michaels, who moaned he couldn't even find a "Two Seasons" hotel somewhere near the U of I.

When bean-counter Ted Phillips was promoted to Bears President and CEO in February of '99, there was guarded optimism over his new business card. Addition by subtraction—with Mike McCaskey removed—likely was the reason observers fore-cast bluer skies in BearNation. And Phillips delivered, quickly striking a deal with Mayor Daley and the Park District to renovate Soldier Field. Sadly, the result was so nightmarish, the new Soldier Field deserves exclusive billing on this "list."

1. The new Soldier Field opens on Monday, September 29, 2003 (a 38-23 loss to Green Bay).

If Captain Kirk would have ordered a Lake Shore Drive set-down for the Starship Enterprise, it would look like our city's foot-ball stadium. It looks like somebody's bad dream. It is the "Spaceship on the Lake." It sucks. It's rounded with peculiar overhangs. Asymmetrical. Cold. And all to protect the precious historical columns outside the stadium. This was a terrible idea. I'd love to meet the idiots who looked at an artist's rendition of the new Soldier Field in '02 and said "Yeah! We gotta do that!" Furthermore, because the mental midgets who stamped approval on this project were so short-sighted, Chicago will never host a Super Bowl. We needed a large venue with a retractable roof. If a cow town like Milwaukee has this technology, why can't we? Millions of dollars will never flow through Chicago com-merce because they botched this project. Once inside, the "new" Soldier Field is comfortable. More restrooms and concession stands. More of the spoils that go with new edifices. The aesthetics outside, however, are nothing shy of horrific. Soldier Field is Chicago's most outlandish scenic blight. And by a landslide.

It would be stupid for Joe Fan to pick a fight with pretty much any large, angry man, especially those who are trained to dismantle other human beings. It is also unwise to assume "smaller" men can't absolutely eviscerate a bigger dude in a street fight. Here's a five-pack of former Chicago non-boxing athletes who, in boxing jargon, would be light heavyweights. They don't have the biggest names in their respective team's histories, but they're guys you will remember. And guys you should remember to avoid if ever confronted by one of them.

5. Norm Van Lier, Bulls. Stormin' Norman was a pal. And a guy I recall fondly when I think of his 5½ years in a Bulls uniform ('72-'78). At 6'1" and only 180 lbs., Van Lier earned his NBA keep by being a bitch on defense. Three times he was a league first-team, All-Defensive team selection. Van Lier grew up outside of Pittsburgh and learned to scrap his way to play college basketball at not-exactly-center-ring St. Francis. He was an NBA long shot who made it because of his penchant for, in Van Lier language, "putting a foot up your ass." I love Norm.

4. Aaron Rowand, White Sox. Key member of the Sox '05 championship team. Rowand is fearless as a center fielder, as evidenced by his broken face when playing a ball hit to the fence when with the Phillies. Like others on this list, he is an approachable, decent guy. A man's man. If he weren't playing professional baseball, he could tear out trees with his bare hands. He's a ripped 6'1", 200 lbs., who wishes he played in the NFL. An outstanding athlete at Cal State-Fullerton, Rowand was the White Sox's first-round pick in '98. Best year with the Sox was '04, when he hit .310 with a career-high 24 homers. I bet Rowand could have kicked Frank Thomas' ass had they ever clashed.

3. Jocelyn Lemieux, Blackhawks. If you think lucid thoughts, you avoid engaging in pugilism with professional hockey players. Lemieux, the younger and less-talented brother of former NHL Stanley Cup champ Claude Lemieux, was a relentless forechecker and fierce take-the-body winger for the Hawks between '89 and '94. Favorite Lemieux moment: Norris Division Finals, Game 6 in St. Louis. The smaller Lemieux pummeled Blues tough guy Harold Snepsts after the long-time Hawks antagonist cross checked him behind the Blues' net. Joc landed a bunch of jackhammer right hands to Snepsts' ugly face, then scored an inspired two-point takedown. Check it out on YouTube.com. Lemieux's spirit was a big contribution to the Hawks President's Trophy winning squad in 1990-91.

2. Dave Duerson, Bears. A 6-foot-1, 215-lb safety who went to four straight Pro Bowls between '86 and '89. Won rings with the Bears in '85 and with the Giants in '90. Double D had his previously good name dragged down when he lost his cool and roughed up his wife in a South Bend hotel in '05. The domestic battery charge forced Duerson's resignation from the Notre Dame Board of Trustees. I first met Duerson when I was taking a dollar and an ID at the front door of a dance club in Muncie, IN, Duerson's home town. I was a junior at Ball State and he had just finished his rookie year with the Bears. I have always liked Dave. A great guy, despite his obvious indiscretion several years ago. And if I were picking sides for a UFC cage match with guys in my weight class, Duerson is one of the first names I'd choose. As much as any incredibly bright-minded guy I've met, Duerson possesses the ability to flip the switch to "the dark side."

1. Glenallen Hill, Cubs. The muscular, unattractive Hill did two stints with the Cubs, hitting 59 of his 186 career dingers with the North Siders. Several of those bombs have yet to land. Glenallen was a butcher as an outfielder, earning the nickname "The Juggler." He also was dubbed "Spiderman" because he suffered from arachnophobia. Amidst a nightmare about spiders, Hill crashed out of bed and fell down a staircase, leading him to the 15-day disabled list from the tumble. I would not want to be the spider if Hill were chasing me. Hill was 6-foot-2 and easily carried his 210 lbs. A very frightening man who always looked pissed off, Hill is the only guy on this list I didn't get to know. And yeah, it's likely because I steered clear of him in the Cubs' clubhouse in '98 when I was a Wrigley regular. I sought refuge near the locker stalls of fan favorite Mark Grace, Rod "The Shooter" Beck and versatile southpaw Terry Mulholland. Hill was a beast.

Favorite Names :: by Gene Honda

Note: Most Chicago fans wouldn't recognize Gene Honda by his face, but they certainly would know his voice. Honda has been the long-time PA voice for the White Sox, Blackhawks, DePaul basketball and the NCAA Final Four. Here he provides his favorite names to announce at the ballpark or in the arena.

10. Carlton Fisk. A tough name. The short last name makes it hard to emphasize. That just made it more of a challenge.

9. Jocelyn Thibault. I'm a goalie, so there had to be at least one goalie in the list.

8. Ron Karkovice. Names with a lot of "hard" sounds are fun to say. Letters like P-C or K-T-D.

7. Quentin Richardson. Good things happened at a DePaul game whenever I said his name.

6. Cal Ripken Jr. Although he was a visiting player, you always felt a sense of class when you announced him.

5. Shingo Takatsu. Being of Japanese origins, there was a sense of pride in announcing him. There was also some pressure, since I don't speak Japanese, to do the name correctly.

4. Nikolai Khabibulin. OK, so there are two goalies on the list! Seriously, there is a challenge in getting all the European names in the NHL correct.

3. Ozzie Guillen. Ozzie was a rookie my first year as PA for the White Sox. It was as much fun to say his name as it was to watch him play.

2. Robin Ventura. He and Karkovice—for the same reasons.

1. Frank Thomas. I guess I've become known for that name. What makes it tough for the future, is that it will be very hard to use that same inflection for just any player. Frank was very unique.

The 10 Worst Guys in Chicago Sports :: by Terry Boers

Note: Terry Boers has dissected Chicago sports for more than 30 years as a columnist for the *Chicago Sun-Times* and long-time sports-talk host for WSCR-AM 670. It is not a good thing to get on Terry's bad side, as these Chicago athletes have discovered. Here is Terry's list of worst guys.

10. Joakim Noah. Still a relative newcomer to the city, Noah was dressed like Bozo on the day the Bulls drafted him and he's been quite the clown ever since. Just a handful of games into his rookie year he tried to tell reporters what was wrong with the Bulls before coach Scott Skiles basically told him to shut his pie-hole. After Skiles was gone, Noah screamed at one of the team's assistant coaches at a shoot around and was suspended for a game by interim boss Jim Boylan. Later, his veteran teammates made it two games. Noah still talks a good game, but he's winded if he runs the court for anything more than a couple of minutes. He continues to be late for just about everything, including the team bus.

9. Bill Buckner. All those years he was vilified in Boston shouldn't have bothered anyone who ran across him in Chicago. Even in his best days with the Cubs, Buckner was an unrepentant jerkwad who would go out of his way to make media members' lives miserable, as if we weren't miserable enough just being around him. A few years after he went to Boston, I ran across him in spring training with absolutely no intention of going near him. He broke into a profane tirade. A real charmer.

8. Cade McNown. Here was a guy who famously worked the hotel lobby at the NFL combine telling every team official he encountered that he would be a great pick. The Bears eventually wasted a first-round pick on the mouthy former UCLA star, who proved him to be just what he looked like—a short little fella who never came up big. Teammates learned to loathe him in roughly 15 seconds. He would later admit, after a particularly galling loss to the 49ers, that he had spent very little time studying the game plan. He was probably too busy parking in handicap spaces.

7. Paul Westhead. Although he was born in Philly, Westhead had coached the Los Angeles Lakers to a championship before landing in Chicago to take over the Bulls. He also came with the California cool dripping out of his every pore. He always thought of himself as the smartest guy in the room, even as he was trying to convince the lead-footed Bulls that they could beat every other team in the league up and down the court. Indeed, who'll ever forget all the sprinting championships won by Dave Corzine? Westhead chastised beat reporters who were late for practices and eventually stopped speaking to one of them (that would be me) in February. That was the best day of my life.

235

6. Brian Cox. Another of those free agents the Bears had to have. The linebacker long had a reputation as a loose cannon and a guy who just might not have been quite right upstairs. His time with the Bears was rather unremarkable and he once screamed within earshot of a microphone that a certain radio host could "kiss my black ass." Nice. But everybody was happy when the Bears kissed it goodbye.

5. Sammy Sosa. Talk about holding a city hostage. The muscle-bound Sosa had the slobbering lovers at Wrigley Field adoring his every move, even though he was a butcher in the field and a complete con-man off of it. None of this came without the complete blessing of team management who helped create this attention-seeking monster, who came to believe he was the center of the universe. A Cub teammate finally smashed his obnoxious boom box and then came the Congressional hearings where Sosa brought a translator even though he communicated just fine with the media and teammates. How do you say "garbage" in Spanish?

4. Ben Wallace. Signed to a huge free-agent contract by Bulls' GM John Paxson, Big Ben didn't provide much in the way of help on the court and even less of it off. He wasn't a Bull very long before he tested coach Scott Skiles' authority by wearing his trademark headband, which was a no-no under Bulls policy. Later, he would use his veteran status to undermine Skiles in the locker room, finally reaching the point where Skiles threw up his hands and left. Wallace then proceeded to brutalize interim coach Jim Boylan's tenure before he was finally dealt to Cleveland.

3. Dave Kingman. Surly for the sake of being surly, the Cubs outfielder was prone to long home runs and making everyone he met hate him. He once boxed up a dead rat and sent it to a reporter and later threw a producer from the NBC-TV affiliate into Lake Michigan. When he became Hall of Fame-eligible he put together his own version of a goodwill tour to convince people he was really a nice guy. That tour was a waste of time and so was Kingman.

2. Tank Johnson. Popularizing the "I've got a felon in the basement" lifestyle, he was a menace to his neighbors thanks to his horde of filthy, barking dogs and a stash of weapons that would have made Che Guevara envious. Eventually arrested for the loaded guns, Johnson was later put under house arrest by Bears GM Jerry Angelo, only to go out one night later and watch his thug buddy lose his life in a shootout at a downtown nightclub.

1. Stan Thomas. No less an authority than Bears coach Mike Ditka called his former offensive tackle "the biggest piece of crap" he'd ever seen in all his years of football. Not only was Thomas a complete bust on the field after being drafted in the first round, he was later shot in a rather hazy incident in San Diego. Although he was not seriously injured, the circumstances surrounding the shooting fueled longtime rumors about Thomas's taste in girls.

Top 100 Chicago Athletes of All Time

No book on Chicago sports would be complete without a list of the top 100 Chicago athletes. For starters, we eliminated "Bee-Bee" Richard, Gary Scott, Brad Sellers, Rickey Watts and few others. Extra credit if you know those would-be stars.

Seriously, Chicago has had its share of great athletes and it wasn't easy limiting the list to 100. We tried to spread around the wealth to make sure all the pro-teams were well represented.

We had some ground rules. Athletes had to play their pro or college ball in Chicago. So that eliminated home-grown high school stars like Isiah Thomas and Kevin Garnett, who went on to have success elsewhere. We made an exception for individual sports such as golf, tennis and boxing.

The athlete also had to have his success primarily with a Chicago team. So even though Phil Esposito was once a Blackhawk, all those great years he had with Boston don't count for this list. Obviously, Esposito's brother, Tony, gets a high rating.

The list is very subjective, and when you're comparing different sports, how can you say one player is better than another? We tried to look at the impact the player had on his team. Making the Hall of Fame in your sport also elevated a player's status.

And we probably rated more modern-day players higher than those from the distant past. I never saw Joe Tinker play shortstop, but I did see Luis Aparicio.

Did we leave a few athletes out? Sure. Will you agree with our rankings, especially the top 10? No. That's where the fun begins with this kind of list. You have your list, and I have mine.

Let the debate begin.

100. Dick Allen. He played only three years with the Sox, and was injured for half the year in one of them. Nevertheless, few players had more impact on the team than what Allen did for them in 1972. He posted one of the greatest seasons in Sox history in winning the AL MVP award. An electric player with awesome power, it is a shame he didn't have a longer run with us.

99. Barney Ross. Ross was born in New York, but grew up in Chicago. He had many memorable bouts during the 1930s, becoming the first boxer ever to win titles in three weight classes: lightweight, junior welterweight and welterweight. He went on to become a hero in World War II.

98. Al Secord. The left winger was both a scorer and a fighter for the Hawks. Three times he scored more than 40 goals in a season, including 54 in 1982-83. He also put in some time in the box, picking up a career-high 303 penalty minutes in 1981-82.

97. Johnny Morris. The Bears haven't had many great wide receivers, but Johnny was an exception. Morris had his best year in 1964, leading the league with 93 receptions for 1,200 yards and 10 touchdowns. He would later go on to become the town's most successful sports news anchor.

96. Wilbur Wood. The portly knuckleballer baffled baseball during the first part of the 70s. He recorded five straight 20-victory seasons, beginning with a 22-13 mark and a 1.91 ERA in 1971. Wood was the ultimate workhorse, often pitching on two days rest.

95. Andre Dawson. "The Hawk" came to the Cubs in 1987 as a bargain-basement free agent and promptly won the NL MVP award for a last-place team. Easily one of the classiest players to ever wear a Cubs uniform.

94. Hank Sauer. A popular slugger during the early 1950s for the Cubs. He had his big year in 1952 when he was named National League MVP for hitting 37 homers with 121 RBIs.

93. Lee Smith. Lee Arthur had more than his share of highlights in eight years with the Cubs. A menacing presence on the mound, he had four seasons with 30 or more saves, including 36 in 1987.

92. Dennis Hull. Bobby's brother, Dennis was dubbed "The Silver Jet." However, he was a star in his right. He peaked with 40 goals during the 1970-71 season and scored 298 goals overall with the Hawks.

91. Bill Cartwright. Obtained in a trade for Charles Oakley in 1988, he gave the Bulls a presence in the middle during the first three titles. Even though he never averaged more than 12.4 points per game for the Bulls, he was still a valuable piece to the overall puzzle.

90. Charley Trippi. He led the Chicago Cardinals to their lone moment of glory. The quarterback was sensational during the 1947 NFL title game, scoring two touchdowns to push the Cardinals over Philadelphia. Trippi went on to be elected to the Hall of Fame.

89. Grover Alexander. The Hall of Fame pitcher spent seven years with the Cubs, joining them when he was 31. He still had plenty left as he went 27-14 in 1920 and 22-12 in 1923.

88. Otto Graham. Before he became an NFL Hall of Famer as a quarterback with the Cleveland Browns, the Waukegan native was a star with Northwestern as a tailback. He finished third in balloting for the 1943 Heisman Trophy.

87. Dave Corzine. The native of Arlington Heights helped revive Ray Meyer's DePaul hoops program in the 1970s. The All-American center led the Blue Demons to a 27-3 record in 1977-78. Later, he went on to play seven years with the Bulls. Not great as a pro, but definitely reliable during the early Michael Jordan years.

86. Andrea Jaeger. As a teenager, the native of Lincolnshire rose to be ranked the No. 2 player in the world. She reached the singles final at Wimbledon in 1983. However, a shoulder problem and general burnout curtailed her career. She went on to open a retreat for young cancer patients in Colorado and is the only person in the Chicago top 100 to become a nun. That's assuming Dennis Rodman doesn't get the calling.

85. Paul Konerko. One of the best power hitters in White Sox history, and definitely one of their best leaders. He was the anchor of the 2005 World Series team, hitting one dramatic homer after another, including the grand slam in Game 2 against Houston. It wouldn't be a surprise if the Sox eventually retire No. 14.

84. Greg Maddux. Let it be noted that Maddux began his Hall of Fame career with the Cubs. At the age of 22, he went 18-8 in 1988 and it was off to the races for the pitching master. He won the Cy Young award with a 20-10 mark in 1992. Then, in one of the colossal blunders of all time, the Cubs screwed up a contract with Maddux and let him get away to Atlanta as a free agent. He came back for a second tour of duty in 2004 and still had something left, winning 16 games.

83. Jim McMahon. "The Punky QB" joins Sid Luckman as the only other standout quarterback the Bears ever had. Unfortunately for McMahon, injury problems kept him off the field much of the time. However, when he did play, he made things happen. He had incredible vision and underrated athletic ability. He was a fun player and a memorable character. Too bad he couldn't do more.

82. Keith Magnuson. "Maggy" was one of the most revered Hawks, as evidenced by his No. 3 that hangs in the rafters at the United Center. A fighter, Magnuson got in more than his share of brawls in defense of his team. When he wasn't fighting, Maggy could play a little defense too.

81. Mark Grace. All the girls loved him and all the guys wished they were him. Gracey seemed to have everything going for him. He was a slick fielder, winning four Gold Gloves, and consistent hitter. His total of 1,754 hits was the most of any player in the 90s.

80. Jay Berwanger. The answer to the trivia question: "Who won the first Heisman Trophy?" Berwanger won the award as an All-American running back for the University of Chicago in 1935. Later, he used the trophy as a doorstop for his office.

79. Jim Covert. Jimbo was a classic offensive left tackle. Nobody got past him on the pass, and he was a fierce run blocker for those great Bears teams in the 1980s. He was the top player at his position for a while, earning a trip to four Pro Bowls. Injuries, though, cost him a likely trip to the Hall of Fame. Only if he had been able to play longer.

78. Harold Baines. Baines was quiet off the field, but he made plenty of noise with his bat on it. Baines was a superb clutch hitter, topping out at 113 RBIs in 1985. Owner Jerry Reinsdorf thought so much of Baines, he retired his No. 3 following his trade to Texas in 1989. Baines would come back two more times to wear that number for the Sox.

77. Dennis Rodman. Rodman definitely was the most bizarre player in Bulls history. His off-the-court antics served as a sideshow. But on the court, he came to play. He was a terrific defender and a tenacious rebounder. "The Worm" definitely served a key role in Jordan's last three titles.

76. Pat Stapleton. "Whitey" was a perennial All-Star defenseman for the Hawks in the 60s and 70s. He set an NHL record for most assists by a defenseman with six in a game against Detroit in 1969.

75. Bruce Sutter. The master of the split-finger fastball, Sutter was virtually unhittable during his five years with the Cubs. In 1977, he posted a 1.34 ERA, giving up only 69 hits in 107 innings. The Cubs, though, decided not to give him the big money, and traded him to St. Louis, where he further established his Hall of Fame credentials.

74. Gary Fencik. Fencik had the leading-man good looks to go along with his Yale education along with the demeanor and intellect of a corporate CEO. But on the football field, he had a much different outlook. He and fellow safety Doug Plank were punishing hitters, making more than a few wide receivers edgy about going over the middle. Fencik finished his career with 38 interceptions.

73. Dick "Night Train" Lane. The Cardinals obtained the legendary defensive back in 1954. The Hall of Famer spent six seasons in Chicago before being traded to Detroit in 1960. He intercepted 10 passes for the Cardinals in 1954.

72. Eddie Cicotte. He would have been a Hall of Famer if not for his decision to throw the 1919 World Series. Cicotte's numbers were staggering. He was 28-12 in 1917 and 29-7 in 1919. Yet he will always be remembered as being one of the "Black Sox."

71. Mark Aguirre. The Westinghouse graduate averaged 24.5 points per game during his three years at DePaul. A dominant scorer both inside and outside, he led the Blue Demons to the Final Four as a freshman in 1979. He went on to have a fine pro career with Dallas and Detroit.

70. Hack Wilson. It is unlikely that his single-season record of 191 RBIs in 1930 will ever be broken. Power-packed at 5-6, 190 pounds, he was a devastating hitter. However, Wilson couldn't overcome his battles with the bottle, which limited his career to only 12 years.

69. Phil Cavaretta. The product of Lane Tech, Cavaretta was a fixture at first base for the Cubs for 20 years. He won the NL MVP award in 1945, hitting .355.

68. Jeremy Roenick. JR didn't waste any time becoming popular with Hawks fans. The center was named NHL Rookie of the Year in 1989-90. A center with power, Roenick was a scoring machine. He scored 50 goals in a season twice with the Hawks.

67. Horace Grant. The 6-10 forward from Clemson was a key member of Jordan's "supporting cast." He was a terrific defender and rebounder and could even drop the occasional deuce. He also kept opponents honest if they started pounding on Jordan.

66. Doug Buffone. Buffone had a standout career both in terms of quality and quantity. He recorded more than 100 tackles seven times in his career and led all Bears linebackers with 24 interceptions. He played 14 years, retiring as the all-time leader for games played. He was also the last active player to have played for George Halas.

65. Charlie Root. He pitched 17 years for the Cubs and is the only pitcher to win more than 200 games (201) in their uniform. However, he is best known for giving up the "Called Shot" homer to Babe Ruth in the 1932 World Series.

64. Hoyt Wilhelm. The ageless knuckleballer arrived with the Sox in 1963 at the age of 39. However, he was far from finished as he excelled out of the bullpen during his seven years with the team. In 1967, he went 8-3 with a 1.31 ERA. His success with the Sox helped solidify his status as a Hall of Famer.

63. Chick Evans. The greatest golfer ever to come out of Chicago, Evans became the first amateur to win the U.S. Open and U.S. Amateur in the same year, accomplishing the feat in 1916. He would later found the Evans Scholars, a scholarship program that has sent thousands of caddies to college.

62. Doug Wilson. Wilson enjoyed a stellar career, manning the blue line for the Hawks. He holds the all-time record for goals scored by a Hawks defenseman, putting 39 pucks in the net in the 1981-82 season. He was selected to seven All-Star games with the Hawks.

61. Jay Hilgenberg. Hilgy came to the Bears as a free agent in 1981. Supposedly, he wasn't big enough to handle the duties at center. So much for that. He went on to be a seven-time Pro Bowler for the Bears. He hasn't made it to Canton yet, but he is a Hall of Famer in our book.

60. Richard Dent. Perhaps the greatest eighth-round pick in Bears history. Dent was a dominating pass rusher recording 17 sacks in '85. While some thought Jim McMahon should have been the Super Bowl XX MVP, the honor went to Dent. Still knocking on the door of the Hall of Fame. Hopefully, one day it will be opened.

59. Minnie Minoso. Perhaps the most popular player in Sox history. Minnie gave Sox fans plenty of reasons to love him during his career. He could run and field and he hit over .300 six times during his career with the Sox. He recorded a single at the age of 54 in 1976. His No. 9 was retired by the Sox in 1983.

58. Billy Pierce. The classy lefthander was the leader of the Sox pitching staff during their great run in the 1950s. He pitched 35 shutouts with the Sox, had two seasons winning 20 games and pitched four one-hitters. As a tribute, the Sox retired his No. 19.

57. Chet Walker. "Chet the Jet" was just about the coolest player the Bulls ever had. His moves to the hoop looked so effortless. The graduate of Bradley averaged 20.6 points per game during his six years with the Bulls.

56. Brian Urlacher. It didn't take long for Urlacher to add his name to the list of great Bears middle linebackers. He was the Rookie of the Year in 2000 and was named NFL defensive player of the year in 2005. During his prime, he was capable of completely taking over a game, much like his predecessors in the position, Dick Butkus, Bill George and Mike Singletary.

55. Bill Mosienko. A Hall of Famer, Mosienko posted 540 points with the Hawks during the 1940s and early 50s. Mosienko's most memorable moment came in a 1952 game when he scored three goals in 21 seconds.

54. Johnny Evers. He was the second-baseman of the famous "Tinkers-to-Evers-to-Chance" double play combination. Despite weighing only 125 pounds, he played his way into the Hall of Fame.

53. Ollie Matson. The Cardinals were terrible in the 1950s, but it wasn't because of Matson. The running back began his Hall of Fame career with the Cardinals in 1952, spending six seasons with the team. He was an electrifying runner, scoring nine touchdowns on kickoff and punt returns during his days in Chicago.

52. Ray Schalk. Schalk was a fixture as a Sox catcher for 17 years, beginning with the 1913 season. An excellent defender, he led the league in fielding eight times. He was elected into the Hall of Fame in 1955.

51. Red Faber. Faber was among the last of the legal spitball pitchers. He was the hero of the 1917 World Series, winning three games. All told, he posted 254 victories in a Hall of Fame career.

50. Artis Gilmore. The A-Train is still the only dominant center the Bulls have ever had. Signed from the ABA in 1976, Gilmore averaged 19.3 points per game in seven years with the Bulls. He was a six-time All-Star.

49. Stan Jones. Jones was a Hall of Fame guard for the Bears in the 50s and 60s, earning seven Pro Bowl selections. However, when the Bears needed help on defense in 1962, Jones moved over to defensive tackle, playing the 1963 season at that position.

48. Joe Tinker. The slick-fielding shortstop played 15 years with the Cubs. Five times he led the National League in fielding. Also an excellent clutch hitter, he was elected to the Hall of Fame in 1946.

47. Ed Sprinkle. Nicknamed "The Claw," the two-way player on offensive and defensive was regarded as the meanest man in football during his days with the Bears in the 1940s and 50s. He once said, "if playing tough football makes one a dirty player, I guess I am, but I never did any of the things anyone would constitute as being dirty."

46. Ed Walsh. Big Ed was the dominant Sox pitcher during their early days. He posted an incredible 40 victories in 1908 with a 1.42 ERA. The Hall of Famer had a career ERA of 1.82, among the lowest for pitchers in the 20th Century.

45. Dan Hampton. "Danimal" was an unstoppable force during his career with the Bears. The Hall of Famer couldn't be contained at defensive end, and then smoothly made the transition to defensive tackle, anchoring the heart of the 1985 Bears defense.

44. Steve Larmer. Larmer was the Hawks' iron man, playing 891 straight games during the 1980s, which at the time was the NHL's third longest streak. He was a battler at right wing, scoring more than 40 goals in a season five times.

43. Frank Chance. The "Peerless Leader" was a great player as well as manager. A first-baseman, he was the anchor of the great Cubs teams in the early 1900s. He had four consecutive years where he hit more than .300.

42. George Connor. The former Notre Dame star excelled during his eight years with the Bears. During that time, he was elected to the Pro Bowl at three different positions: offensive tackle, defensive tackle and linebacker. It was at linebacker where he made his biggest impact, eventually leading him to the Hall of Fame.

41. Ted Lyons. After the "Black Sox" scandal, Ted Lyons was one of the few bright spots that emerged during the franchise's dark days. He posted three 20-win seasons en route to winning 260 games, good enough to merit a spot in the Hall of Fame.

40. Mike Ditka. This is about Ditka the player, not the coach. He made his presence felt out of the gate, winning the NFL Rookie of the Year honor in 1961 with 12 touchdowns. Ol' No. 89 had his signature play with a long run in which it seemed every member of the Pittsburgh Steelers tried and failed to bring him down. His outstanding play made him the first tight end to be elected to the Hall of Fame.

39. Ron Santo. You'll be hard-pressed to find another Cub who played with more heart than Santo. He left it all on the field for 14 years with the team. A Gold Glover at third base and a power hitter at the plate, Santo is forever knocking on the door of the Hall of Fame. His legacy, though, is firmly secure with Cubs fans.

38. Joe Jackson. One of the greatest hitters of all time, Jackson had his career ruined by being part of the "Black Sox." Nevertheless, he led all hitters with a .375 average during the World Series he supposedly threw. "Shoeless Joe" was a .356 career hitter, but the scandal cost him a spot in Cooperstown.

37. Max Bentley. He and brother Doug were standout players for Hawks in the 1940s. Max led the NHL in points for two seasons and won the Hart Trophy in 1946; clearly good enough stats to be a Hall of Famer.

36. Doug Atkins. At 6-8, 275 pounds, Atkins was a menacing force on the defensive line for the Bears. A free spirit, he often clashed with George Halas. But on the field, there were few better for the Bears than this Hall of Famer.

35. Ferguson Jenkins. The guy was a stud on the mound. Beginning in 1967, he posted six straight 20-victory seasons for the Cubs. He won the Cy Young Award in 1971 and is the only pitcher to record 3,000 strikeouts with less than 1,000 walks. He sports a Cubs hat on his plaque at Cooperstown.

34. Norm Van Lier. "Stormin' Norman" played just like his nickname implied. He simply was tenacious, refusing to back down to anybody. He was also a terrific point guard, earning recognition in three NBA All-Star games.

33. Carlton Fisk. "Pudge" sports a Red Sox cap in the Hall of Fame, but he actually played longer with the Whites: 12-plus years. He hit a dramatic game-winning homer in his first game with the Sox against Boston and continued to shine from there. He placed third in MVP voting in 1983 and hit 37 homers in 1985. He was a noble warrior for both Sox.

32. Chris Chelios. A double entry here. Chelly grew up in the burbs. Then after becoming a star with Montreal, the Hawks acquired him in a trade for Denis Savard. He was among the best defensemen in the game during his 10 seasons with the Hawks. He also led the team in scoring with 72 points in the 1995-96 season, the only time in team history a defenseman achieved that feat.

31. Mordecai Brown. "Three-Finger" was better than virtually every five-finger pitcher during his day. In the early 1900s, he recorded six straight 20-win seasons. In 10 years with the Cubs, he had a 1.80 ERA, best in team history.

30. Pierre Pilote. The Hall of Famer was the anchor of the defense for 13 years for the Hawks. He was voted to eight straight All-Star games and was a first-team All-NHL selection five times.

29. Jerry Sloan. The "Original Bull" might have been their toughest. A member of the Bulls' first team in 1966-67, Sloan quickly asserted himself as a defensive force. He was named to the All-NBA Defensive first-team four times. He and Norm Van Lier formed one of the best backcourts in team history.

28. Luis Aparicio. Few shortstops ever played the game with the flair of "Little Looie." He and second baseman Nellie Fox arguably formed the best double-play combination of all time. Aparicio was also a weapon on the base path, leading the league in steals nine times. His combination of speed and defense earned him a deserved spot in Cooperstown.

27. Bulldog Turner. His first name was actually Clyde, but his nickname, "Bulldog," says it all. The Hall of Famer was an exceptional two-way player at center and linebacker for the Bears.

26. Gabby Hartnett. The best catcher in Cubs history, he was a six-time All-Star and hit .357 in 1937. Of course, his most memorable moment was the "Homer in the Gloamin," a late-inning homer in the dark against Pittsburgh that helped propel the Cubs to the World Series in 1938.

25. Denis Savard. "Savvy" was the center of the "Party Line" that included Steve Larmer and Al Secord. Savard, though, was always the life of that party. Just when you thought you saw everything from Savard, he would come up with a different move to wow you. He accrued more than 100 points in a season five times with the Hawks.

24. Bob Love. "Butterbean" was the Bulls' first big scorer, averaging 21.3 points per game during his career in Chicago. He was lethal from the outside on the great Bulls teams during the 1970s. He also served as an inspiration later in his life. He overcame a severe stutter to become an active representative of the Bulls in the community.

23. Nellie Fox. Fox was the defining player of the "Go-Go Sox" era. The second-baseman was a 12-time All-Star, won three Gold Gloves and was the American League MVP in 1959. Even though he hit only 35 career homers, Fox showed that doing the little things right could take you a long way. In his case, it was to the Hall of Fame.

22. Bill George. The game's first middle linebacker, George covered the entire field. He stopped the run and recorded 18 career interceptions. The Hall of Famer was the leader of the defense on the Bears 1963 NFL title team.

21. Ryne Sandberg. "Ryno" was the rare second baseman who could hit for power. He led the league with 40 homers in 1990 and won nine straight Gold Gloves. The Hall of Famer will forever be remembered for that day in 1984 when he hit two dramatic late-inning homers off Bruce Sutter in a game that sealed his legend.

20. Mike Singletary. A two-time NFL Defensive Player of the Year, Singletary was the leader of those great Bears defensive teams in the 1980s. He always seemed to be in on the tackle, ranking first or second in that category during his 11 years with the Bears. His dedication was an inspiration to all who had the privilege to be around him.

19. George Mikan. He became basketball's first dominant big-man at DePaul. Ray Meyer transformed the gangly native of Joliet into a force. A two-time college player of the year, he led DePaul to the 1945 NIT title, back when that event was bigger than the NCAA tournament. He would go on to become a legend in the NBA with the Minneapolis Lakers.

18. Tony Esposito. "Tony O" was all that and more during his rookie season with the Hawks, posting a record 15 shutouts in 1969-70. The Hall of Famer always seemed to come up with the big save, winning three Vezina Trophies.

17. Bronko Nagurski. At 235 pounds, Nagurski was a giant in the 1930s, especially carrying the ball out of the backfield. He literally dragged tacklers down the field with him. He was also a brutal hitter at linebacker and a symbol of the Bears during the early stages of their existence.

16. Eddie Collins. One of the greatest Sox players of all time, Collins was acquired from the Philadelphia A's in 1915 for the sum of $50,000, which was astronomic at the time. The Hall of Famer played 12 years with the Sox, hitting .324 or higher seven times.

15. Billy Williams. "Sweet Swingin'" Billy won the National League Rookie of the Year award in 1961 and just kept on hitting. His best year came in 1972 when he hit .333 with 37 homers. The Hall of Famer was also known for his durability, playing in what was then a National League record 1,117 games.

14. Glenn Hall. His nickname was "Mr. Goalie," which pretty much says it all when it comes to Hall. He was the Hawks goalie on their 1961 Stanley Cup team. Hall played in 502 consecutive games, a record that will most likely never be broken for a goalie. He was elected to the Hall of Fame in 1975.

13. Scottie Pippen. He was Robin to Jordan's Batman. Pippen was an extremely versatile performer, often serving as a "point-forward." He had 20 career double-doubles, including four in the playoffs. His long arms made him a lock-down defender, as he was a seven-time member of the NBA's All-Defense team. Jordan knows he doesn't win six NBA titles if he doesn't have Pippen by his side.

12. Gale Sayers. "The Kansas Comet" exploded on to the scene and then seemingly was gone in a flash. He played in only 68 NFL games. But the impression he left in that short time was more than enough to enable him to be the youngest player ever inducted into the Hall of Fame. You wonder what might have been if he had stayed healthy. At least we can be thankful we had him for as long as we did.

11. Luke Appling. "Old Aches and Pains" was a superstar during the 30s and 40s. The Hall of Fame shortstop had a career batting average of .310, with a high of .388 in 1936. He still was going strong at the age of 42, hitting .301 in his last full season with the team.

10. Stan Mikita. Perhaps the most respected player ever to wear the Hawks uniform. And after Hull, probably the best. Mikita spent 21 years with the Hawks, possessing a flair as a playmaker that made him one of the best centers of all time. He won the Hart Trophy twice and led the league in scoring three times. His No. 21 was the first ever to be retired by the Hawks, a fitting honor.

9. Sid Luckman. Luckman remains the only true great superstar the Bears ever had at quarterback. The fact that he still holds the biggest records for a Bears quarterback, accumulated in what was not a passing era, remains a tribute to his talents. It also is an indictment to the many quarterbacks who have followed him.

8. Red Grange. "The Galloping Ghost" was a driving force in legitimizing pro football in the 1920s. Fresh out of Illinois, Grange and the Bears played to huge crowds in barnstorming tours across the country. His last great play occurred on defense: In the 1933 NFL title game, he made a game-saving tackle against the Giants to preserve the victory for the Bears.

7. Frank Thomas. Easily the greatest hitter in Sox history, Thomas was the entire package at the plate. He could hit for average and power. A two-time MVP, he put up numbers early on that compared to Babe Ruth and Ted Williams. However, Thomas' knack for creating controversy never allowed him to be fully embraced by Sox fans. Still, he will be wearing a Sox cap when he is elected to the Hall of Fame.

6. Sammy Sosa. Yes, he had some major flaws. He was a "me-first" player and then there is the issue of steroids. But his numbers are staggering. Three times he hit more than 60 homers in a season. He had nine years when he drove in more than 100 runs, including 160 RBIs in 2001. The Cubs and their fans reveled in Sammy when he was star and then tossed him aside when things got bad. His legacy will always be tarnished in Chicago.

5. Dick Butkus. The best middle linebacker of all time, if not the best defensive player ever. Butkus had an unrelenting desire to devastate anything and everything that got in his way. Too bad a knee injury limited his career to only nine years. However, it was more than enough to have his legend sealed in Canton in 1979.

4. Ernie Banks. Just being called "Mr. Cub" pretty much says it all. Nobody embraced the spirit and joy of playing at Wrigley Field more than Banks. And let's talk about his numbers for a second. He hit 512 homers, back when reaching 500 homers was a rare feat. He won back-to-back MVPs, becoming the first National League player ever to receive that honor. He hit 47 homers in 1958 and drove in 143 runs in 1959. The only thing lacking on his resume was a pennant, but it didn't alter how he was viewed by Cubs fans. To them, he will always be a cherished icon.

3. Bobby Hull. There was nothing like the "Golden Jet" during his heyday in Chicago. An amazing combination of speed and power, Hull was majestic at full throttle with the puck on his stick. The records are formidable: He became the first player to score more than 50 goals in a season. He scored 50 or more goals in a season five times for the Hawks. He had 24 career hat tricks and won the Hart Trophy twice. For 15 years, he thrilled the fans at the Chicago Stadium, leaving memories that will last a lifetime. More than enough to be placed in the NHL Hall of Fame in 1983. Thanks, Bobby.

2. Walter Payton. Mike Ditka always considered Payton the "greatest football player I ever saw." The coach had plenty of people who agreed with him. Payton was the entire package: elusive, powerful, the rare running back who enjoyed inflicting pain on defenders. Just to refresh your memory, go back and look up some of his old highlights. It will provide a vivid reminder of just how good he was. Hall of Fame class of '93.

1. Michael Jordan. The numbers, please. He averaged 31.5 points per game with the Bulls. He was a five-time NBA MVP, a figure that should be greater. He led the NBA in scoring 10 times. He was the NBA defensive player of the year in 1987-88. He was an NBA All-Star Game MVP three times. And the most important stat of all: He led the Bulls to six NBA titles, winning the Finals MVP each time. All hail "Air Jordan."